STOP SELLING VANILLA ICE CREAM

STOP SELLING
VANILLA
ICE CREAM

The Scoop on Increasing Profit by Differentiating
Your Company Through Strategy and Talent

Steve Van Remortel

GREENLEAF
BOOK GROUP PRESS

Published by Greenleaf Book Group Press
Austin, Texas
www.gbgpress.com

Distributed by Greenleaf Book Group LLC

For ordering information or special discounts for bulk purchases, please contact Greenleaf Book Group LLC at PO Box 91869, Austin, TX 78709, 512.891.6100.

Design and composition by Greenleaf Book Group LLC
Cover design by Imaginasium
Cover illustration by Final Art Studio

Publisher's Cataloging-In-Publication Data
(Prepared by The Donohue Group, Inc.)

Van Remortel, Steve.
    Stop selling vanilla ice cream : the scoop on increasing profit by differentiating your company through strategy and talent / Steve Van Remortel. -- 1st ed.

    p. ; cm.
    Issued also as an ebook.
    Includes bibliographical references.
    ISBN: 978-1-60832-387-6

    1. Strategic planning. 2. Manpower planning. 3. Reengineering (Management) 4. Marketing--Management. 5. Success in business. I. Title.

HD30.28 .V26 2012
658.4/012   2012941180

Part of the Tree Neutral® program, which offsets the number of trees consumed in the production and printing of this book by taking proactive steps, such as planting trees in direct proportion to the number of trees used: www.treeneutral.com

TreeNeutral®

Printed in the United States of America on acid-free paper

12 13 14 15 16 17   10 9 8 7 6 5 4 3 2 1

First Edition

CONTENTS

PHASE 4: STRATEGY IMPLEMENTATION

WHY YOU MUST STOP SELLING VANILLA ICE CREAM

Are you selling vanilla ice cream?

Consider for a moment the features of this familiar product. It's a safe bet you've had it alongside your favorite dessert, beneath a mouth-watering dollop of chocolate syrup, or accompanying a bowl of fresh fruit. Vanilla is the perfect accompanying flavor, because it will never overpower the main attraction.

However, if everyone were content to eat vanilla ice cream, Baskin-Robbins never would have created its 31 Flavors marketing concept, offering a different flavor for every day of the month. Do you think that iconic retailer would have grown to boast almost 6,000 stores around the world today if all it sold was vanilla ice cream? Of course not.

Interestingly, vanilla remains Baskin-Robbins's top-selling flavor, but the company has gone on to create more than one thousand ice cream flavors since World War II, according to the company's website (www. baskin-robbins.com). Founders Burt Baskin and Irv Robbins realized early on they couldn't just sell vanilla ice cream and hope to enjoy long-term success. They quickly saw the fantastic impact that a constant flow of innovative flavors would have on attracting customers to their stores—not just once, but over and over again. This variety became the differentiating factor that set Baskin-Robbins apart in the ice cream market.

Chances are, you're not in the ice cream business, but your industry has its own version of vanilla. What is that basic product or service offered by every one of your competitors? What is the feature that has become almost a commodity item, forcing you to compete on price and affording you minimal profit margins?

You can't completely stop selling your industry's version of vanilla ice cream. After all, there are certain basic, indispensable products and services that every industry has, and everyone in that industry is going to have to offer them if they expect to stay in business. Even Baskin-Robbins still sells vanilla, right? But even when an ice cream company does sell vanilla, more than 90 percent of the time something is put on it, in it, or underneath it. The same should be true of your services and products.

You must differentiate yourself from competitors. In order to thrive in good times and bad, you must go beyond the regular, expected offerings that everybody else in your business has. Like Baskin-Robbins, you had better be selling something more interesting, more valuable, and enticing—something that sets you apart. Otherwise, you'll find limited success in your market. Indeed, if you find that you are consistently negotiating on price, there's a good chance that you're selling only vanilla ice cream. If your clients or customers don't see any difference between what you're offering and what your competitors are offering, why wouldn't they go where they can get the best price? We do it as consumers every day. We choose to go to certain stores or restaurants because they provide something we want and cannot get anywhere else. So if we do that as consumers every day, why would we not turn that same mind-set toward our own businesses?

THE STOP SELLING VANILLA ICE CREAM PROCESS

As president and chief strategist of SM Advisors, a strategy and talent management company, I've been able to observe the best practices of hundreds of companies interested not only in earning their customers' business but also in retaining and meriting a premium for it. The experience I have gained in leading more than one thousand planning sessions for companies in over three hundred different industries has helped me focus on the best of the best. I've developed a lean yet robust process that I've distilled and refined into proprietary tools and processes that generate the greatest probability of success. These actionable, practical methods make up the Stop Selling Vanilla Ice Cream process. With this book, you are literally holding in your hands the fruits of decades of personal, hands-on experience, multiplied by the hundreds of companies I've assisted in realizing more of their potential for higher earnings and greater industry impact.

This book is for and about the entrepreneur in each of us. No matter where you are in your career or where your company is situated within your industry, you'll learn some things by reading this book that you can incorporate into your business *today*.

However, I'm not offering a quick fix with little staying power. *Stop Selling Vanilla Ice Cream* isn't the latest feel-good-quick read for business travelers in a hurry. On the contrary, this process is built upon some of the latest research and incorporates the most powerful strategic planning methodologies and behavioral assessments in the marketplace. Whether you are a manufacturer trying to break into new markets, a service company trying to differentiate itself, or a nonprofit trying to deliver your mission, this book can help you create custom-built solutions for your unique challenges and leverage them for long-term, measurable success.

The most successful organizations offer something special that sets them apart. For me and my associates at SM Advisors, that differentiating factor is the Stop Selling Vanilla Ice Cream process; it enables us to provide something to our clients that they can get in only one place, and for which they are willing to pay extra. Want to know why they're willing? Here's the answer: More than 90 percent of the companies SM Advisors works with experience an increase in profitability and/or sales in their first year.

HOW DOES IT WORK?

The Stop Selling Vanilla Ice Cream process gets results because it focuses on two key fundamentals of every successful organization: strategy and talent.

After working with so many organizations to help them build strategies, teams, and execution plans to improve profitability, I've learned that no two situations are alike. But one thing shared by every company—indeed, every organization of any size—is the central importance of strategy and talent. Think about it: What problem could you possibly face in your business that couldn't be overcome by a combination of a focused strategy and the right talent in the right positions?

In fact, I'll go out on a limb and say it this way: There is no difficulty any viable enterprise can confront that cannot be surmounted by

- ✔ improving its strategy;

- ✔ optimizing its talent.

The combination of simultaneously taking your strategy and talent to the next level is what makes this process so unique and powerful.

Once I realized this truth, I began designing a process to build high-performance teams that execute differentiated strategies. That process is the foundation of this book, and you can find additional tools, templates, and assessments to help you implement it at www.stopsellingvanillaicecream.com.

Creating the perfect marriage between strategy and talent liberates your company to soar, to set itself apart from competitors and begin creating what Ken Blanchard and Sheldon Bowles term "raving fans." In the language of the process described in this book, this dual focus allows you to start selling mint chocolate chip ice cream (or fill in your own personal favorite flavor—as long as it's not vanilla!), radically differentiating your company's product or service from the vanilla served by your competitors.

THE FUNDAMENTALS OF STRATEGY AND TALENT

There are five fundamentals of the process that help define the organization's route from square one—where you are today—to greater prosperity and effectiveness:

1. **Differentiation.** Deliver a competence that creates a clear differentiation for your organization. Don't sell vanilla ice cream. Instead, sell mint chocolate chip, and make it tastier and creamier than your competitors'. Make your differentiation so clear that your customers consistently choose you over your competition and are willing to give you more business and pay you more for your products or services.

2. **Tangible Value.** Don't just say you're the best—prove it. Your organization must consistently reinforce the tangible value, in dollars, that your competence delivers to current and prospective customers.

3. **Talent Management.** Implement a talent management system that enables your organization to identify, select, develop, and retain the talent and skill sets necessary to execute and deliver your competence and plan. Optimizing talent to build a high-performing team is critical to improving communication, improving company-wide decision making, and increasing profitability.

4. **Tactical/Department Plans.** Develop and execute action plans that work "on" the business in each department of your organization rather than simply working "in" the business with regular daily duties. The action plans created in the strategic planning process are distributed to the appropriate department plans. As each department completes its action plans, the success of the organization accelerates.

5. **Plan Execution.** Implement a plan execution program to ensure an organizational culture of discipline that focuses on accountability. The journey doesn't end with the completion of a plan; it's only the beginning! Execution is the hard part, but that's what results in sustained top-line and bottom-line growth.

It's important to understand at the outset that strategy is an evolution, not a revolution. It takes time and perseverance to achieve your vision. In my experience, companies that try to get everything done all at once often end up getting very little accomplished. In the early stages of the process you will identify the top five to seven strategic challenges you want to resolve as a result of the plan. Based on our results, all companies that follow the process resolve their identified strategic challenges. The most successful companies, however, keep sharpening the tip of the pencil, building momentum year after year as they make step-change success and continuous improvement part of the organizational culture. Those who understand the need to follow a process and distinguish themselves from the crowd will master the markets in which they compete, while those who don't will fade. The phrase "Those Who Plan — PROFIT!®" is the battle cry for our team at SM Advisors and characterizes the ultimate result for our clients and those who implement the process.

If strategy is the map that shows you where you want to go, then talent is the transportation that gets you there. In the work we do with our clients, one of our chief objectives is to help them implement a talent management system that focuses on identifying, selecting, hiring, developing, and retaining the talent required to deliver their competence and strategy.

You'll learn how to develop and manage your talent to "Build the team to achieve your dream™" by using state-of-the-art behavioral assessments and talent management processes. We have found, time and again, that the trust, accountability, and improved communication among team members that results from this part of our process create an incredible breakthrough for the organization. In this book, I'll show you how to implement a Talent Management System into your company that will get your organization on the path toward financial success and greater industry impact.

CHANGING THE BUSINESS LANDSCAPE

The worldwide recession that began in 2007 ended forever the days when businesses could prosper despite offering little more than middle-of-the-pack products and services. While nobody likes a recession, it's also true that economic hard times create opportunities for companies that are dedicated to rising above the crowd. Organizations that differentiate themselves from their competition thrive regardless of the economy, while those who remain content with the status quo struggle to survive. The fact is that your customers' buying criteria have evolved to the point where average just isn't good enough anymore and never will be again. Indeed, you've probably noticed that shift in your own purchasing decisions. During the latest business downturn, the most successful entrepreneurs and business leaders understood they needed a new approach. They survived the recession by realizing there had to be a better way—a more effective way—to outplan and outperform the competition. That's what I will share with you.

By this point, you may have concluded that your business is in the same position that most companies find themselves in: You're stuck in a flat, leveling, or even declining sales pattern. It's also possible that, like many of the companies I work with, you find yourself working harder, even expanding your client or customer base, and still not making any money. You lack balance in your life because you are putting in so many hours—but for what? Or it may be that you've realized there are roadblocks to progress within your company—sacred cows—that are limiting your ability to grow and prosper.

If one or more of these situations describes your organization, you're far from being alone. Perhaps a big part of the reason so many companies struggle is that *an estimated 70 percent of organizations do not invest the time and effort necessary to develop and execute an annual business plan.* Many business leaders put more effort into planning a successful long weekend or their retirement than for the vehicle they rely on to fund those plans—their business.

Even more surprising is the fact that *fewer than 10 percent of the companies that do develop an annual business plan are able to define clearly how they're going to differentiate themselves from their competition.* In other words, they fail to determine the single most important reason a customer would choose to do business with them rather than their competition.

Also, *fewer than 10 percent of all businesses develop and execute departmental (tactical) plans.* This is even harder to understand once you realize that these plans are where strategy blossoms into action.

Does your experience follow these trends? Let me ask you a few questions:

✔ Do you develop and execute an annual business plan?

✔ Can you clearly define how your organization differentiates itself from its competition? Is it a real differentiation?

✔ Do you develop departmental plans to work on the business, such as operations, sales, marketing, human resources, or manufacturing plans?

This challenge is not a condemnation of you, me, or the other gifted entrepreneurs and business leaders who successfully drive our economy; rather, these questions point out the reality that most people simply don't know exactly how to develop and execute a business plan. Many of us struggle to get our "in the business" work done every week, much less put time aside to work *on* the business.

Now, by using the common-sense principles and guidance in this book, you can help your organization move to the head of the class: you can be among those few visionary leaders who not only know where they want to go but have a solid, workable plan for getting there and putting the team in place to make it happen.

HOW TO USE THIS BOOK

In *Stop Selling Vanilla Ice Cream*, I've provided you with what is essentially a field guide for organizational success. In these pages and on the companion website at www.stopsellingvanillaicecream.com, you'll find easy-to-use templates, forms, questionnaires, behavioral assessments, and action plans that take strategic planning out of the realm of theory and into the practical, no-nonsense arena of making your enterprise the one that stands out against the competition.

Most organizations don't have plans for differentiating themselves from the competition because they simply don't know how to do it. The straightforward, effective process outlined in this book changes all that. Using the principles and procedures outlined here, you and your leadership team or departmental associates can now craft and execute a strategic plan and also ensure that you have the right people in the right places to make it work. In other words, the question becomes not "Can we do it?" but rather "When do we get started?"

Another tremendous benefit of this process is that it seamlessly integrates strategic and tactical planning with talent management. By utilizing the strategies and tools I'll give you in this book, you can not only establish how you will differentiate yourself from the competition, but you will also learn how to make sure you have the right team in place to achieve your goals. Remember: There's no obstacle facing your organization that can't be overcome by the combination of strategy and talent. The unique approach of this system helps you focus on both.

The greatest payoff of an effective differentiated strategy and talent management system is, of course, that it allows your enterprise to optimize its potential in all aspects, from financial goals to becoming the leader in your industry. One of the greatest thrills I get is seeing the improvement in the lives of the people in the organizations that successfully implement the Stop Selling Vanilla Ice Cream process. In many ways, then, the success of this process is measured by the success and enriched lives of the people who make it happen.

Therefore, in the pages of *Stop Selling Vanilla Ice Cream*, you'll follow the progress of Connecting Cultures, a company providing interpreting services. As Rashelle and her team dive headfirst into the strategic planning process and build a skill set–aligned team to accomplish strategic objectives, I predict you'll recognize something of yourself or members of your organization. In fact, you will get to know these people on a deeper level than you may be accustomed to from reading other business books. As you read, the process and its results will become real for you . . . because it was real for them. This is a true story, not a parable, and I encourage you to put yourself in their shoes to understand how to complete the process.

This case-study approach is vital not only to communicate the ABCs of our strategic planning and talent management processes and system but also to give you and your team a simple example to follow as you execute the process. I would encourage you to read the book and then execute the process as you read it a second time with your team members. It will also demonstrate that every one of our techniques and methods is thoroughly field-tested, practical, and actionable. I'm not going to be giving you a lot of high-flown theory or fluff—what I like to call a philosophical-theo-retical rampage. Instead, I'm going to show you—in real-world, human terms—how your enterprise can use the process and templates to begin differentiating itself dramatically from competitors, significantly increas-ing sales and profitability.

Throughout each chapter, I'll pose some questions that will challenge you to consider the principles under discussion and apply them to your own organization. I urge you to not shy away from the implications of these questions. Time and again, my experience with client organizations has shown that once you start asking the right questions, you will begin getting the answers you really need. One of my goals for this book is to help you start asking those questions.

Finally, at the end of each chapter, I'll define the action plans for imple-menting the process in your organization. After all, as its name implies, the Stop Selling Vanilla Ice Cream process is about what you *do*, not just what you *know*. The principles and directives in this book are intended to lead to better, more decisive actions. I'll help you put in place a plan that will allow you and your organization to achieve an entirely new level of success and prosperity.

Since *Stop Selling Vanilla Ice Cream* is your field guide to organizational success, I urge you to retain your individual copy; you will probably want to jot some notes in the margins or into your e-book reader.

LET'S GET STARTED!

If you recognize yourself, your organization, your division, or your depart-ment in the struggles I've described, this book is for you. It will help you create a simple and executable plan to implement the strategic fundamen-tals in your organization. It will help you build the team to achieve your dream and execute your plan. It will focus your limited time and resources (human and financial) on action plans that will generate the greatest impact on the success of your business.

Stop Selling Vanilla Ice Cream will provide you with the tools, templates, and assessments necessary to increase the level of strategic thinking in your organization and institute a culture of accountability that will engage individuals at all levels of the organization. Once this process becomes a regular part of your annual business cycle, your team will look forward to the planning process every year.

Remember the statistics: Most businesses aren't doing any kind of annual strategic planning, which means chances are good that your competition isn't doing any, either. This is your opportunity to seize the advantage. Take action by moving away from selling vanilla ice cream to a point of clear differentiation.

My vision is that this book will inspire you to champion the need for strategic planning and talent management in your organization, regardless of your position. I encourage you to share copies of the book with your teammates, check off the action plans at the end of each chapter as you complete them, and use the templates from the website to implement the process. I'm confident the process will help you develop and execute a more effective business plan, sending you on a course toward achieving your professional and personal goals. It's all about creating a better life for you and every person in your organization.

Ready to get started? Let's go to work on building your future.

The Scoop

1. On a scale from 1 to 10, how great a differentiation does your organization have from your competition? (10 = clear differentiation; 1 = no differentiation and selling vanilla ice cream)

2. On a scale from 1 to 10, how well does your organization optimize its talent? (10 = a strong talent optimizing system; 1 = no investment in talent management)

THE POWER OF STRATEGY + TALENT

For Rashelle, owning her own business felt like a treadmill of nonstop work. She is the cofounder and president of Connecting Cultures, Inc., a family-owned business based in northeastern Wisconsin that specializes in providing interpreting programs for the health care industry. Price negotiations, low profitability, a lack of process and structure, and the challenges of defining appropriate roles for her team were creating tremendous stress for her. The constant need to manage some internal crisis or another was hindering her efforts to pursue the new business that the company so desperately needed. She knew they needed help to improve operating efficiency and financial results.

The first time I met Rashelle, I expected a level of skepticism. Bobbie, who is Rashelle's mother as well as her business partner, delivered that in spades. As I began talking to them, Bobbie silently observed the discussion, providing a reserved balance to Rashelle's unbridled enthusiasm and extroverted nature. I asked Rashelle to tell me the story of how Connecting Cultures came to be. What was it about the business that got her adrenaline pumping? What made her get up in the morning, eager to get to work?

Rashelle took a deep breath, collected her thoughts, and launched into her life story. I soon found out that Connecting Cultures wasn't just a business to Rashelle; it was the core and summation of who she was.

She had always been a hard worker, she told me. "I became interested in foreign languages and studying abroad in high school. I was hooked on the idea of traveling and seeing the world." Deciding on an exchange program in Argentina, Rashelle spent a year living in the city of Mendoza. "I loved speaking Spanish, and by the time I came back to Wisconsin, you couldn't tell the difference between me and my Argentine friends."

Rashelle said that not long after her return to the States, one of her friends told her about an interpreting agency in her home area. "I accepted the company's job offer, and without any training, they sent me to the home of a hospice patient. I met the nurse at the client's home, and that was it. I was hooked." For two years she worked for different agencies.

Possessing generous quantities of both passion and confidence, Rashelle decided that she wanted to start her own interpreting business. She was expecting her first child, and she longed for the freedom to be able to set her own hours and make her own decisions about how to provide the best possible service to her clients. "We started Connecting Cultures out of a small room in my parents' basement, ten years ago. From the beginning, Bobbie took care of the business end of things, and I had the creative vision."

Connecting Cultures landed an important contract with a regional health care system. "We had to figure out how to take a business that started with two people and turn it into a business with numerous employees and all the challenges that entails," Rashelle said, describing the struggle that so many small to midsize companies face.

Six years into the relationship, business volume from that client stopped growing. "We always knew we would need to diversify our customer base," Rashelle explained, "but I didn't know how to sell or break into a new market because I had never done it before. So we moved up to Green Bay, which is the nearest major health care market to where we were living. If I was going to go after this new market, I wanted to be there."

Rashelle was able to land a major new client despite her inexperience in a sales role. "It was challenging to take on this new business when I knew internally we weren't ready for it. When you have chaos inside the company and you're putting out fires all day, it's hard to go out and get new business; you know inside that you might not be able to deliver."

Rashelle told me they had hired several employees, including interpreters for new language populations. However, she admitted that she had difficulty making appropriate hires and sometimes granted promotions more for loyalty than for appropriate skill sets and experiences.

> *Growth and profitability aren't always linked. Is your organization's growth leading to greater profitability, or are you just working harder, for little return?*

Emotionally spent, Rashelle's tone dropped along with her shoulders. Bobbie nervously took a sip from her coffee and waited for what would come next.

"Connecting Cultures has arrived at this point without much planning. I'm sick of just having gut feelings," Rashelle said. "I would like to have the training to understand the business fully and manage it better. There's a lot of pressure knowing my business is supporting all of those families. Ultimately, the way I run this business will affect their primary breadwinners. I can't escape the fact that this is a business, and I need to look at it from a fiscal perspective. I'm going into a realm in which I'm very uncomfortable."

"What is it about Connecting Cultures that leaves you with a good feeling at the end of the day?" I asked. "I assume that beyond the day-to-day duties of getting your work done, you enjoy a level of satisfaction from running your business."

"You're right, Steve," she said, her tone immediately more upbeat than it had been seconds earlier. "Interpreting makes me proud. It makes me happy. It leaves me with a sense of knowing I did something good. When it comes to health care, everyone deserves to know what's going on with themselves or their family member. The clients are nervous and not thrilled to be there. You get into a rhythm where you're able to empower the doctors and patients to build lasting relationships, and to do it without having an interruption. It feels great to help with that process."

As I listened to Rashelle describe her business, the challenges they were facing, and her love for her work, I became excited. I could see that

Connecting Cultures was in a good position to succeed and that Rashelle was an ideal leader who was willing to move forward. "I look for three things in a business owner," I said, "and you've got them all, Rashelle. You have a passion for what you do; you have a sense of business competence; and you're open to learning how your organization can improve."

Like many small- and midsize-business owners, Rashelle grasped that she had something potentially big in her hands, but she didn't really know what to do with it. She was green in terms of business acumen, yet her passion and technical ability put her in a perfect position. More important, I could tell Rashelle knew she needed help and was ready to listen.

If the previous paragraph describes any part of you, the Stop Selling Vanilla Ice Cream process can offer all the help you need.

STRATEGY, TALENT, AND A PROCESS FOR OPTIMIZING BOTH

I always ask potential clients this question: Can you name one aspect of your business that strategy or talent wouldn't be able to address? I have never received a yes answer. Strategy and talent play such critical roles that it's virtually impossible to separate them from the overall performance of the business. That's why a focus on strategy and talent are at the core of the Stop Selling Vanilla Ice Cream process.

The process has several distinct components. Ideally, it is a multiyear process in which the focus gradually shifts from strategic development to tactical execution. The first year involves identifying and resolving the four to six biggest challenges the company faces.

For a moment, picture yourself and your management team in a boat on a small lake. The planning team's job is to get that boat going as fast as possible. At this point, however, you can't move very quickly because there are a number of large rocks—challenges—sticking out of the water. The process helps you identify and remove those rocks, leading to an organization that moves forward at a faster pace.

The next year, you can lower the water level of the lake to reveal a few more boulders. In subsequent years, you'll have to deal only with small pebbles, because the annual planning processes will have removed the large boulders. That's when an organization like Connecting Cultures might be in a position to acquire a company or expand into a major new market. But companies that try to make those moves before they're truly ready often fail — there are too many boulders blocking their path.

Here's another way of looking at it: Think of this process as preparing your ship for battle. We may not leave the harbor the first year, because we'd get our butts kicked. However, once we have the two key fundamentals — strategy and talent — in place, we will be able to leave the harbor, engage the competition, and win not only the battle but the war.

But the most critical year in the process is year one, so that is the focus of this book. I'll walk you through the four phases of the process: planning process preparation, building the team and strategy development preparation, strategy development, and strategy implementation. The figure shown on the following page maps the process and the specific steps along the way.

Phase One: Planning Process Preparation

Phase one is focused on building a team that can guide the boat across the lake. Each team member goes through a series of behavioral style assessments, which are handled online and are available to you with the code found in this book. Then the advisor, either internal or external, interviews each member in order to determine and understand the specific issues the team will need to address. The interviews provide all the content for the process, so that it is efficient and lean. It's important that you collect information from more than just the company owner or CEO, because others may have insight that person doesn't. The focus of the process from a talent evaluation perspective is to put people in positions where they bring the greatest value to the company. When people are in the best positions, they love their jobs and bring the greatest value to themselves and the company, especially when motivated by a pay-for-performance compensation plan.

PHASE ONE: PLANNING PROCESS PREPARATION

Select the planning team and advisor (Ch. 3)

Team completes preplanning questionnaire and behavioral assessments (Ch. 4)

Advisor interviews each planning team member (Ch. 5)

PHASE TWO: BUILDING THE TEAM AND STRATEGY DEVELOPMENT PREPARATION

Finalize current strategic challenges and complete team-building exercise (Ch. 6 and 7)

Conduct internal analysis and market analysis to create insights to prepare for strategy development (Ch. 8 and 9)

How to define your competence, strategy, and target markets (Ch. 10)

PHASE THREE: STRATEGY DEVELOPMENT

Finalize competence, define target markets, and perform competitive analysis (Ch. 11, 12, and 13)

Define tangible value of competence, evaluate brand strategy, and develop mission statement (Ch. 14)

Develop detailed strategic vision and the transitional issues to achieve it (Ch. 15 and 16)

PHASE FOUR: STRATEGY IMPLEMENTATION

Address organizational structure, skill sets, and new processes and systems to achieve vision (Ch. 17)

Develop annual company goals (Ch. 18)

Create detailed department plans (Ch. 19)

Establish organizational buy-in, plan execution meetings, and create a culture of accountability (Ch. 20)

STOP SELLING VANILLA ICE CREAM®

Phase Two: Building the Team and Strategy Development Preparation

Phase two is the strategy development part of the process and involves the entire planning team. Each team member will present his or her behavioral survey results to the rest of the team to build stronger team communication and cohesion. Then the team moves forward on an internal analysis of the company's values, strengths, weaknesses, and financials. The next step is an external analysis involving market research. As ideas come up about actions the company might take as part of its strategy, they're recorded and used later in the process to develop departmental plans. Completing the team development exercise and the internal and external analyses prepares the team (lays the foundation) to develop the optimal strategy.

Phase Three: Strategy Development

With this knowledge in hand, the planning team breaks into smaller homework teams and works for a period of time, usually a few weeks, on developing ideas for the company strategy. When the team comes back together, everybody should be ready to identify the organization's competence and its target markets; discuss the competition's areas of competence; brainstorm action plans to strengthen his or her own competence and make it tangible to the target market; develop a brand and positioning strategy; and create a mission statement and vision for the next two to three years. The outcome of phase three is the teams defining the key aspects of its strategy.

Phase Four: Strategy Implementation

The final phase is strategy implementation and departmental planning. You'll address organizational structure, skill set voids that need to be resolved (as identified by the talent management system), processes and communication systems you need to implement, and a business-planning calendar. You'll also develop company goals for the next year and methods of measurement. This leads naturally to a discussion of departmental plans, responsibilities, and time lines, including a brainstorming session on action plans to achieve each company goal.

All the strategic planning, discussion, and departmental planning in the world mean nothing unless an organization actually takes action to move its business forward. To ensure this takes place, the process includes a plan execution program that systematically guides an organization toward its vision. The monthly review process creates an ongoing culture of discipline and accountability in the organization.

CONNECTING CULTURES TAKES THE NEXT STEP

The second time I met with Bobbie and Rashelle, Bobbie was more forthcoming, took a more active role, and described her state of mind. "We started with just Rashelle, me, and a part-time Hmong interpreter. After we passed the first full year in business, we were thrilled. But we didn't know exactly what we were doing—we were just winging it. I don't think we truly understood the value of planning."

"You're not alone, Bobbie," I said. "That's why about 70 percent of companies never take the time to write an annual business plan. One of the main reasons to plan is to zero in on a specific competence that your company does better than anyone else in the markets in which you compete . . . to make sure you're not just selling vanilla ice cream."

As I continued to describe what Rashelle and Bobbie could expect from the coming process, I could sense excitement growing in both of them. Their eyes widened and they sat up straighter in their seats. I believe they began to see a light at the end of their tunnel: a light they hadn't known could exist only a few minutes earlier. They seemed to understand that the road may be long, but at least they would have a process to point them in the right direction.

This process would be intense and require an investment, but I told them that their return on investment would be significant.

Rashelle voiced concern that going through the process would require taking people away from their desks for planning meetings, and she wondered if the company would be able to handle it. I reminded Rashelle that the scenario she just described is exactly the reason for going through a strategic planning process as comprehensive as Stop Selling Vanilla Ice Cream. After all, if nothing ever changes . . . nothing will ever change. Rashelle knew this, but she still needed a dose of reinforcement.

"The process on which we're about to embark will help you create a singular, realistic vision that will guide all of your decisions," I said. "You'll develop a cohesive team that focuses on that vision, and you'll gain a competitive advantage over your competition."

"You'll find that we'll resolve the real issues—the big boulders in your lake—and call out the sacred cows that are holding you back. A successful strategy relegates your competition to a state of virtual irrelevance. It enables you to determine your organization's future before someone else does it for you. The end result goes beyond moving your business forward; it also generates measurable improvement in your personal lives."

In the kind of connection shared only by people who can finish each other's sentences, Bobbie and Rashelle glanced at each other with unmistakable expressions of excitement. "Let's do it," Rashelle said, and we were on our way.

The Scoop

1. What are the primary struggles of your company?

2. How would the combination of improving your strategy and talent help address these struggles?

3. Are you and your organization/division ready to Stop Selling Vanilla Ice Cream?

Action Plans to Complete the Process

☐ Download and finalize the strategic planning outline for your organization.

PHASE 1

PLANNING PROCESS PREPARATION

SELECTING THE PLANNING TEAM

The Stop Selling Vanilla Ice Cream process is democratic, not dictatorial—which is why it works so well. The goal is to get as many people as possible engaged in working "on" the business rather than simply working in it on day-to-day issues. The more minds focused on developing and implementing a differentiating strategy, the higher the likelihood of success.

In many ways, this first step of selecting a planning team and an advisor is the most important in the process. This group of individuals will transform into a high-performance team under the process leadership of the advisor. Who makes up the planning team will define the direction of the company and the success of the process.

These are the agenda items I discussed with Rashelle in our first official meeting. She was spared the challenge of identifying the right advisor because she was working with me and the SM Advisors team. However, she still had to identify her planning team, prepare the team members for their first responsibilities, and communicate the purpose of the process to the team and to the rest of the organization.

CHOOSING AN ADVISOR

The Stop Selling Vanilla Ice Cream process is the ideal vehicle to keep visionaries, like Rashelle, on track while providing welcomed structure for the more tactical members of the team. But it also requires a great deal of upfront work from the company leader, advisor, and the team. If you are the process advisor, prepare for your role to range from cheerleader to strategist to taskmaster. It's important to keep the process professional, honest, open, and informal, to ensure optimal participation. Because of the significance of the role, I use the term *advisor*, whether this person is an internal team member or an external consultant.

When deciding who should lead the process, know that the advisor must be trusted, approachable, and able to effectively read people in order to lead the team through honest and open dialogue. The advisor must extract information from the team members, regardless of how introverted or reluctant to address hard truths the members are. The behavioral assessment tools give the advisor the ability to do it. As you'll see throughout the book, introverted team members like Bobbie typically are not as forthcoming by nature, yet when they talk, their words can speak volumes. And even for extroverts like Rashelle, it's not always easy to admit to shortcomings in themselves or the business.

In this role, the advisor has private, confidential discussions with each team member. The advisor can never breach the confidentiality of team members before, during, or after the process. If the advisor doesn't maintain that confidentiality, it jeopardizes his or her credibility with the planning team, which would make him or her significantly less effective during the process. When I explain this concept to company leaders, they understand it and are fine with it. They simply want to know what the team is thinking, and the advisor plays a key role in providing that perspective within the bounds of credibility and confidentiality. If there is one golden rule the advisor must always follow, it is to maintain the anonymity of who said what.

It also helps to review the responsibilities of the advisor in order to make the best decision about who will lead the team through the process. First, gaining majority agreement on all strategic decisions and accomplishing every agenda item are the more obvious advisor tasks, as well as recording notes and preparing a written plan for the next meeting. In my role, I focus on keeping things simple and executable. Make sure that the advisor you choose can execute the process effectively.

In some companies, it might seem like the best person to lead the planning team and the process is the owner or CEO. Each organization has to weigh the advantages and disadvantages of both for your specific situation. The advantages of the owner or CEO leading the way are that the process is perceived as more important, the leader is typically more strategic/visionary, and the leader can channel the necessary resources and focus to drive the process to completion. However, there are disadvantages: the owner or CEO could overpower the process, could be more focused on the process rather than the plan, and may significantly influence and bias the plan. As a result, most of the plan might be developed by the leader with very little input or buy-in from the rest of the planning team or organization.

It is also important to understand the interaction between the advisor and the leader of the organization:

- ✔ The advisor and leader need to interact consistently and effectively throughout the process.

- ✔ The advisor and leader should read and discuss the book in advance to ensure they both have a clear understanding of the process. The process outline available at www.stopsellingvanillaicecream.com can be used to guide the process.

- ✔ The advisor needs to provide counsel and advice to the leader along the way on how to optimize the process and bring the team together. He or she can speak to specific issues but never identify who said what in confidential discussions with team members.

- ✔ The leader and advisor need to build a relationship of trust because they will be having candid conversations throughout the process. The leader will likely look to the advisor for coaching and recommendations throughout the process. And at times, the leader can be the cause of some of the challenges the business is facing; the advisor has to have the ability to be professionally candid with the leader and help him or her improve.

When I worked for EnzoPac, a food manufacturer, my first year we followed the strategic planning process on our own — without an advisor — and generated a decent amount of success. We didn't realize it at the time, but instead of being part of the process, we were driving the process. The second year we hired an external management consultant to lead the effort using all our methodologies. The difference in perspective generated a night-and-day improvement. Over the next five years, EnzoPac grew from a $5 million company to a $30 million company. This proves that executing the Stop Selling Vanilla Ice Cream process with an internal or external advisor will bring significantly more value than completing the process without one. So make the best decision possible and move forward.

> *Is there an individual in your organization who is trusted by his or her peers, maintains objectivity in tough situations, and is effective in terms of organization and process? This person might be right for the role of advisor.*

Like all other decisions, who should lead the Stop Selling Vanilla Ice Cream process should be thoroughly discussed with those who are going to take part in it. The advisor plays a critical role in the success of the process, so be thoughtful in deciding who it should be. Use the deliberation as a topic to galvanize the team and reinforce that this process is going to be effective.

IDENTIFYING THE TEAM BEST SUITED FOR THE CHALLENGE

Identifying the team members who will participate in the planning process is an important first step. "The planning team doesn't necessarily have to be the same group as the company's leadership team," I explained to Rashelle at our first official meeting. "It typically is, but on occasion, organizations will pull in other people. You have to decide who's going to bring value to the planning process and be a key player in implementing the strategy. Those are the kinds of people you want on the planning team."

Initially, I encourage companies to err on the side of having more employees involved in the planning process than fewer. This generates more strategic ideas and increases the buy-in from across the organization, because there are more ambassadors for the plan. However, I've worked with organizations that have had teams as small as a single person and as large as nineteen.

I believe it is important for each department to directly or indirectly have a representative on the team, with an optimal total of five to eight people.

Try to include strong strategic thinkers on the team. I worked with one CEO who believed only one out of ten people are able to think strategically. Most people are wired to think tactically, focusing only on what's on their desk that day. Because of this, it's common for business owners to struggle with who should be on the planning team.

Strategic thinkers can see the end result, the vision of a process. They can describe in vivid detail what they think the organization should look like at some point in the future, say in two or three years. It comes easy to them. Where they often struggle and need to rely on other team members is in developing the discipline necessary to execute their vision and make it a reality.

Difficult decisions arise when people in positions of responsibility or authority may not be appropriate fits for the planning team. Consider any collateral damage that might result from leaving certain individuals off the team and speak to them in advance of the process. They typically will understand the rationale for the makeup of the team. Not all members of the organization can participate. And let's be real: this process is going to entail a lot of extra work, and that is not what some employees may want right now. It is important to communicate with these individuals in advance in most cases, and show them the respect they deserve.

In some cases, the company leaders know exactly who should be on the team, but if not the advisor can provide helpful input. The leader may create an interviewing team first, and based on the interview and the answers to the questionnaire each potential team member completes before the first planning session, the advisor can identify which people will bring the greatest value to the process and provide a recommendation to the leader. When it is openly communicated from the start that the planning team will emerge from the interviewing team results, those who don't end up on the planning team are typically fine with it: they were happy to provide initial input on how the company can improve and strategies it should implement moving forward. Essentially, they felt heard and part of the process. What is it the advisor is looking for in planning team members? Those who can step back, look at the big picture of the company, and develop a vision for its long-term success.

Once the interviews are finalized and you select your planning team, you should avoid any further changes. In the first session, the team completes the "getting in their underwear" team development process, and once you have built that team you want them to complete the process together. The team development exercise brings a cohesiveness and unity that would be diminished if you brought a new team member on after the first session.

> *Who are the most strategic thinkers in your organization, including people in leadership positions and those who are not?*

Ideally, the planning team will not include members of your board of directors. Their job is to approve the plan and hold the management team accountable, while it's the management team's role to develop and execute the plan. However, nonprofit organizations occasionally will include board members in the planning process.

Finally, a few key points to keep in mind: You'll be sharing sensitive financial information, so make sure you can trust all team members to maintain confidentiality outside the group. If there are any future stars in the organization, you might want to include them on the team, or at least on the interview team.

After some discussion, Rashelle decided the Connecting Cultures planning team would include herself and Bobbie; Kyle, the company's relatively new operations manager; Eric, who handles information technology issues; and Erin, a longtime employee who serves as the company's training coordinator and quality director. Rashelle thought these individuals would offer a variety of behavior styles and job duties yet share an ability to see the bigger picture beyond their specific tactical area.

PREPARING THE TEAM

The momentum for initiating the Stop Selling Vanilla Ice Cream process was beginning to grow with Connecting Cultures' leadership. Now it was time to ramp up the level of engagement with the individual members of the planning team. The first homework assignment for team members calls for the completion of a set of interview questions and an online behavioral survey. But first each member of the team needs to understand the purpose of the process and that the organization is moving forward with it. They particularly need to grasp the importance of the initial steps toward building a powerful planning team.

"The quality of the preparation of your team, throughout the process, equates to the quality of the planning sessions, which equates to the quality of the strategy," I explained to Rashelle. "It's your job as the leader of the company to make sure that happens. It's easy for people to agree to get things done while they're sitting around a planning table, but it's just as easy for them to put things on the back burner once they return to their daily activities." Helping each team member understand the important role he or she might play on the planning team is a great way to improve participation and engagement.

ACTION PLAN REGISTER			
ACTION PLAN/ TASK DESCRIPTION	Owner	Due Date	Date Completed
Action plan item 1			
Action plan item 2			
Action plan item 3			

PLANNING PROCESS			
Planning Meeting 1			
Planning Meeting 2			
Planning Meeting 3			

Go to www.StopSellingVanillaIceCream.com to download the Action Plan Register template.

The action plan register on the previous page (available at www.stop sellingvanillaicecream.com) is the most simple and effective tool the team members will use, and it's the first step in creating accountability. It keeps all planning team members informed of their responsibilities — their action plans to complete for the next step in the process. After each session the action plan register is updated, and then it's reviewed at the beginning of the next session to ensure everyone completed his or her assigned tasks. The register inherently creates clear accountability: when an action plan is written down with somebody's name and a completion date next to it, it almost always gets done. An easy-to-use reference, the register also can serve as the agenda for the next meeting.

While the action plan register is a fantastic way to keep the team accountable throughout the process, when a team is first chosen, the leader also needs to explain the process and its purpose to team members. Rashelle first met with key people in the company who would not be part of the planning team to explain the purpose of the efforts and to explain the makeup of the planning team. Those meetings went well. She then met with each team member to explain why and how the process would be implemented and her expectations for the team. After those initial meetings, Rashelle and I met with the whole team to review the entire process and the action plan register to launch the first three steps of the process— the interview questionnaire, the online survey, and the interview.

One of my golden rules of strategic planning is you do not create content during planning sessions—you make decisions regarding the content. I made this point with Connecting Cultures' planning team during our first meeting. I wanted to help them understand the purpose of the early steps, particularly the interview, and the importance of the action plans— the homework—assigned to them throughout the process. The interview questionnaire, behavioral assessments, and interviews are not a system for judging employees. They are a system for gathering information, or content, on the company so that the planning sessions can be focused on developing the most impactful plan based on that information.

I gave each team member a list of interview questions (you can download a template at www.stopsellingvanillaicecream.com) to complete before our face-to-face interview. As you can see, questions range from general ones about job duties and percentage of time spent on primary tasks to opinions about the organization's strengths, weaknesses, and major challenges. More specific questions probe into opinions regarding the direction the company is taking or should be taking, and any frustrations the individual is feeling. This questionnaire and the interview enable the advisor to get a grasp on possible strategic issues, general morale, and personal communication styles.

PRE-PLANNING QUESTIONNAIRE

Completed by _____
Date _____

1. Tell me about your job in terms of where you spend your time (in percentages). Supply your job description.

2. Have you ever taken part in a strategic planning process? If yes, how did it go?

3. What are your personal expectations from this planning process?

4. What do you perceive to be the major strengths and weaknesses of the company?
   Strengths: _____
   Weaknesses: _____

5. a) What market research information do we need to collect and study to make the most informed strategic decisions? For example, market share, industry growth, effect by baby boomers, etc.
   b) What relevant trends are developing in the world/state/region/ industry right now?

6. a) Does the company have a clearly defined strategy?
   b) What is it?
   c) Does the strategy need to be changed? Why?

7. What is the competence of the company? (A competence is what the company does best or should be doing better than anyone else in the markets in which it competes. It is why your customers buy

or should buy from you over the competition.)

8. What do you feel are the major strategic issues and sacred cows (sensitive issues) that need to be resolved?

9. List your top two to three competitors and describe what you think their strengths, weaknesses, and strategies are.

Competitor	Strengths	Weaknesses	Strategy/Competence

10. What are the greatest opportunities (external) for your company? For example, new services, geographic areas, markets, target markets, etc.

11. What is your vision for the company? In your opinion, what should the organization look like in three years (size, expertise, products, services, etc.)? How do you see yourself being a part of it?

12. Are their any skill set voids in your company? Are you missing key skills to accomplish your vision?

13. What is your greatest frustration in your current position?

14. In your opinion, what should the major two or three company goals be for the next twelve months?

15. What could be major obstacles for new strategy implementation? What could be done to improve the execution of the plan?

Go to www.StopSellingVanillaIceCream.com to download the Interview Questionnaire template.

Completing the questionnaire prior to the interview allows the team members to think through their answers. Having these written answers to the questions allows the advisor to consolidate information and feedback to facilitate the most effective process. For example, the advisor consolidates all the company weaknesses identified by the team members during the interviews. Then during the discussion of the internal analysis later in the process, the team can make decisions on and discuss how to resolve the weaknesses derived from the interviews, rather than wasting time trying to come up with the weaknesses during the session. Again, the information is consolidated into one document, so the individual responses remain anonymous.

I ask that team members bring their completed forms to the face-to-face interviews and not discuss their answers with anyone. I want them to feel confident that their answers will remain confidential. That is why it is critical to select the right advisor for the process. It's important for each member to be completely forthcoming, without fear of consequences. There are no right or wrong answers. The point is to dig into their perspective of where the organization has come from and where they believe it should go, to pinpoint the rocks in the water—the strategic challenges that are commonly identified by virtually every team member.

The combination of the assessments and interviews gives the advisor all the content he or she needs to build the optimum planning process that will resolve your company's specific strategic challenges.

KEEPING THE WHOLE ORGANIZATION IN THE LOOP

Up to this point, Connecting Cultures' decision to pursue improvement through the Stop Selling Vanilla Ice Cream process had been discussed at the management level, but the rest of the organization was not yet in the loop. That needed to change immediately.

"We can't be quiet about this process until we present the plan to the company, and then expect them to believe us," Bobbie said. "We have to keep them informed along the way."

"You're absolutely right," I said. "It's imperative that the rest of the organization feels the same level of excitement that you do, even if they're not involved in the actual strategic portion of the process. They will see the results of this process, and it will be important for them to buy into what the planning team presents. They need to know this process isn't about downsizing; it's about growth."

"I think we absolutely need to send something out," Rashelle said. "When we're developing and driving where the company is going, communication needs to come from us. We just need to let them know we're working on designing the future of our organization to ensure long-term competitiveness."

"Be sure to communicate that they will receive regular updates and that their input is valuable," I reminded her.

The mode of communication depends on the culture and structure of the organization. Some organizations like to communicate more in person while others rely on technology. Rashelle chose to write an e-mail because Connecting Cultures has interpreters all over the state who rarely come into the office. After some input from me, here is the e-mail she sent out to the company:

Hello to you all!

I want to make you aware that several members of the Connecting Cultures team will be unavailable for a few days during the course of the next couple of months. We will be holding strategic planning meetings with Steve Van Remortel at SM Advisors to develop the next phase of our company's growth. Connecting Cultures has seen consistent growth over the last ten years, and we will continue that growth with a clear plan that will have measurable outcomes.

One of the things that came from our preliminary interviews was our need to better communicate with all of you. As we travel through this process, we will be providing regular updates as to our progress and how we're working to build a stronger future for Connecting Cultures. We will also be looking for more and more of your input as we get deeper into the process.

As is customary with Steve, we will come away from each meeting with homework leading up to our next planning session. Those homework assignments will include ideas on how to be different and better than our competition, as well as our vision of what we want the company to look like in two to three years.

We are very excited about this process and anticipate great things. If you have any questions or comments regarding the work we're doing, please feel free to discuss them with one of us. As SM Advisors says, "Those Who Plan—PROFIT!"

Thank you in advance for your time and patience.

Rashelle

"Assuming you're ready to get started, Rashelle, let's have your team take the assessments and fill out their interview questionnaires, and then I'll schedule everyone for their interviews," I said.

"We're as ready as we'll ever be," Rashelle replied. "There may never be a perfect time to devote resources to a project like this, but it's something we have to do if we're ever going to get to the next level."

The Scoop

1. Is there a person in your organization who could objectively and effectively lead a change process like the one I'm describing? If not, is there an advisor you know or you've worked with in the past who might be a good candidate for leading the process?

2. Which leaders or managers in your organization may not be ideal for the planning team? How will you address that with them?

3. How will you get the planning team excited and energized about the process? How will you reassure them that the assessments and interviews are to collect content and are not opportunities to judge their work or their opinions?

4. How will you keep your organization in the loop? How will you communicate with all employees?

Action Plans to Complete the Process

- ☐ Select an advisor.

- ☐ Define who is on the interviewing and/or planning team. ·

- ☐ Talk to those individuals who are not on the planning team.

- ☐ Finalize the interview questionnaire and distribute it to the planning team.

- ☐ Set the interviewing schedule with the advisor.

- ☐ Notify the organization of the planning process and its objectives.

OPTIMIZING YOUR TALENT

It is extremely helpful to the overall Stop Selling Vanilla Ice Cream process—and any company's future success—to gain a better understanding of the team members' individual strengths and behavior styles.

"What do behavioral assessments have to do with strategic planning?" Rashelle challenged. "It's not like it will affect what our competence should be, will it?"

"Oh, you'd be surprised," I replied with a smile. "You'll learn something about yourself and every person in that room. We'll use the behavioral assessments as the foundation of individual development plans after completing the strategic planning process."

Remember, there isn't one aspect of your business that strategy or talent can't address. The Talent Management System ties together these two critical elements of the process. It focuses on identifying, selecting, hiring, developing, and retaining the talent required to deliver your competence and strategy, and it will generate numerous benefits for the organization:

✔ **INCREASED PROFITABILITY**—The number one factor leading to organizational success is a skill set–aligned, high-performance team that succeeds regardless of the challenges it faces. Profitability increases because the system eliminates costly hiring mistakes that average three to five times annual salary, reduces hiring costs (hiring, training, turnover), increases retention of the right talent, and increases productivity.

✔ **INCREASED COMPANY-WIDE COMMUNICATION**—Individuals who understand the variety of behavioral styles people exhibit are more effective in communicating and working with other people.

✔ **IMPROVED TEAM PERFORMANCE**—The team development process cultivates the characteristics of a high-performance team. It focuses on the strengths of the team and creates awareness of weaknesses and tendencies with the goal of improving communication and identifying gaps to fill. One of my favorite experiences as an advisor is watching the team become a "true" team right in front of my eyes.

✔ **BETTER DECISION MAKING**—A balanced team considers all dimensions of a decision, which ultimately leads to the best decision for the organization.

✔ **WORLD-CLASS SELECTION PROCESS**—The Talent Management System creates a detailed selection process that dramatically increases the accuracy and confidence of your hires. Interviews with specific strategies for each candidate are more productive and take less time because you know the candidate through the behavioral tools and their resume before you ever meet him or her.

✔ **SKILL SET ALIGNMENT**—This involves matching the natural talents of the individual to the requirements of the position. It finds the best person for each seat on the bus.

✔ **STRATEGIC FOCUS**—The system minimizes people issues, which enables leadership at all levels to work more "on" the business rather than in the business. This generates continuous improvement and helps the organization do more with less.

The objective of the Talent Management System is to provide a more comprehensive picture of individual and general team tendencies so we can communicate more effectively and build the team to achieve your dream.

There are three parts of the assessment: behavioral style, workplace motivators, and a soft skills inventory. Behavioral styles measure how you work, while workplace motivators provide a glimpse at why you work. And soft skills are what help you get things done. (At the end of the chapter you'll find details on how to order your complimentary behavioral assessment.)

The assessment results create a starting point for open discussions about the strengths, communication styles, and growth opportunities of each individual, the planning team, and the business as a whole. The assessments help team members understand how they can bring the greatest value to the organization and to their own individual development. Combined with the interview questionnaire described in the previous chapter, the assessments build the foundation for attacking the organizational strategy component of the process. Having the right talent in the right positions is a critical element to the long-term success of your company.

From a short-term perspective, the assessments also help the advisor understand what to expect from each planning team member and from the team as a whole. The assessments reveal which team members will try to control a meeting or a discussion, and which members will be most comfortable staying in the background. The latter will need encouragement to share their opinions. The Talent Management System also produces two team wheels from the completed assessments, illustrating at a glance how individual workplace behaviors and motivators disperse across the spectrum of possible style types.

BEHAVIORAL STYLES: DISC

The behavioral style component of the Talent Management System measures how an individual responds to various situations. It is called the DISC behavioral profile. The major developer of the DISC language was Dr. William Moulton Marston in the early 1900s. DISC is an acronym for Dominance, Influence, Steadiness, and Compliance. These are the four primary behavior modes, and each is scored on a scale of 1 to 100, with 100 being the high end and 1 the low for that characteristic. High or low doesn't necessarily translate into "strong" or "weak," since one can argue for the relative strength of different types of behaviors.

"A common misperception of the behavioral assessments is that they're a personality profile," I told Rashelle. "That's like referring to the space shuttle as a glider. Unlike most systems, which divide people into general groups with shared traits, this system delves deeply into an individual's thought processes to reveal not only his or her natural style of behavior but also the style he or she adapts to in the workplace. Your natural style is determined by about age seven and typically won't change dramatically for the rest of your life. It's who you are and how you're wired. DISC is an assessment, not a test, and there is nothing right or wrong about the results."

D = Dominance (How you respond to problems and challenges)

A low number on the Dominance bar suggests a more reflective and laid-back response to challenges, while a high number reflects a more aggressive response.[1] People with high D assessment scores tend to be decisive and forceful. I call them the gas pedals of the organization. They are ambitious, independent, and confident, with a high desire to win. They're good problem solvers who are bottom-line oriented. High Ds typically have very active minds that generate a lot of creative and visionary ideas, but they may lose interest in projects quickly after the initial challenge fades. They can have a tendency to lack tact and listen poorly, dominating others and overstepping authority. High Ds typically have a shorter wick on their temper and may show anger more than other styles.

"The strong D behavioral style may seem rather harsh to the lower Ds with whom the strong Ds interact," I said. "Their value to a team comes in their ability to initiate activity, challenge the status quo, and have a

---

1. The description of the DISC assessment is synopsized from *The Universal Language DISC: A Reference Manual* by Bill J. Bonnstetter and Judy Suiter (Target Training International, 2004) and various training programs.

forward-looking perspective with an innovative mind-set. Donald Trump is an example of this type of person. People with low D scores tend to take a more cautious approach and are conservative by nature. They are more agreeable and peaceful."

I = Influence (How you influence others to your point of view)

The Influence bar displays an introverted style on the low end and an extroverted style on the high end. Rashelle is a prime example of someone with a high I assessment score. People with high I scores tend to influence others with their verbal skills and warmth. They love to interact and want people to like them. They're very trusting and optimistic. Their behavioral strengths include an ability to be conversational, open-minded, and convincing and enthusiastic while being personable. They may rely too much on verbal communication and not pay enough attention to details. They often plan time poorly and act impulsively, don't always listen well, rely more on emotion than logic, and have a tendency to trust indiscriminately. Their problem-solving approach is to be appeasing.

"Their value to the team lies in their optimism and enthusiasm, creative problem solving, and ability to motivate others toward goals," I noted. "They have a positive sense of humor and negotiate conflict well, verbalizing with articulateness. Oprah Winfrey is an example of this type of person."

"That sounds like me," Rashelle said. "Sometimes those traits work in my favor, and sometimes they don't."

People with low I scores tend to be more reflective, calculating, and introverted, and they influence more with logic and facts. They typically are very skeptical of people at first.

S = Steadiness (How you respond to the pace of the environment)

The Steadiness bar reveals a fast-paced comfort zone on the low end and a more methodical approach on the high end. People with high S assessment scores tend to listen well to others and like to serve. They prefer to focus on one or two things at a time. They're slow to change and appreciate closure, appearing relaxed, calm, patient, and loyal. Their strengths lie in their team focus, ability to be patient and empathetic, and strong logical-thinking skills while being driven to task closure.

"High S people sound like they would be a valuable part of a team," Bobbie said.

"They are," I responded, "but like all of the style high scorers, they have their limitations. These individuals appear to have little sense of urgency, internalize others' comments, and are resistant to change. They have a tendency to not tell you what they're thinking. They don't delegate as much as they could and tend to be too people-focused. Their approach to problem solving is observing, reflecting, and avoiding. Their value to the team centers on the ability to be a dependable team worker, putting in effort for a leader or a cause.

"They're great listeners, good at reconciling factions and calming people down. They finish what they start and favor loyal, long-term relationships. Laura Bush is an example of this type of person. People with low S scores tend to be impatient, impulsive, and restless. They are comfortable having multiple balls in the air and prefer a very fast-paced work environment."

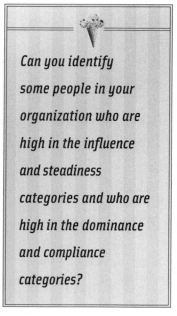

Can you identify some people in your organization who are high in the influence and steadiness categories and who are high in the dominance and compliance categories?

C = Compliance (How you respond to rules and systems)

A low number on the Compliance bar shows low attention to detail, while a high result predictably indicates high attention to detail or quality. People with high C assessment scores tend to be precise, analytical, and systems oriented. They have a high attention to detail and love collecting data. They are thinkers and rule followers, often effective questioners with a focus on quality. "Their limitations include being worrisome and exacting, and they establish high standards that often lead to them being harsh on themselves and others," I explained. "They tend to get lost in the details and avoid risk. They evaluate, plan, and investigate, coming across to others as highly critical. Their value to the team lies in their ability to be objective thinkers who maintain high standards. They're conscientious and diplomatic, often asking the right questions. They're task-oriented, feeling most comfortable clarifying, gathering information, criticizing, and testing. Albert Einstein is an example of this type of person. People with low C scores can be independent and stubborn, avoid detail work, and are tolerant of risk."

"There are a lot of variables in those assessment combinations," Rashelle noted. "Are there any general observations you can make that can simplify things a little bit?"

"People with assessment scores that are higher in the I and S categories tend to be more people-oriented, while the high D and high C people tend to be more task- or results-oriented."

"You mentioned natural and adaptive styles. What does that mean?" Rashelle asked.

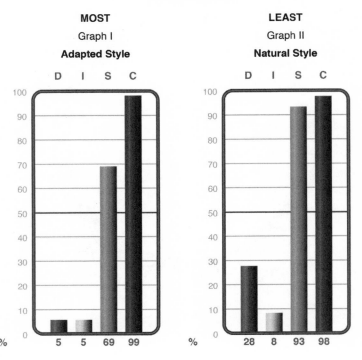

DISC EXAMPLE

MOST	LEAST
Graph I	Graph II
Adapted Style	**Natural Style**

D	I	S	C		D	I	S	C
% 5	5	69	99		% 28	8	93	98

"Some people act pretty much the same at home as they do at work, while others switch gears and adapt to different behavioral traits to be successful in their position. This adaption can be a conscious effort made by the individual, but in many cases it's subconscious. In other words, people don't realize they are adapting. Adaption requires a lot of energy and can cause a great deal of stress and fatigue over the long term. Imagine an introvert having to be the point person on sales calls or an extrovert having to sit in a cubicle all day. It can lead to job discontent and even costly personnel turnover if the person leaves the organization. Any behavioral style can be successful in any position, but significant adaption can take a lot of energy and may cause stress for that individual."

"That will be even more interesting to see," Rashelle noted. "It might be the source of some of our issues."

The Talent Management System plots the results of team members' DISC assessments on a Behavioral Style Team Wheel, shown here, providing a visual depiction of where each member resides on the behavioral

BEHAVIORAL STYLE TEAM WHEEL

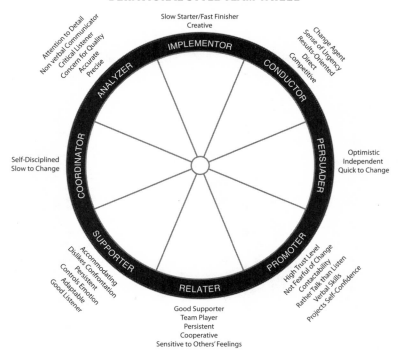

spectrum. For planning teams, the wheel maps both the natural and adaptive styles of each team member. A balanced team will have natural styles evenly distributed around the wheel.

"The Behavioral Style Team Wheel is important because it clearly illustrates the balance of the team and identifies possible skill set voids," I explained. "It also illustrates significant adaption by any team member, and it helps you understand each other's styles and perspectives while ideally coming to value them."

A balanced assortment of behavioral styles on the planning team benefits the organization by providing multiple perspectives to a decision or opportunity. If everyone looks at a problem from the same perspective, chances are good the organization will miss out on some viable alternatives. Achieving a balance of behavioral types around the team wheel is an important factor in creating a high-performing team.

"For instance, D and C behavior styles may not consider the people side of an issue and thus display little empathy for those affected," I explained to Rashelle. "Instituting a new work shift schedule may make sense on a production level, for example, but it would negatively impact workers' personal lives. Conversely, the I and S people may never consider making such a change because of the impact on workers, regardless of how much sense it makes from a business perspective. Both sides of the issue deserve consideration, which leads to the best decision. The best chance of that occurring would be with multiple behavior styles present on the planning team."

"It will be interesting to see where our planning team members fall on the wheel," Bobbie said. "I can already make some guesses. I think you'll find our behavior styles will be one extreme or the other, with few middle-of-the-road scores."

"It's perfectly okay if that's the case," I said. "The key to success is leveraging the strengths of each individual, and the behavior assessment reports will help us do just that."

WORKPLACE MOTIVATORS

The second set of results from the Talent Management System illustrates the six basic workplace motivators that each of us possesses. These are the drivers behind our actions and decisions at work. They're what motivate us to act the way we do. Understanding the workplace motivators for planning team members is as important as understanding their behavioral styles.

Unlike the behavioral style components, which stay relatively unchanged from age seven, our workplace motivators can change as our life circumstances change. Here are the six workplace motivators:

- ✔ **THEORETICAL**—The primary driver is the discovery of knowledge and an appetite for learning. The primary motivation is to learn.

- ✔ **UTILITARIAN**—Money is a big motivator. A person with a high score has a passion to efficiently gain return on investment of time, resources, and money.

- ✔ **AESTHETIC**—The primary driver for these individuals is form and harmony. A high score indicates a desire for balance and unity. They value the creative side of life (music, arts, etc.). They appreciate the beauty in things and how visually appealing the environment is. They have a primary interest in the artistic episodes of life.

- ✔ **SOCIAL**—Those with high scores here gain satisfaction from helping people and eliminating conflict.

- ✔ **INDIVIDUALISTIC**—The primary interest is power and winning, however the individual defines it. A high score indicates a passion to achieve position and then to use that position to influence others and get ahead in the world.

- ✔ **TRADITIONAL**—This driver measures an individual's desire for a system of living. A strong tendency indicates a passion to pursue higher meaning in life through a defined system of living, principles, faith, or set traditions. These individuals appreciate rules and feel most comfortable abiding by them. Their actions and decisions are driven by that system of living.

Employers and employees can benefit from understanding these six motivators. Certain positions within an organization lend themselves to individuals with strong tendencies in specific areas. For example, salespeople should be strong in Utilitarian, while quality directors often score high on the Traditional scale. Knowing what motivates an employee from the start can eliminate time wasted in a position he or she simply doesn't enjoy. Likewise, matching an employee's job duties more closely to what motivates him or her to perform at high levels makes for a more engaged and satisfied team member.

"What if the report shows we're all motivated the same way?" Rashelle asked. "I don't think we are, but I'm curious."

"The chances of that are very slim, simply because people are different," I said. "However, we may find that more than one person shows a strong tendency in the same areas. Remember these assessments measure many behavioral and motivational variables, so while two people may be similar in one way, they likely will be different in other ways.

WORKPLACE MOTIVATORS GRAPH EXAMPLE

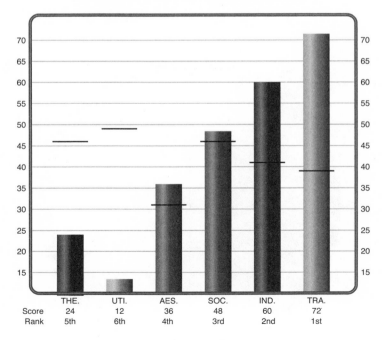

	THE.	UTI.	AES.	SOC.	IND.	TRA.
Score	24	12	36	48	60	72
Rank	5th	6th	4th	3rd	2nd	1st

—— national mean

"High and low motivation scores are equally important, since they indicate a strong or low level of passion in a particular category. Common sense tells us an unmotivated team member won't be very productive and isn't likely to remain with the organization for long, at least not in the current position," I continued. "Satisfying each team member's top motivators is critical in that it helps ensure he or she enjoys work and has a high level of job satisfaction and loyalty."

> *Do you believe you understand what motivates each of the people on your leadership team, or in your organization?*

The Workplace Motivators Team Wheel shown below shows the primary and secondary motivators of each team member. The wheel clearly illustrates what motivates each person on the team and enables the company to implement systems that ensure each individual remains motivated and engaged. Accurate motivational systems help organizations maximize employee retention.

WORKPLACE MOTIVATORS TEAM WHEEL

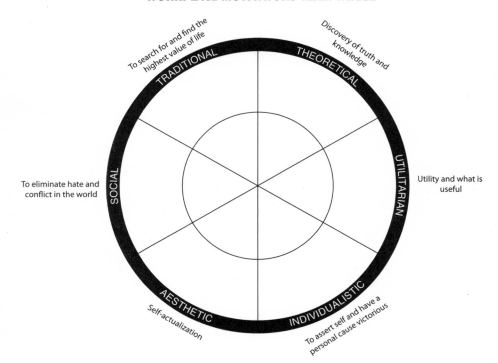

The outside ring of the wheel represents an individual's No. 1 motivator, and the inside ring represents his or her No. 2 motivator. While not as important as having a balance of behavioral styles, it's important for the organization to recognize and satisfy the motivating factors present on the team.

"We'll talk about some of the key points we can take out of this session, not only for the individuals, but also for the team," I told Rashelle. "This is about getting the right people in the right positions. By the time we're done, you'll know how to communicate with different behavioral styles much more effectively than you do now."

PERSONAL TALENT SKILLS INVENTORY/SOFT SKILLS INDICATOR

The third component of the Talent Management System is the Soft Skills Indicator, which measures your clarity and understanding of the world and yourself. Where you have high clarity and understanding you have a higher capacity for soft skills. For example, if you have high clarity and understanding of other people, you have the capacity for high soft skills when it comes to people. Those soft skills could include interpersonal skills, evaluating others, empathy, and so on. The higher your score on each factor, the higher the soft skills capacity you'll have in that particular factor.

The Soft Skills Indicator measures the clarity and understanding a person has in regard to external systems (world view) and internal systems (self view).

The three external factors (your world view) measured in the Soft Skills Indicator are:

✔ Understanding others

✔ Practical thinking

✔ Systems judgment

The three internal factors (your self view) are:

✔ Sense of self

✔ Role awareness .

✔ Self-direction

The category with the highest score is the anchor point, from which the person interprets reality. The category with the lowest score is the factor for which the individual has the lowest clarity, often a good starting point for a development plan. One objective of the development plan is to increase the clarity for the individual, which leads to the capacity for stronger soft skills in that area. The survey also measures your bias toward each factor, whether you undervalue, overvalue, or feel neutral about each factor.

PERSONAL TALENT SKILLS INVENTORY/SOFT SKILLS INDICATOR EXAMPLE

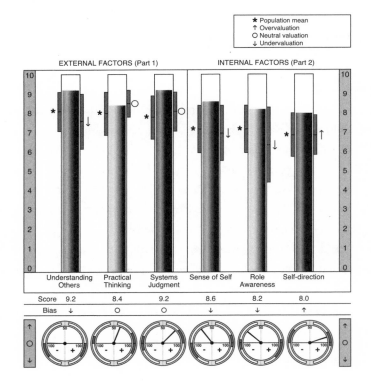

"It seems to me that these are all important skills," Rashelle said to me when I explained the tool. "Shouldn't everybody place high value on them?"

"Undervaluing or overvaluing isn't necessarily a bad thing or a good thing; it just provides one more insight into how you think. The Soft Skills Indicator is one of the most effective coaching and development tools in the marketplace today. Increasing an individual's soft skills often takes her from being an average-performing to a high-performing team member. The team members are often blown away by the accuracy of the assessments, and the level of candor from team members during discussion of their Soft Skills Indicator scores is incredible."

At www.stopsellingvanillaicecream.com, you can download a detailed guide for reviewing and interpreting the assessment results.

USING THE TALENT MANAGEMENT SYSTEM FOR BETTER HIRING

Aligning an employee's soft skills, behavior style, and motivation within the company leads to increased job satisfaction, reduced turnover, enormous cost savings, higher productivity, and increased profits. Organizations typically hire people for the hard skills required for a specific job (for example, accounting skills), but often fire them for a lack of soft skills (for example, inability to lead others). By the time an organization goes through the interview process with a candidate, hires him, goes through the pain of realizing he's not working out, and then suffers through the process of termination so they can start the interview process all over again, turnover becomes very expensive. It can be three to five times the annual compensation for the position.

"We've seen that happen, and it's a tremendous stress for everyone involved," Rashelle said. "Not only is that person doing the job poorly, but he or she also takes me away from my job because I have to deal with the issues created."

"Exactly," I said. "Especially in a smaller organization like yours, the ripple effects of a bad hire can multiply quickly."

A benchmarking process can help organizations clearly identify what a top performer looks like in each position; benchmarks are set in education, experience, behaviors, values, task preferences, and soft skills. The process provides clarity and awareness about each job function, enabling the organization to build a skill set–aligned team and hire the right people the first time. Once the benchmark is completed, you can compare the assessments of all candidates against the benchmark through a gap report, which shows where each candidate has gaps against the benchmark. There is no perfect candidate, so all candidates will have gaps. The question to ask is, are the gaps in the most critical areas of the benchmark? Benchmarking not only increases the chances of hiring the right person, it also creates the foundation for an individual development plan for the new hire to address potential growth opportunities, based on the gap analysis.

Benchmarking also creates a line of communication that leads to candid dialogue regarding facts rather than opinion. That is especially helpful in the hiring process, where the human resources and leadership teams can eliminate potential biases and ensure they evaluate candidates using the same standards. A thorough benchmarking process and dedicated follow-up will enable your organization to make more accurate hiring decisions, which will lead to a higher performing team with lower turnover and fewer associated costs.

Do you currently map or benchmark the behavioral style, motivators, and soft skills necessary to be successful in each position in your company?

"Team members will see their Talent Management System personal assessment results within the next few weeks," I told Rashelle when I was done explaining the three components. "First, we'll need to schedule individual meetings to go over the pre-planning questionnaire responses and each person's assessment results. Later, each team member will present their results to the group as part of a team development exercise in the first team session."

"Part of me wants to see my results and part of me would rather not," Rashelle said. "But I can see where having a better understanding of what makes each of us tick would be helpful in creating a more efficient team."

"Rashelle, imagine the advantage of knowing the soft skills of one of your employees or job candidates, and being able to match those skills to job duties that put that person in the best position to succeed," I said, taking note of her widening eyes.

"That would be incredibly valuable for us," Rashelle replied. "I'm not convinced we have all of our pieces positioned correctly in the puzzle, myself included. I can't wait to see our results."

The Scoop

1. How effective is your current talent management process? How would your company benefit from implementing a more rigorous talent management system?

2. What value do you think you would gain by understanding your behavioral style, workplace motivators, and soft skills, and those of each member of your team?

3. What was the last hiring mistake you made? How can your organization improve its hiring process by using behavioral science to make the right hire the first time?

Action Plans to Complete the Process

☐ Have each member of the planning team take the behavioral assessments in preparation for the interview and debriefing with the advisor.

☐ Order your complimentary assessment.

☐ Complete the preplanning questionnaire.

How to Order Your Complimentary Assessment

To help you implement the Stop Selling Vanilla Ice Cream process in your organization, we are excited to offer you a complimentary assessment as the owner of this book. Recognizing the depth and volume of information that the assessments provide, we have developed a thoughtful and responsible process that provides you with the information you need to understand and apply your assessment results to optimize your performance and that of your organization. The complimentary assessment includes your Behavioral Style (DISC), Workplace Motivators, and Soft Skills Indicator. These assessments are scientifically validated to be 85 percent to 90 percent accurate. I have used them thousands of times and can vouch that they enrich people's lives.

The results of the Behavioral Style and Workplace Motivators assessments, particularly given the depth of the accompanying thirty-plus page report and the "how to interpret" guidance it offers, are fairly easy to process. Consequently, we will provide you the Behavioral Style and Personal Motivators results immediately following completion of the assessments. They offer incredibly valuable information and insight while allowing you to implement the Stop Selling Vanilla Ice Cream process. The Soft Skills Indicator results, however, are more complex but enlightening because they are rooted in behavioral science. As a result, accurate interpretation requires training, certification, and debriefing experience. To take full advantage of this offer and to optimize your planning process and strategy and talent in your organization, the Soft Skills Indicator results are essential. To receive the results of the Soft Skills portion of the assessment, we require that you schedule a forty-five minute, one-on-one debrief with a certified talent development advisor. During this debrief, via phone or Skype, the advisor will thoroughly explain your assessment results (including the Soft Skills Indicator), answer any questions you have, and define several development opportunities for you to optimize your professional and team performance. To cover our costs of a certified professional analyst, there is a nominal charge of $95, paid in advance of the debrief.

Keep in mind that the other detailed assessment results are entirely FREE and still allow you to complete the Stop Selling Vanilla Ice Cream process in your company. The debrief is simply an option to optimize your planning process. It is a valuable coaching session that will lead to a development plan for you and a strategic and talent management process for your organization. Our sincere intent with this process is to provide you the most advanced and accurate assessments and debriefing to optimize your performance as well as your team and organization. It would be professionally irresponsible for us to put your Soft Skills Indicator results out there without providing a certified debriefing. As a business owner and leader myself, I can say with confidence that this is the most cost-effective approach for you to implement a process that optimizes the strategy and talent for your organization.

Remember the track record of the Stop Selling Vanilla Ice Cream process—over 90 percent of companies increase sales and profits in their first

year after implementing the process with SM Advisors. You can c.
that same level of success because you now have the process and assess
ments to do it. Those who plan, profit!

To get started on your assessments, follow these steps:

1. Go to www.stopsellingvanillaicecream.com/free-assessment-
   request and enter your personal assessment code of 51234 and your
   e-mail address. Upon receipt of your request, we will send you a
   link that you will use to take your assessments.

2. Follow the instructions carefully in completing the survey.

3. Recognizing the confidentiality and depth of the results, we follow
   a strict protocol in delivering the assessment results to you, which
   is as follows:

   a) Your assessment results will be shared only with you.

   b) We will e-mail you your Behavioral Style and Workplace Moti-
      vators report along with our "How to read the assessments"
      packet.

   c) We will provide a link for you to set up your assessment debrief-
      ing if you choose to do so.

You can discover more information on how to implement the fundamentals of strategy and talent into your organization at www.stop
sellingvanillaicecream.com and www.smadvisors.com. You can speak to a
member of our team at 920-884-8442.

PLANNING TEAM INTERVIEWS

Interviews are one of the biggest process steps for the advisor. After all the interviews are complete, you'll have a very good idea as to where challenges and opportunities exist for the organization. The interviews and assessment results provide the content to build the entire planning process. They set the stage for everything that follows, from how to leverage available skill sets and behavioral styles to identifying organizational strengths and planning the future direction. This approach gets all the real issues on the table, which allows the planning process to be very efficient and resolves the challenges holding the organization back.

The interviews provide a cross-functional, honest appraisal of the state of the organization from the perspective of each team member. The interviews typically bring up a number of items that are worthy of discussion with the planning team. The goal is to identify those four to six strategic challenges, the boulders in the lake, that are limiting the company's potential. But it's also an opportunity to discover a host of other smaller unresolved issues or ideas that can be addressed throughout the process.

As you follow the Connecting Cultures planning team's journey, it is important that you gain a clear picture of these individuals so you can understand how an organization moves through the Stop Selling Vanilla

Ice Cream process. You also may recognize some of the issues that challenge this team in your own organization.

PLANNING AND STRUCTURING THE INTERVIEWS

Kyle was a relatively new hire as Connecting Cultures' operations manager. His addition came about as Rashelle began to notice a growing inability to tend to day-to-day operations while creating the growth she desired. Because he was somewhat new, I was looking forward to discussing his perspectives on the company. And his behavioral assessments told me that if we didn't find a way for Kyle to leverage his natural behavioral style at work, he might burn out.

While planning team meetings are held off-site, the interviews with the Connecting Cultures team members would take place on-site in a conference room. Since this is the first engagement with the process for most of these individuals, it's important to create a comfortable environment and minimize some of their anxiety. We start off with a quick overview of what to expect from the day's proceedings, kind of a, "Here's why we do these interviews, now give me everything you've got." I tell them we'll spend the first hour going through their completed questionnaire, and the second hour reviewing their behavioral assessment results and discussing individual growth opportunities. I emphasize the anonymity of their comments—and I make sure to maintain that anonymity in any comments I share with the planning team or with company leaders. As mentioned in chapter 3, this is a critical consideration in deciding who will facilitate the process.

In the first hour of the interview, the point is not for the team member to read aloud his or her responses to the questions about the company. The goal is to dig deeper. The questionnaire is a starting point for a conversation designed to explore the nuances and details behind the responses (why did the person respond the way she did), get the team member to open up even more about her opinions (what else does she have to say), and encourage her to think strategically about the future of the company (to get excited about the rest of the process). You can do this by walking through the responses and asking probing, clarifying questions. But you must also leverage the information you have about the person's behavioral style to adjust your approach and make each individual comfortable.

The last question of the first hour is an important one for gauging the person's level of engagement in the organization and his passion for the business. I ask each team member to reveal his personal dream of where the organization should proceed and how he sees himself being a part of it. An experienced advisor can tell when an individual is providing honest, heartfelt answers—the individual truly gets it—and when that person is throwing out a bunch of words. When the latter occurs, it is incumbent upon the advisor to ask questions that dig beyond the charade and get to the core thoughts of that team member.

From there, I move on to a discussion of the behavioral assessment results. The primary visual we use to illustrate an individual's behavioral assessment report is a series of charts we refer to as a Talent Tracker™. The Talent Tracker tracks a person's development to success. This visual tool includes the key graphs from the behavioral assessments (you can download a guide to creating your Talent Tracker as well as the Behavioral Style and Motivators Team Wheels at www.stopsellingvanillaicecream.com). Each planning team member is trained on the assessments during the process, so he or she can look at a Talent Tracker of another person and quickly understand that person's behavioral style. And as the talent management system is implemented into the organization, the planning team members educate the other employees on how to read a Talent Tracker. This key communication tool often ends up on cubical walls and office doors as a method of sharing an individual's style to others in the organization. You'll see Talent Trackers for each of the Connecting Cultures' team members throughout this chapter.

I begin the discussion of the assessment with planning team members by first reviewing the DISC natural and adaptive behavioral styles. I describe what DISC means and talk about any significant differences between their natural and adaptive styles and how that might be taking a toll on them. We then discuss the general characteristics defined by their results, the value their style brings to the organization, and areas for improvement. I reference key points from the report generated as a result of the assessment. From there, we move to the workplace motivators graph. I define each motivator and discuss the ordering of their motivators and explore the top one or two motivators in some detail. Finally, we discuss the Soft Skills Indicator, reviewing their level of clarity in their life on each of the three external factors and the three internal factors. These three assessment discussions set up the perfect foundation for a brainstorm of individual development opportunities. These opportunities will be formalized once the strategy of the company and the individual departmental plans are finalized. I end the discussion by giving the person a list of questions to help her prepare for the behavioral style presentation to the team. (I'll share the Behavioral Style Presentation outline in chapter 7).

Let's explore how an interview typically progresses through my scheduled time with Kyle. I had already reviewed Kyle's assessment results and knew that his natural style shows him strongest in influence and compliance, with a moderate dominance and extremely low steadiness. When he comes to work, he scales back his dominance and influence, and ramps up his steadiness and compliance. Kyle's primary motivating factors are individualistic (a passion to achieve position and use it to influence others) and utilitarian (economic). That comes as little surprise for a young professional with a wife and two young children.

A young man with a natural ease with people, Kyle began talking immediately upon taking his seat. "This is ideal timing to go through this process. Rashelle is a visionary, but there was no one at the steering wheel. That's where my position came in. We're a good yin and yang to each other. It makes for a successful work dynamic. We communicate well and find a way to come to common ground."

I jumped in for a moment to explain the purpose of the interview and then asked, "What types of frustrations do you feel about how your position has evolved?" I knew Kyle's behavioral style would make him comfortable answering such a direct question.

"Frustrations?" he replied, using the moment to collect his thoughts. "When I came into the company, the challenges were all brought to the table, but the complexity or depth of those challenges wasn't something that could be explained. I think this business has moved a lot faster than I could ever have expected.

"Changing Connecting Cultures to a more professionally run organization requires a diligent path. Half of my job is tending to the team and the other half is moving the company forward. I see the operational side and understand what the dollars and cents say, and I enjoy blending those two together. I have no problem pushing on the gas as long as I feel like everyone is on board."

"Talk about some of the weaknesses you've observed so far," I said. "Where do you see opportunities for improvement?"

"We have a great deal of expertise and talent, but historically the organization has viewed our business as only interpreting," he continued. "It's actually a by-product of an entire process that is focused on delivering a service. If our interpreters—who are the front line of our organization—don't understand what adds value to our customers, beyond the actual interpreting appointment, then they're not looking for opportunities to make relationships stronger. They're not looking for ways to make the company more productive. Our challenge is how to take the idea of being a partner—a full-service organization—to our customers and embed that vision in the culture to help our interpreters know there's more to the business than just interpreting.

> *Which people in your organization would have the most strategic insight to offer about opportunities and challenges? How would you encourage them to be forthcoming with their opinions?*

"In many respects, our interpreters operate as independent contractors," he continued. "We don't have a touch point every day. That makes it tough to send a consistent message about the business. We need to figure out a process of marketing to our own staff; we need internal brand alignment."

Kyle certainly had a grasp of the business despite his relatively short tenure in the organization. His written responses indicated that Connecting Cultures needed to increase profitability, build capital reserves, develop sustained personal relationships with clients' key decision makers, define interpreter performance metrics, improve language quality management, and maximize the company's ability to market its language service knowledge.

"The greatest challenge I've had all along is that I see what the company can be, and we could be miles ahead of where we are now. But first, we have to build people into their roles. Right now, I have to tell my managers how to manage. We're a small company that has grown into a bigger company, and a lot of people are in their positions because they've grown with the company. I've spent more time developing people than I would have in other environments. That's fine, but it takes time to do that."

The Stop Selling Vanilla Ice Cream process predicates itself on the ability to find differentiation for organizations to excel in the marketplace. Kyle was about to verbalize a potential strategy to do just that.

"We had two clinics that wanted to take their interpreting services internal. In other words, they wanted to try to do it themselves and hire their own interpreters. That showed the need to diversify our revenue streams and the need to add other services, like training external interpreters to leverage the strength of our internal training program. But we're still coming to the table and saying we only provide interpreting services: 'This is what we do. Take it or leave it.' Instead, we could be saying, 'If you have internal staff, let us train them to make sure your quality matches ours. Let us give you some tools to make sure they're being used as efficiently as possible. Let us help you define a plan that's going to be the most cost effective.'

"The real opportunity in consulting is to open doors to do what we do best. It's about rebranding ourselves to be more than just an interpreting service. We have more to offer. And there's no one in the marketplace that says, 'Tell me about your business. Tell me what you need. We will customize a solution to fit those needs.' We know how to do that, but we haven't found the metrics to show the customer how partnering with us will be valuable. There isn't anything that says, 'When you do this, you will get this.' We're missing the follow-through in our sales and marketing. We can increase our closing ratios by being able to quantify results, and that would enable Rashelle to sell with confidence."

"That's some great insight, Kyle," I said. "You envision that Connecting Cultures' competency is not just interpreting anymore. It's not, 'Is there an opportunity?' It's actually, 'Which one?' When the team becomes market-intelligent, your strategy will follow it."

Kyle concluded, "As demand for interpreting services increases, health care facilities will evaluate whether outsourcing is best for their interpreting needs or whether they should provide the service internally. In my opinion, the market lends itself to more of our customers hiring their own staffs, and we have an opportunity to help them do that. Let's not wait for a competitor to do that first."

I've found that people typically answer the written question regarding their dream for the company and how they see themselves being a part of it in one of two ways. They either write in complete sentences with a conversational tone, or they fire off a bullet-point wish list. Kyle was the latter. The two most critical points were to build a national presence and diversified revenue streams, particularly through offering training to health care providers and independent interpreters; and to develop empowered and engaged employees who see and respect the big picture of the business and have an opportunity to grow.

After discussing these goals, we turned to Kyle's Talent Tracker, shown on the next page, and behavioral assessment results. The first pair of bar graphs illustrates the adapted and natural behavioral styles of the individual, with a box beneath that lists his strengths and value to the team; the middle bar graph illustrates what motivates the individual, along with a list of do's and don'ts for effective communication; and the final bar graph illustrates the capacity for soft skills the individual possesses, with a list of actions the individual can take to increase his performance and value to the team. One look at Kyle's assessment graphs shows he does a considerable amount of behavioral adaption when he comes to work. As mentioned, he adapts his natural style to scale back his dominance (D) and influence (I) and increase his steadiness (S) and compliance (C) at work.

The report's Success Insights Wheel plots Kyle's natural style within the persuader sector, but he adapts across the wheel to the analyzer sector at work. Kyle is adapting his natural style at work in order to be more successful in his position. His adapted style lends itself to an analytical approach and a desire to be a good team player. Adaption may be conscious or subconscious. Conscious adaption is when a person knowingly adapts her style, while subconscious adaption is being unaware of the adaption. My guess is Kyle feels the need to make these adjustments at this point in his tenure with Connecting Cultures in order to be effective, but it's not something he will tolerate over the long term. That much adaption tends to be emotionally exhausting over time, creating stress and fatigue. Most people who adapt this much know their job takes a lot out of them. They are often drained by the end of the week, but they think it is from simply working so hard. When you explain the adaption, a lightbulb turns on.

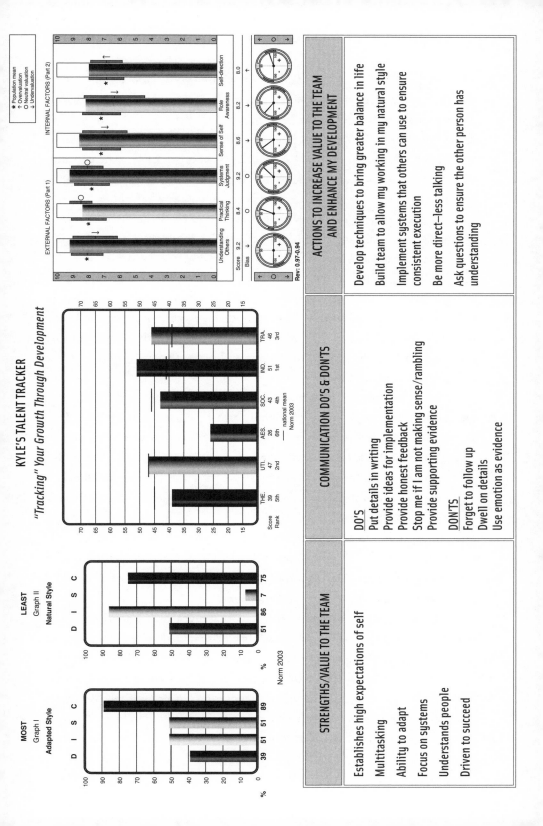

KYLE'S TALENT TRACKER

"Tracking" Your Growth Through Development

MOST — Graph I — Adapted Style

D	I	S	C
39	51	51	89

Norm 2003

LEAST — Graph II — Natural Style

D	I	S	C
51	86	7	75

Norm 2003

	THE.	UTI.	AES.	SOC.	IND.	TRA.
Score	39	47	26	43	51	46
Rank	5th	2nd	6th	4th	1st	3rd

— national mean

EXTERNAL FACTORS (Part 1) / INTERNAL FACTORS (Part 2)

	Understanding Others	Practical Thinking	Systems Judgment	Sense of Self	Role Awareness	Self-direction
Score	9.2	8.4	9.2	8.6	8.2	8.0
Bias	→	O	O	→	→	←

* Population mean
↑ Overvaluation
O Neutral valuation
↓ Undervaluation

Rev: 0.97-0.94

STRENGTHS/VALUE TO THE TEAM

Establishes high expectations of self

Multitasking

Ability to adapt

Focus on systems

Understands people

Driven to succeed

COMMUNICATION DO'S & DON'TS

DO'S
Put details in writing
Provide ideas for implementation
Provide honest feedback
Stop me if I am not making sense/rambling
Provide supporting evidence

DON'TS
Forget to follow up
Dwell on details
Use emotion as evidence

ACTIONS TO INCREASE VALUE TO THE TEAM AND ENHANCE MY DEVELOPMENT

Develop techniques to bring greater balance in life

Build team to allow my working in my natural style

Implement systems that others can use to ensure consistent execution

Be more direct—less talking

Ask questions to ensure the other person has understanding

They begin to realize *why* their current position takes so much out of them and are truly excited to understand this critical factor. We can then have a discussion about how they can minimize their adaption in the future. My discussion with Kyle went just like this. The lightbulb turned on for him.

One of Kyle's strengths is also a weakness in terms of how he communicates with coworkers. He's an extroverted intellect. He's very talkative and has an extensive vocabulary. The problem comes when the people he's communicating with don't have the same verbal skills he does. It's not a matter of him being smarter; it's just that he's not succinct when he communicates details. He can t-a-k-e t-h-i-s l-o-n-g to say something that should takethislong.

Kyle has strong clarity of thinking and he's motivated to get ahead in the world. He's a really smart guy but not very experienced. Rashelle and Bobbie knew that when they hired him, but they couldn't afford to hire someone with more experience. They understood there would be some learning curve along the way.

On the positive side, Kyle takes no time at all to get into gear. He buries himself in details until he has enough information to make a decision. He's a good guy with no major shortcomings, and his ability to slow down his pace at work helps him to become more of a team player. That's okay for now, but recall that long-term adaption causes stress, fatigue, and tension.

"Kyle, your adaption at work to increase your C and your attention to detail is likely a result of your focus on the details of the day-to-day operations. It would be in your best interest to return to your natural style sooner than later," I said. "My challenge for you is to begin thinking of ways to adjust your role so you spend less time buried in tactical duties and more time in decision making and leadership."

Kyle nodded with a resigned expression that revealed an underlying skepticism regarding the short-term feasibility of that challenge. "That's going to be easier said than done," he said, "but it is a direction I'd like to pursue."

Given Kyle's high level of self-confidence and his willingness to speak, I asked whether he would be willing to present his behavioral assessment (and fall on his sword early) in the first session. It would be a first step in his development. He agreed without hesitation.

STRATEGY INSIGHTS

Kyle's interview was fairly typical. He didn't hold back, and he offered a wealth of information about strategic opportunities and challenges for Connecting Cultures. The trick in any interview is to separate issues that are just items on somebody's personal agenda from the actual strategic issues. That wasn't much of an issue with Kyle, but the strategic challenges automatically rise to the top when you hear multiple interviewees raise the same concerns or hopes for the company. For Connecting Cultures, I was looking for those issues that at least three of the five planning team members raised.

Erin, who has been with Connecting Cultures for seven years and is now the training coordinator and quality director, raised some of the same issues as Kyle, but because of her work with the interpreters, her perspective was slightly different. "There is an 'us versus them' mentality from the interpreters toward the management," she explained. "I think the interpreters feel that we don't do enough to recognize their skill. Interpreting is a calling; it's a vocation. They need more one-on-one contact with department managers, to have somebody tell them how they're doing. We've identified continuing support and ongoing training as the parts we need to further develop in our interpreting process," she said. "The busy nature of the job is part of our challenge.

"We seem to have great ideas but no follow-through," she continued. "It's hard for us to be consistent in keeping things moving. Kyle helps, but it's hard to do when you've got entire walls falling down around you. It's too easy to get pulled into daily operations issues. We also need better communication across the organization and within departments."

Through Erin, I also learned about the strength of the company's quality control and training, a strength that Kyle wanted to leverage and expand through consulting. "We groom our interpreters through the training process. Our levels for interpreters are novice, intermediate, advanced, and senior. Interpreters move through these levels via field experience and continuing professional development. I develop these programs to ensure our customers and their patients continually receive great services regardless of the person, language, or seriousness of the encounter."

When I asked about the interviewing and hiring process, what Erin described further clarified how Connecting Cultures' focus on quality was a possible differentiator. "Sometimes there's a shock-and-awe reaction. If they've applied for an interpreting position elsewhere, it's different than the application process with us. We do language screenings that test for basic interpreting skills and foundational knowledge of medical terms in two languages. If the language screening goes well, then we go through several pages of questions in person to determine their skills and ability to perform this work."

Erin listed her two major corporate goals for the next year as diversifying interpreter service delivery methods and implementing continuing education/quality support externally. Looking out further, her dream included having the company recognized as an industry leader and expert on a national level, with the financial stability and freedom to pursue that endeavor.

The issues that Kyle and Erin identified were supported by what I learned from Bobbie, Eric, and Rashelle. These three shareholders in the company have real issues with role definition, and that can trickle down through the organization, creating confusion, lack of communication, and lack of strategic direction. While it's partially a talent management issue, it's also a strategic issue because it affects the direction and focus of the company as a whole. Even more important than role confusion was the lack of focus on sales. Everybody was running from that responsibility.

Bobbie admittedly is a shareholder searching for a more defined role in the company. She was accustomed to intimate involvement in the business at virtually every level. Then Kyle entered the picture as the operations manager, and suddenly Bobbie perceived that her role was changing and perhaps her status was diminishing. Officially, she serves in account management. In actuality, she handles many accounting and business office functions, addresses internal personnel issues, and acts as a sounding board for Rashelle.

Bobbie sees the ability to train interpreters as a critical service line for Connecting Cultures, especially since some competitors already are going down that path. She sees her and Rashelle's current responsibilities within the sales function as the primary barrier to developing the training and consulting components of the business. She would like to see Kyle take on more of a sales role now that he has a good handle on the business and possesses a sales background. She claims the reason she hasn't sold anything lately is because she doesn't feel a personal buy-in, especially because of the company's current pricing model.

"It's something I have to work on, I guess," she said with almost a defeatist tone. "My mind-set is I don't understand it, so why spend the time on it? Rashelle is filling in where I'm pulling back. What concerns me is she wants to sell only to elephants, but that has a long sales cycle and we could starve in the meantime."

Rashelle's written response to the first item on the questionnaire regarding job duties spoke volumes about the seriousness of the sales problem and role confusion: "Mostly unfocused and putting out fires as they arise. Need to generate job description to give me direction. No selling."

"Why is it you don't want to do sales, Rashelle?" I asked. "Your skill set and passion for the company make you a natural for that role."

"I think the reason I have challenges with sales and marketing is that sitting in a sales situation gives me a lot of anxiety," she replied. "I want someone to show me how to do it. My frustration is I don't understand the process. Give me the process and show me how to do it, and then I can execute on it."

"The good news, Rashelle, is that this process and the resulting strategic plan will lay the foundation for a proactive sales and marketing plan, and the development of tools for selling the competence of Connecting Cultures," I said. "The process will build your confidence in sales situations, and consequently increase revenue."

Rashelle provides a good example of how some leaders can be good at performing day-to-day activities, but they don't take the time to be strategic. Her greatest strength lies in visualizing how the interpreting industry will be five years from now. That's why her business has the potential to be significantly different and better than it is today. Executing it and delivering it is a different thing.

TALENT INSIGHTS

Most planning team members are excited to see their assessment results. I believe that people have a natural desire to improve and enjoy a better life. And in many companies, the team members are simply happy to finally talk to somebody about their development opportunities and give their perspective on where the company should go.

Occasionally, a team member discounts something that the assessment reveals. When this happens, it's usually a specific statement in the report, and I try to get the person focused on the big picture results. I might remind him or her that the assessments have been scientifically validated at 85 to 90 percent accuracy. But generally, planning team members are amazed at the accuracy of the results and are ready to dig in on growth opportunities.

Erin's behavioral assessment reveals that she is an introvert and will likely not be as outgoing as Kyle. During the interview, I had to adapt and throttle back my natural instincts for a very direct communication approach to have any chance at a successful interaction. Her DISC scores from her behavioral assessment are almost off the charts: extremely low for dominance (D) and influence (I), and extremely high for steadiness (S) and compliance (C). The assessment reported: "Erin likes having others initiate the conversation. She can then assess the situation and respond accordingly. She may guard some information unless asked specifically about it. She will not willingly share unless she is comfortable with the knowledge she possesses about the topic." Her assessment also indicates she highly values systems and rules, and also wants others to follow them. Her extremely high motivating factors scores in the areas of traditional and social reflect her desire for a system of living (her faith) and assisting others.

Rashelle had told me she considered Erin one of the most valuable and loyal employees in the company. I took the opportunity to plant a seed of challenge with Erin. "Bringing up some of these scores will help you create more soft skills and become a higher performing employee and person. It's about recognizing where your strengths are and the things you can do better. My sense is Connecting Cultures needs you to use this process as an opportunity to step up and be more vocal in your role as a company leader," I said. "I assume it's very frustrating for you to feel a lack of structure and a constant battling of fires within the company, is that correct?"

"Yes, it is," she replied quickly. "But I don't know if I'm comfortable taking on the role of a vocal leader. That's not who I am."

"I understand it may be somewhat outside of your comfort zone—and I'm not suggesting you change who you are and suddenly become the

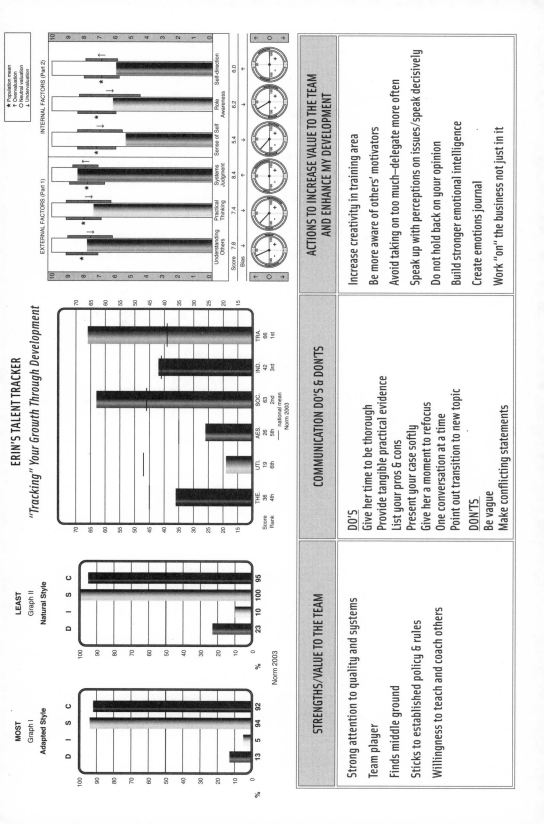

ERIN'S TALENT TRACKER
"Tracking" Your Growth Through Development

MOST
Graph I
Adapted Style

LEAST
Graph II
Natural Style

EXTERNAL FACTORS (Part 1) — Understanding Others, Practical Thinking, Systems Judgment

INTERNAL FACTORS (Part 2) — Sense of Self, Role Awareness, Self-direction

★ Population mean
↑ Overvaluation
O Neutral valuation
↓ Undervaluation

	Understanding Others	Practical Thinking	Systems Judgment	Sense of Self	Role Awareness	Self-direction
Score	7.8	7.4	8.4	5.4	6.2	6.0

STRENGTHS/VALUE TO THE TEAM

Strong attention to quality and systems

Team player

Finds middle ground

Sticks to established policy & rules

Willingness to teach and coach others

COMMUNICATION DO'S & DON'TS

DO'S
Give her time to be thorough
Provide tangible practical evidence
List your pros & cons
Present your case softly
Give her a moment to refocus
One conversation at a time
Point out transition to new topic

DON'TS
Be vague
Make conflicting statements

ACTIONS TO INCREASE VALUE TO THE TEAM AND ENHANCE MY DEVELOPMENT

Increase creativity in training area

Be more aware of others' motivators

Avoid taking on too much–delegate more often

Speak up with perceptions on issues/speak decisively

Do not hold back on your opinion

Build stronger emotional intelligence

Create emotions journal

Work "on" the business not just in it

Norm 2003

voice of the organization—but you've got a lot to contribute as the company moves forward," I said.

I was eager to see which Erin would show up at the planning sessions—the introvert who would be content to observe the proceedings or the budding leader who would take the opportunity to step forward and contribute on a higher level.

The Stop Selling Vanilla Ice Cream process also presented an opportunity for Bobbie to refine her role. She was at a fork in the road with her career at Connecting Cultures. She was unsure of where she fit into the organization. She was either going to withdraw further and drop out of the picture altogether, or the process would reenergize her.

Bobbie's natural style is heavy on steadiness (S) and dominance (D), and moderate on influence (I) and compliance (C). She does a fair amount of adapting at work, reducing her steadiness and dramatically cranking up her dominance. Like Kyle, her adaption puts her in a position that often becomes stressful over time. Part of Bobbie wants to drive, while another part wants to be a team player. The assessment had this to say about Bobbie's general characteristics: "Bobbie likes to know what is expected of her in a working relationship and have the duties and responsibilities of others who will be involved explained." Her feelings about her unclear role in the company were clearly in line with this.

"You have a lot of gifts to bring, Bobbie, but sitting on the sidelines is not the answer," I told her. "When you start checking out, you're not bringing value to anybody. Now we just need to define the tasks and roles that fit your skill set."

"I know," she replied. "And I don't feel good when that happens, either. What do you think I should do?"

"I'm confident we'll have the answers as we progress through this process. In the meantime, start thinking of where you and your skills can bring the greatest value to Connecting Cultures. Chances are we'll find the answers there. Because typically where you bring the greatest value to the company, you also bring the greatest value to yourself."

Like Bobbie, Eric had a problem with role clarity at Connecting Cultures, but there were much bigger issues to address. In fact, Rashelle had pushed for me to have a serious conversation with Eric, a real heart-to-heart to find out if he wanted to have a role in the organization at all.

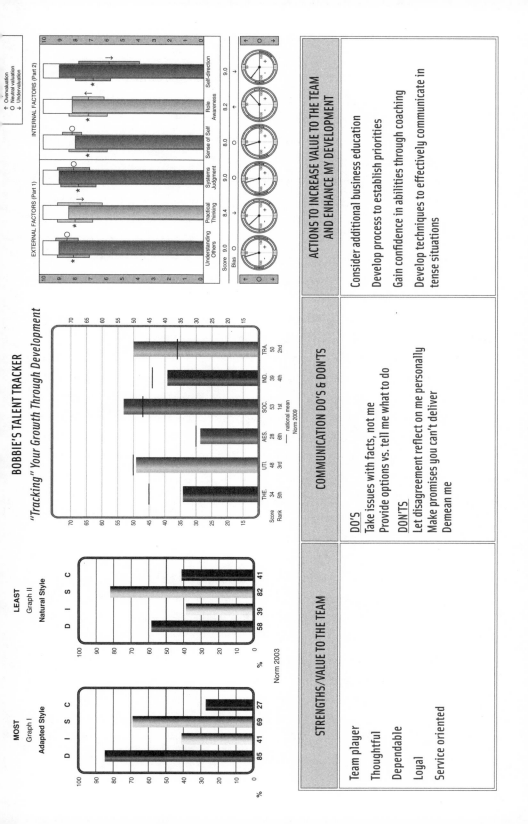

BOBBIE'S TALENT TRACKER
"Tracking" Your Growth Through Development

MOST
Graph I
Adapted Style

D	I	S	C
85	41	69	27

Norm 2003

LEAST
Graph II
Natural Style

D	I	S	C
58	39	82	41

Norm 2003

	THE.	UTI.	AES.	SOC.	IND.	TRA.
Score	34	48	28	53	39	50
Rank	5th	3rd	6th	1st	4th	2nd

national mean ——
Norm 2009

EXTERNAL FACTORS (Part 1)

	Understanding Others	Practical Thinking	Systems Judgment	Sense of Self	Role Awareness	Self-direction
Score	9.0	8.4	9.0	8.0	8.2	9.0
Bias	O	→	O	O	←	→

INTERNAL FACTORS (Part 2)

↑ Overvaluation
O Neutral valuation
→ Undervaluation

STRENGTHS/VALUE TO THE TEAM

Team player
Thoughtful
Dependable
Loyal
Service oriented

COMMUNICATION DO'S & DON'TS

DO'S
Take issues with facts, not me
Provide options vs. tell me what to do

DON'TS
Let disagreement reflect on me personally
Make promises you can't deliver
Demean me

ACTIONS TO INCREASE VALUE TO THE TEAM AND ENHANCE MY DEVELOPMENT

Consider additional business education
Develop process to establish priorities
Gain confidence in abilities through coaching
Develop techniques to effectively communicate in tense situations

It's not easy to make the owner's spouse a viable member of the organization. Even if he isn't a leader, people see him as being one, and Eric wasn't wired to be an effective leader. He fills the role of Connecting Cultures' information technology coordinator, which includes managing computer and phone systems. However, he doesn't manage any staff. His behavioral assessment reveals an extreme level of verbal dominance, with little to no recognition of other people's styles and speeds of operating. He's also very confident, which can be a volatile combination. His high natural dominance (D) score of 100 combined with a low steadiness (S) score creates the impression of a bull in a china shop. Eric's not shy about telling you just how wrong you are, so be ready for incoming fire if you find yourself on the opposite side of an issue or if you're simply not moving fast enough to keep up with his desired pace. He's a really smart guy, just not an effective communicator at this point in his career.

Not surprisingly, Eric's low compliance (C) score reveals that he is fine with following instructions to complete a task but not with following directions for which he doesn't see the point. He has a general disdain for completing tasks such as detailed paperwork. "Eric, I see you didn't fill out much of the written questionnaire," I said to him when I saw that he had only answered one question. "Why is that?"

"I don't know," he replied with a shrug. "I'm not much for doing things like that."

Eric's Workplace Motivators scores also showed a tendency toward the extreme, led by a high score for theoretical (the drive for knowledge) and low scores for social (helping people) and traditional (a defined system of living). His Soft Skills Indicator showed high clarity of thinking but a relatively low level of role awareness and self-direction. Eric is uncertain about his current roles within the organization, and it's clear he is struggling to see where he fits in long-term.

His behavioral style suggested he might react positively to a direct challenge, and I didn't hold back in delivering the message. "Eric, if you're going to function as a valuable member of the team going forward, we'll have to find some projects where you can follow a plan and work at your own pace," I said. "That would minimize the interpersonal conflicts that arise when you deal with other team members."

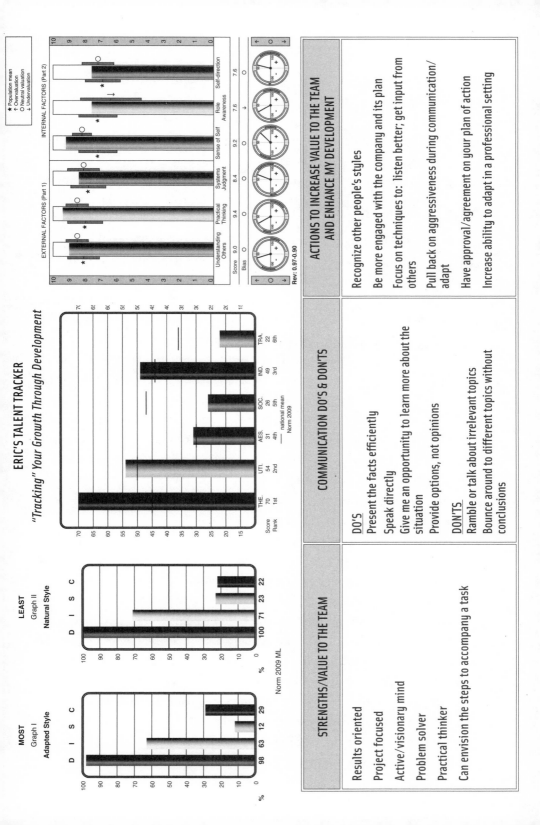

ERIC'S TALENT TRACKER
"Tracking" Your Growth Through Development

MOST — Graph I — Adapted Style

	D	I	S	C
%	98	63	12	29

LEAST — Graph II — Natural Style

	D	I	S	C
%	100	71	23	22

Norm 2009 ML

	THE.	UTI.	AES.	SOC.	IND.	TRA.
Score	70	54	31	26	49	22
Rank	1st	2nd	4th	5th	3rd	6th

— national mean
Norm 2009

EXTERNAL FACTORS (Part 1)

	Understanding Others	Practical Thinking	Systems Judgment	Sense of Self	Role Awareness	Self-direction
Score	9.0	9.4	8.4	9.2	7.6	7.6
Bias	O	O	O	O	→	O

INTERNAL FACTORS (Part 2)

Rev: 0.97–0.90

* Population mean
↑ Overvaluation
O Neutral valuation
→ Undervaluation

STRENGTHS/VALUE TO THE TEAM

- Results oriented
- Project focused
- Active/visionary mind
- Problem solver
- Practical thinker
- Can envision the steps to accompany a task

COMMUNICATION DO'S & DON'TS

DO'S
- Present the facts efficiently
- Speak directly
- Give me an opportunity to learn more about the situation
- Provide options, not opinions

DON'TS
- Ramble or talk about irrelevant topics
- Bounce around to different topics without conclusions

ACTIONS TO INCREASE VALUE TO THE TEAM AND ENHANCE MY DEVELOPMENT

- Recognize other people's styles
- Be more engaged with the company and its plan
- Focus on techniques to: listen better; get input from others
- Pull back on aggressiveness during communication/adapt
- Have approval/agreement on your plan of action
- Increase ability to adapt in a professional setting

"That sounds good," he replied. "Give me something to do, get out of my way, and I'll get it done."

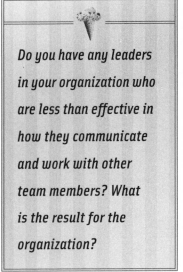

Do you have any leaders in your organization who are less than effective in how they communicate and work with other team members? What is the result for the organization?

I sensed Eric could be an asset if he changed the way in which he communicates. The planning process will help Eric become a more effective communicator, and more important, will bring him role clarity. The best-case option might be for him to write an IT plan, and then make it happen. We need to lay the groundwork for him to be successful. After we finished reviewing his assessment results, Eric and I brainstormed several growth opportunities for him that will significantly increase the value he brings to the organization and himself.

The company leader is the last interview, so it was time to talk with Rashelle. "Rashelle believes in getting results through other people and prefers the team approach," I read from her assessment report, and glanced up to see Rashelle nodding in agreement. "She prefers working as a participative manager and likes freedom from many controls. She may leap to a favorable conclusion without considering all the facts. Because of her trust and willing acceptance of people, she may misjudge the abilities of others."

Rashelle's behavioral style displays the maximum score for influence (I), moderately high scores for dominance (D) and steadiness (S), and an extremely low score for compliance (C). Those scores changed only slightly for her adapted style at work. Her primary workplace motivators are utilitarian (money), which is not uncommon for a business owner, and theoretical (an appetite for learning). Not surprisingly, her Soft Skills Indicator showed lower clarity in her practical thinking. Based on my time with her, that's not surprising, because she is a visionary who is not big on details. However, she measured very high for self-direction, indicating a clear image of her future.

"Your vision of where you're going is crystal clear. You're able to paint the future; you just struggle to pave the road to get there. That's what the planning process is going to do."

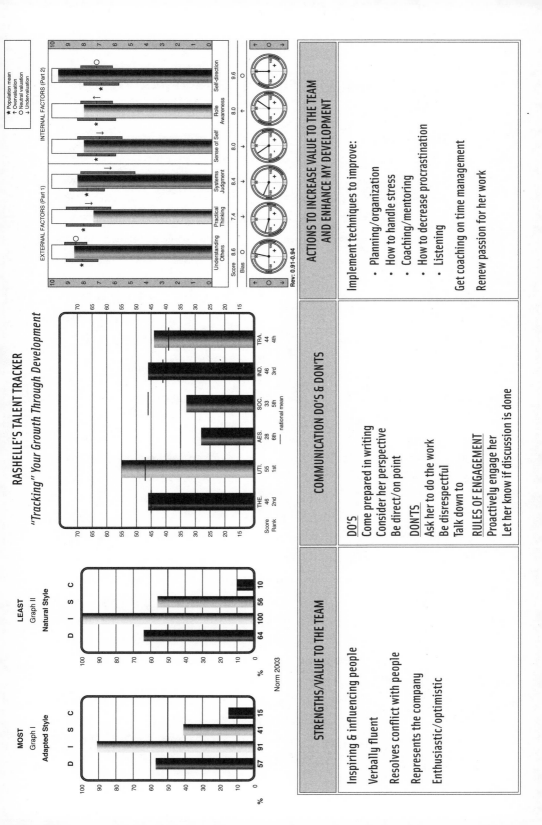

RASHELLE'S TALENT TRACKER
"Tracking" Your Growth Through Development

MOST
Graph I
Adapted Style

D I S C
57 91 41 15

Norm 2003

LEAST
Graph II
Natural Style

D I S C
64 100 56 10

	THE.	UTI.	AES.	SOC.	IND.	TRA.
Score	46	55	28	33	46	44
Rank	2nd	1st	6th	5th	3rd	4th

— national mean

EXTERNAL FACTORS (Part 1)

	Understanding Others	Practical Thinking	Systems Judgment
Score	8.6	7.4	8.4
Bias	O	↓	↓

INTERNAL FACTORS (Part 2)

	Sense of Self	Role Awareness	Self-direction
8.0	8.0	9.6
↓	←	O

Rev: 0.91–0.94

★ Population mean
↑ Overvaluation
O Neutral valuation
↓ Undervaluation

STRENGTHS/VALUE TO THE TEAM

Inspiring & influencing people
Verbally fluent
Resolves conflict with people
Represents the company
Enthusiastic/optimistic

COMMUNICATION DO'S & DON'TS

DO'S
Come prepared in writing
Consider her perspective
Be direct/on point

DON'TS
Ask her to do the work
Be disrespectful
Talk down to

RULES OF ENGAGEMENT
Proactively engage her
Let her know if discussion is done

ACTIONS TO INCREASE VALUE TO THE TEAM AND ENHANCE MY DEVELOPMENT

Implement techniques to improve:

- Planning/organization
- How to handle stress
- Coaching/mentoring
- How to decrease procrastination
- Listening

Get coaching on time management
Renew passion for her work

ANALYZING THE INFORMATION AND PREPARING FOR NEXT STEPS

The interviewing process has given me all the information I need to customize a planning process to resolve Connecting Cultures' strategic challenges. As I reflect back on the individual interviews, it's apparent this team has the talent to accomplish what it needs to do. However, some of the team members may be stuck in roles that are better suited for others, or we may need to find ways of springing people free to concentrate more on a portion of their duties. This process will help Rashelle construct a team in which all the necessary talents and abilities are in place. The Connecting Cultures team members are inexperienced in terms of business acumen, so a plan will help them tremendously. The Talent Management System increases the likelihood of putting the right people in the right positions to succeed, leading to a high-performing organization.

The extremes in behavioral assessment scores indicate a potential powder keg with regard to emotions and feelings. One of the objectives is to bring more emotional intelligence and balance to the organization. Passion is a desirable attribute, but understanding it and regulating the emotion is what makes it powerful. Using that knowledge for your benefit is what leads to personal and professional success, however you define it.

The advisor's role is to sift through the individual issues to identify the four to six strategic challenges that truly are impeding an organization's progress. The first step I take is to compile the information in a way that will be useful as we move through the process. I take the answers to each question on the questionnaire and put them on a single page for quick reference during different discussions. I call this "building the deck." I also create a list of ideas and unresolved issues that came up during the interviews. Then I review all the comments and extract the four to six issues that seem to present the biggest strategic hurdles.

Finally, I prepare information on the organizational and team assessment to share first with the leader of the organization and then with the planning team. (I'll share the outcomes for Connecting Cultures in the next chapter.) It's important to give leaders a heads-up as to what may lie ahead. The more we can eliminate surprises, the more productive the process will be. You complete the review by finalizing the strategy development planning process needed to resolve the four to six strategic challenges you just agreed upon.

When I met with Rashelle and Kyle, I could tell that they were both a little anxious to hear what I had discovered. As always, I maintained the confidentiality of my interviews, but I described the overall issues I had heard from the team. Then I reminded them of the purpose behind the work that was to come.

"As with most company leaders, your desire is to drive growth through this process, Rashelle," I said. "We'll leverage what we've learned about the team and company to develop your competence, turn that competence into a comprehensive strategy, and then execute that strategy successfully."

"I'm really looking forward to that, Steve," Rashelle said.

We concluded the meeting with a brief overview of what to expect at the first planning session. I asked both leaders to bare their souls in front of the group when presenting their behavioral assessments in order to establish an open and candid environment. I refer to this as falling on your sword. It's important for leaders to show vulnerability and imperfection in a setting like this to increase their own credibility as well as encourage others to be open and candid in evaluating their own behavioral style and skill set.

"Keep in mind that the level of quality of preparation equates to the quality of the session, which equates to the quality of the strategy," I said. "It's your job as the leaders to make sure preparation gets done. It's the hard part of being a leader and it's not glamorous."

I shared the Action Plan Register (homework assignments) that showed tasks for the next phase. Together we assigned the tasks:

- ☐ Complete the questions to present your behavioral style to the team at the first meeting—All planning team members

- ☐ Prepare the first draft of the company values and beliefs; prepare opening remarks—Rashelle

- ☐ Prepare a financial analysis, including financials for the current year and historical sales and profits—Kyle

- ☐ Work with Rashelle to create a market research summary, including a market analysis of what trends are taking place in the health care interpreting industry—Kyle

- ☐ Obtain demographic information from census data and larger school districts—Rashelle

☐ Create a competitive competence analysis using the competitive competence template (available in the resources section at www .stopsellingvanillaicecream.com)—Rashelle

"If we remove the four to six largest rocks," I asked, "will it be a good year?"

"Absolutely!" Rashelle said with a smile. "That's what we're counting on."

ACTION PLANS TO PREPARE FOR PHASE #2			
PROJECT DESCRIPTION	Owner	Due Date	Date Completed
Complete the questions to present your behavioral style to the team at the first meeting	All	8/18/XX	
Prepare first draft of company values and beliefs and present at first session	Rashelle	8/18/XX	
Prepare financial analysis and be prepared to present at first session	Kyle	8/18/XX	
Work with Rashelle to create market research summary and be prepared to present at first session: What trends are taking place in the industry?	Kyle	8/18/XX	
Obtain Green Bay School District and Heart of the Valley School demographics	Rashelle	8/18/XX	
Complete competitive competence analysis and be prepared to present at first session	Rashelle	8/18/XX	

PLANNING PROCESS			
Planning Meeting		8/18/XX 8:30 a.m.	
Planning Meeting		9/9/XX 8:30 a.m.	
Planning Meeting		9/29/XX 8:30 a.m.	

The Scoop

1. How would your organization benefit from your managers and selected employees speaking one-on-one with an internal or external advisor about their perspectives on the strategic issues facing the company?

2. How would your organization benefit from understanding the behavioral styles of managers and selected employees? How would the employees benefit?

3. What do you think are the current challenges your leadership or planning team face in terms of how they work together and communicate with each other?

4. What do you think are the four to six strategic challenges (boulders) that are holding your organization back?

Action Plans to Complete the Process

☐ Ensure all members of the planning team complete the questions to present their behavioral style to the team at the first session.

☐ Assign owner and due date for financial analysis.

☐ Assign owner and due date for market research summary.

☐ Assign owner and due date to complete first draft of competitive competence analysis.

☐ Set date and off-site location for first strategic planning meeting.

☐ Are there any other details that need to be discussed to prep for the first session and move to phase 2, which is the strategy development process?

BUILDING THE TEAM AND STRATEGY DEVELOPMENT PREPARATION

6

A PROCESS FOR RESOLVING STRATEGIC CHALLENGES

A sunny and pleasant spring morning greeted the Connecting Cultures planning team members as they arrived for our first meeting. The weather helped everyone start the day in an upbeat mood, despite the fact there was a fair amount of nervous energy. Rashelle was eager to jump into the day and arrived on time. Of course, her colleagues were quick to point out that fact and it generated a healthy laugh.

Once everyone fills their coffee cups, picks a seat, and gets situated, it is time to begin. This initial meeting will lay an important foundation for the rest of the process. It's important that the team agrees on the rules of engagement, or how they will interact during the planning meetings and going forward as a team. It's equally if not more important that we review everybody's expectations for the process and lay out the strategic challenges that came through in the interviews. These challenges will be a primary point of focus for the rest of the process, so the team needs to carefully consider them or adjust them as necessary.

ESTABLISHING THE RULES OF ENGAGEMENT

The room has been set up to create an atmosphere of openness and positive energy. I've found it most effective to arrange the planning team members in a horseshoe configuration so everyone can see each other, leaving one end open for a projector and presenters to take center stage.

We held the planning sessions in SM Advisors' conference room so Connecting Cultures' meetings were off-site. I recommend this approach so that team members aren't as likely to engage in their tactical world of daily duties. I've found it very difficult to keep their focus on the task at hand if meetings take place at the workplace or if participants have ready access to their portable devices. This is an important detail we can't overlook. The withdrawal from daily activities can be particularly difficult for small business planning teams, where fewer backup people are available to handle issues that arise during the course of the day.

But before the work can begin, it's crucial to set the right tone and approach to the process. "Good morning, everyone, and welcome to the Connecting Cultures strategic planning process," I said. "I'm going to begin by reviewing the agenda for the first phase of the process, and then I would like Rashelle to set the stage for today with some opening remarks." I quickly reviewed the agenda and then Rashelle spoke.

"I'm really excited," Rashelle began, her voice filled with enthusiasm. "This conversation will be dynamic because we have all the players in the room and things have been happening already. I hope we're all constructive, honest, and forward. I may talk a lot, but everybody's opinion is valued, and I hope we can be respectful and listen to each other.

"There is a lot of opportunity here, and we've worked very hard for ten years to get to this point. For the little bit of vision that we've had, we're finally starting to look beyond where we are, and I'm excited to see where this takes us."

After opening remarks by the leader, the advisor lays out the ground rules for the session. Covering details such as break times, restroom locations, and lunch plans eliminates sources of uncertainty and helps participants inch closer to a relaxed state of mind. I distribute the Strategic Plan Binders that include a left-side pocket for parts of the plan we have completed and a right side for the work still in process. I keep my working list of unresolved issues handy so I can quickly add items or cross them off. And as always, I'm prepared to write down any action plans that may arise based on the team discussions.

"There are two ways you can approach these sessions," I said to the group. "You can think like a member of the leadership team or like a department manager. I would encourage you to think like a leader—it's what's best for the company. This may not always match up with your specific department needs. The first and only priority of this process is developing a focused strategic plan for Connecting Cultures."

The advisor should remind the team about the purpose of the process by discussing some of the reasons companies should plan. These are basic to the process yet helpful to introduce at this point in laying the foundation for the team:

- ✔ Build a selected competence: become better at your competence than anyone else in the markets you compete and create a real differentiation for your company

- ✔ Create one realistic vision to guide all decisions

- ✔ Develop a cohesive and focused team

- ✔ Resolve the real issues and sacred cows

- ✔ Create measurable improvement in employees' professional and personal lives

"As you move further into the execution of your strategy, the focus will move from strategic development to tactical development and execution," I said. "Eventually, and this may take a couple of years, you'll just tweak your strategy and get into department planning right away, until of course you hit a point when you need to revise your strategy due to a significant change in the market or the competitor base. The most profitable companies are those that become experts at department planning. As each department completes tactical plans and moves the company forward by working *on* the business, it has a multiplying effect and the company just takes off."

Strategic to Tactical Continuum

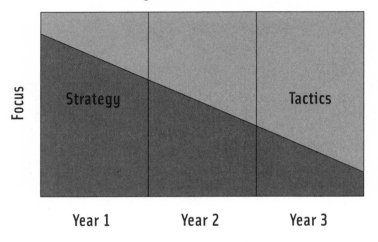

Next, we covered some basic guidelines for the planning sessions, including important ground rules of team communication. These are important points to put on the table to encourage open yet respectful discussion.

- ✔ Put yourself in your teammate's shoes; actively listen to the finish and then probe for clarity. You do not have to agree with what a person says, but you must understand it.

- ✔ What is said in the planning sessions stays in the planning sessions, unless we agree otherwise. "There has to be an understanding that you can talk about anything in these meetings and not worry about the organization finding out about it tomorrow," I said.

- ✔ Challenging a teammate's idea is healthy; attacking the teammate is not. If a person challenges your idea, try not to take it personally. Healthy conflict and debate is a sign of a high-performing team.

- ✔ Build team trust by professionally handling any disagreements one-on-one with the individual but outside the group. If the rest of the organization notices a rift, it deteriorates what the team is trying to accomplish. Understand that it all starts at the leadership team level. The organization will emulate how the team communicates, works together, and performs.

- ✔ There are no untouchables or sacred cows. All issues must be addressed. Speak your mind or forever hold your peace. This is the place to put it all on the table.

✔ All teammates have equal responsibility for the development and execution of the plan. Come to each meeting prepared. At the end of each phase, we'll review the action plan register that will keep us on task with homework assignments to complete prior to beginning the next phase.

✔ Turn off your cell phones.

✔ Have some fun. Build a team, not barriers!

"Ninety percent of the decisions should be made by the leadership team, but every once in a while Rashelle will want to play what I call her presidential prerogative card. You don't want that trump card to come out very often, Rashelle. It needs to be available, but use it sparingly or the rest of the leadership team won't engage." Rashelle gave a nod, showing her understanding that one of Connecting Cultures' shortcomings is a lack of consistent structure behind its decision making.

TEAM MEMBER EXPECTATIONS

One of the interview questions that team members answer is what are their individual expectations of the planning process. It is important to review these answers with the team (anonymously, of course) so that everybody is focused on meeting those expectations. When we consolidate answers to questions, we don't delete repeated items or change the wording because we want to truly understand what the exact expectations are.

"As your advisor," I said to the team, "I will review your expectations consistently and at the end of the process to ensure we have met them. Here are the expectations the Connecting Cultures team members had."

✔ Instill a vision in the organizational culture to get everyone on the same page

✔ See more regional/national growth

✔ Expand our training program

✔ Create a budget and make sound financial decisions

✔ Define clear goals for the upcoming year, attain team consensus for those goals, and establish a road map on how to attain those goals

✔ Develop internal brand alignment to include a sales and marketing plan that everyone can understand and confidently execute, and that encompasses all services

✔ Create a solid plan and steps to move the company to the next phase of business

✔ Establish a professional image

✔ Increase sales and profitability

✔ Develop a concrete sales plan that encompasses all of Connecting Cultures' service offerings

✔ Establish monthly goals to grow services

✔ Define the company's true strengths and where it can diversify

"That's a big list," Bobbie observed.

"Yes, it is. But it's totally doable," I responded. "There's not one of these expectations that we won't attack during the course of this process."

OBSTACLES TO PLANNING

Despite the fact that strategic planning usually makes sense to the majority of an organization's leadership team, a common set of obstacles can stand in the way of making it happen, including the following: people view future direction from their own perspective; there is no one, single vision; operational (day-to-day) thinking dominates management's time; organizations let outside forces shape their strategy; people are reactive rather than proactive; and a tainted view of planning exists, usually from a previous bad experience.

Because of these obstacles, it's not uncommon early in the process for planning team members to voice some skepticism concerning their organization's ability to capitalize on the journey they're about to embark on. Connecting Cultures was no different. It is helpful to allow these concerns into the conversation so we can address them immediately. Let's get them out there so we can talk them through.

As a result, we look at possible obstacles specific to the company. One of the interview questions asks about the obstacles the company could face in developing and executing the plan. Again, we consolidate the answers from the questionnaire and then discuss them with the team. The most common issue mentioned by the Connecting Cultures team was communication.

"Part of this process should be about how all of us communicate with the staff," Rashelle said. "As a leadership team, you pass off a lot of that to Kyle or me. We're all leaders. We should create a platform for us to share those things. We all need to be engaged so communication is not dependent on the management team."

"I struggle with *what* to communicate," Kyle said. "I'm reluctant to handle too much of the communication responsibility because I feel like I'm enabling the department managers to not communicate. We need to understand which things each role should communicate."

"That's where I'm really lacking," Bobbie stated. "I hear on a daily basis from customers, but I never tell the interpreters what I'm hearing—good, bad, or indifferent. That needs to change."

Rashelle and Kyle also discussed the difficulty of getting everybody on the same page.

"Everyone is in his or her own bubble in our company. It's the nature of the business," Rashelle said. "Ultimately, the interpreters are out running their own show based on the work we do. We were a cohesive team in the beginning, but when we grew, that flew out the window. There's a severe disconnect once they go out into the field."

"But if they saw where we are heading, they would feel more a part of the team," Bobbie replied.

"It's not like we can have everyone in the office join a quick huddle," Kyle said. "We don't have those opportunities. So how do we make sure this effort is sustainable? What's happened before is we come up with great ideas, and then everyone disperses and goes out to achieve. I've never worked in an environment that is so naturally disconnected. We have full-time employees, but they are independent workers who happen to come to the office on occasion. I think we have to get creative."

Internal communication would be an obvious target for improvement as we progressed through the process. Improved communication comes through the organizational structure, and that's something we would work to solidify.

STRATEGIC CHALLENGES AND OPPORTUNITIES

I had already presented to Rashelle and Kyle the four to six strategic challenges synthesized from the interviews, but the rest of the team needed to discuss them as well. "These are the most important strategic issues we are going to resolve as part of this process," I explained. Team members almost unanimously noted six major challenges facing Connecting Cultures. In other words, the biggest boulders in the lake that the next year's business plan must work to remove included the following:

1. **Clearly define and gain agreement on Connecting Cultures' competence and strategy.** How are we going to differentiate ourselves from our competition? What are the key strategies and action plans to make it happen?

2. **Increase role clarity by developing and implementing an organizational structure with skill set–alignment and with clear responsibilities, expectations, and accountability.**

3. **Create a platform for a proactive sales and marketing plan designed to increase revenue and profitability, and expand Connecting Cultures' customer base.** The Stop Selling Vanilla Ice Cream process resolves the strategic sales and marketing issues and lays the foundation for the Business Development department plan.

4. **Implement an effective and sustainable companywide communication system that ensures each employee understands the plan and his or her role in delivering it.** The leadership team must have the ability to communicate effectively with the rest of the organization without scheduling a bunch of meetings. A well-defined organizational structure can make that happen, regardless of how large or geographically diverse the workforce.

5. **Develop and execute department plans to work "on" the business and build a stronger organizational team.** Team members will step up by developing their own department plans and executing on those plans. A fundamental difference between a company that's profitable and one that's not is department planning. It's taking the strategy to action. A positive snowball effect begins to emerge as each department completes their plan and moves forward.

6. **Develop a plan execution process to implement a culture of discipline and consistent accountability.** This is a process, not an authoritative person who holds team members accountable. The strongest form of accountability is to the team. When you say you're going to get something done, it has to happen.

"If we resolve these strategic challenges as part of this process, will it be a great year?" I asked.

The team was unanimous. If they could overcome these challenges, they believed the future of the company would be bright. "We haven't accomplished that much in five years, much less one year," Rashelle said.

"This process could become the defining moment for this team and the company," I replied. "So let's dive in."

The Scoop

1. Are the rules of engagement for how the planning team is going to interact with each other clear to all team members? Any discussion?

2. What are the possible obstacles to your company that could hinder the implementation of this plan? How do we minimize their impact?

3. Do the strategic challenges include the top four to six strategic challenges facing the organization?

Action Plans to Complete the Process

☐ Finalize the strategic challenges of the organization that will be resolved through the focus of this process.

BUILDING THE TEAM TO ACHIEVE YOUR DREAM

The team development exercise is the first step in building a high-performance team, and I'm always curious to see how these sessions play out. This exercise is about getting everyone in his or her metaphorical underwear—there should be no pretenses remaining. The exercise uses the assessments, a behavioral style questionnaire, and a unique process to instill the characteristics of a high-performance team into your organization.

Recall the second phase is all about building a foundation for strategy development; a high-performance team is necessary to optimize success. It's difficult to develop an effective strategy—and your success will be limited—if you don't first work on your team. The strengths and weaknesses of the individuals will play a major role in strategy development, and matching the natural talents of each individual to the requirements of specific roles results in powerful skill set–alignment. Once you have a brilliant strategy, having the right people in the right positions executing the plan is the most effective path to success.

Patrick Lencioni brilliantly described the struggles of under-performing teams in his book, *The Five Dysfunctions of a Team*:

✔ Absence of trust

✔ Fear of conflict

✔ Lack of commitment

✔ Avoidance of accountability

✔ Inattention to results

According to Lencioni, team dysfunction doesn't happen overnight. These issues simmer and mature over time until they become an elephant on the back of an organization. Avoiding, or at least minimizing, the effect of these pitfalls is a primary objective behind the team development process. The behavioral style presentations are the first step in that direction. Having discussions about these typical team issues creates an environment in which resolution can occur and the team is set free.

After this process, you'll be able to proceed professionally and candidly because there will be no more barriers. If you have something on your mind, you will feel free to express it in a respectful and professional manner. Candid discussions increase efficiencies by reducing confusion. This helps your organization grow through the power of individual development and continuous improvement.

I could sense that the uniqueness of the Stop Selling Vanilla Ice Cream process was beginning to have an impact on the Connecting Cultures planning team. They were coming together quickly as a cohesive unit, ready to take the next steps.

PRESENTING BEHAVIORAL STYLES

"Now that the administrative groundwork is behind us, it's time to get to work," I said. "It's time to present your behavioral styles."

The team members groaned, chuckled a little bit, and then shifted anxiously in their seats. Several glanced without purpose at their notes, seemingly avoiding eye contact with each other.

"We really have to do this, huh?" Rashelle asked rhetorically.

"Yes," I replied, "and I'm sure you will do a great job leading the way."

The behavioral assessments and presentations provide important insight regarding the team dynamics you will see play out during the course of the process. For a group with dynamic behavioral assessment scores like the Connecting Cultures planning team, I suspected we could see some emotional fireworks and passionate give-and-take between the participants.

The behavioral presentations are structured around the following statements, although the discussion of the last statement regarding the vision for the team is held until after each person presents his or her behavioral style:

Behavioral Style Presentation Outline

1. I learned the following strengths of my behavioral style that positively impact the team:

2. I learned the following growth opportunities of my behavioral style that could increase the performance of the team:

3. I feel others in the organization perceive my style as:

4. To communicate most effectively with me, I ask that you do/not do:

5. I am going to take these steps in my development in the next twelve months to increase my performance and build a stronger and higher performing team:

6. a) My vision for the planning team interactions is:

   b) The characteristics or processes of a high-performance team that need to be implemented in our team are:

You can download the Behavioral Style Presentation Outline template at
www.stopsellingvanillaicecream.com.

Dealing with the emotional and mental energy challenges that pop up along the way is inherent in the process, and it's up to the advisor to help the group persevere. A great first step in creating a candid and interactive environment is to have the leader present her behavioral style first. And based on Rashelle's behavioral style I knew that she would create an open and honest tone for the discussions.

I opened the proceedings by offering some background on what the participants may see in themselves and others around the table. I then provided a brief overview of the behavioral assessments, including a description of the four primary behavioral styles—dominance, influence, steadiness, and compliance. Since participants have already seen their own assessments, this overview helps set the stage for what they're about to hear in the individual presentations.

"I can't wait to see what we learn from this," Rashelle said. "I know we have good people, but I'm concerned we might not be in the best positions for our individual strengths."

"Each team member will have fifteen minutes to present his behavioral style to the group," I said. "The main objective of the exercise is to increase understanding of each other's behavioral styles in order to more effectively communicate and work with each other. One of the specific outcomes of the process is an awareness of how an individual needs you to communicate with them versus how you want to communicate with them. This is a key to effective communication. Each of you will complete an individual development plan as part of the department plan later in the process."

I had asked Rashelle and Kyle to take one for the team by going first and highlighting their own opportunities for improvement. This approach helps the rest of the planning team become more forthcoming and willing to assign credibility to the process after seeing the leaders admit they're less than perfect.

"Clearly understanding who we are is the first step in our individual development journey," I explained. "The moment we reach this understanding, we will have already improved. We can't work on something if we don't know what it is. This needs to be an exercise in self-improvement and mutual understanding, not a contest to see who can defend their behavioral styles the strongest."

"I'll go first," Rashelle announced. "Like most people, I thought I knew a lot about myself already, but this assessment exercise revealed things I wasn't aware of before. And seeing my behavioral style on paper really

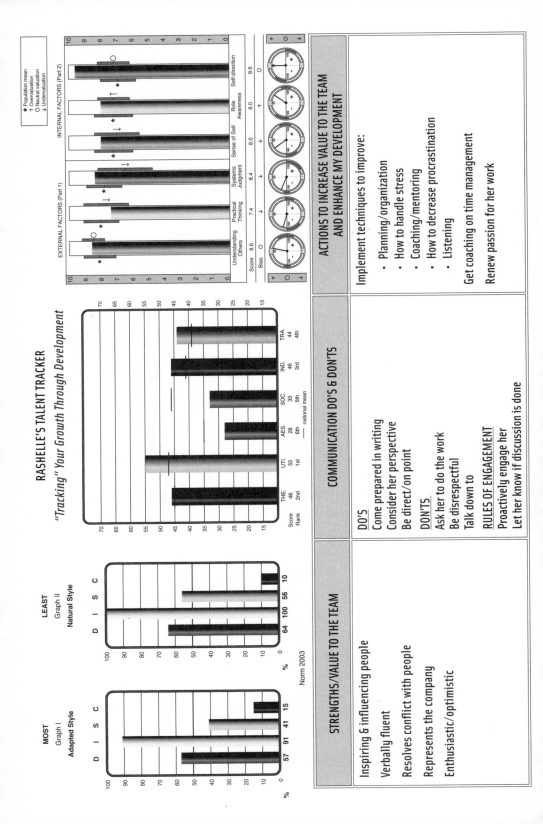

RASHELLE'S TALENT TRACKER

"Tracking" Your Growth Through Development

MOST
Graph I
Adapted Style

D	I	S	C
57	91	41	15

Norm 2003

LEAST
Graph II
Natural Style

D	I	S	C
64	100	56	10

	THE.	UTL.	AES.	SOC.	IND.	TRA.
Score	46	55	28	33	46	44
Rank	2nd	1st	6th	5th	3rd	4th

— national mean

EXTERNAL FACTORS (Part 1)

	Understanding Others	Practical Thinking	Systems Judgment
Score	8.6	7.4	8.4
Bias	○	→	→

INTERNAL FACTORS (Part 2)

	Sense of Self	Role Awareness	Self-direction
	8.0	8.0	9.6
	→	←	○

★ Population mean
↑ Overvaluation
○ Neutral valuation
↓ Undervaluation

← ○ →

STRENGTHS/VALUE TO THE TEAM

Inspiring & influencing people

Verbally fluent

Resolves conflict with people

Represents the company

Enthusiastic/optimistic

COMMUNICATION DO'S & DON'TS

DO'S
Come prepared in writing
Consider her perspective
Be direct/on point

DON'TS
Ask her to do the work
Be disrespectful
Talk down to

RULES OF ENGAGEMENT
Proactively engage her
Let her know if discussion is done

ACTIONS TO INCREASE VALUE TO THE TEAM AND ENHANCE MY DEVELOPMENT

Implement techniques to improve:

- Planning/organization
- How to handle stress
- Coaching/mentoring
- How to decrease procrastination
- Listening

Get coaching on time management

Renew passion for her work

helped me understand myself better." Rashelle's enthusiasm seemed to settle some of the nerves around the table.

I presented a brief overview of the core aspects of Rashelle's behavioral style, and then she held everyone's attention as she launched into her presentation. She began by discussing her strengths, the first statement on the list.

"I learned I am very motivated about Connecting Cultures and the decisions that affect it," she said. "I have an influencing personality that can inspire staff and customers to come along with me, and I have strong problem-solving skills that can create solutions to short- and long-term challenges. I have a strong vision that creates a guiding direction for today and our future growth. Since I am very decided on these things, it takes a lot of convincing for me to make a change. My decisions have reason behind them, although sometimes I may not communicate them well."

After strengths, she addressed her growth opportunities. "This process helped me understand the growth opportunities I have that could increase the performance of my team. I could benefit from some coaching on time management, because I know I need to become more organized and a better planner. I also need to become less impulsive and consider others' workloads. Evaluating other opinions, especially if they're stronger than mine, would allow me the ability to help support all of you in your work rather than just focusing on myself."

"That's an excellent observation, Rashelle," I said, offering some positive feedback in the midst of her self-critique. "What other growth opportunities did you uncover?"

"I need to do a better job at handling stress," she continued. "I lose perspective and want to find quick solutions immediately, regardless of how it will affect things overall. I'm a huge procrastinator. That's where my shoot-from-the-hip style comes from. I don't have balanced decision-making skills, or at least I feel I can improve on that."

"How do you feel others perceive your style?" I asked, moving the presentation along.

"I feel others perceive me as being a strong leader," Rashelle stated. "Those who work closely with me see me as driven and opinionated about what I want, and most everything has an urgency. I think they'd like to see me provide more support and direction, and become more engaged with them individually and the work they do."

I asked the team how they thought the organization perceived Rashelle's style, which generated some respectful but interesting discussions. These progressed naturally to a discussion of the best ways to communicate with Rashelle.

"I realize I have some specific rules of engagement that help people communicate with me," she said. "First of all, I ask that you understand we will reach a happy medium, but there may be things I won't move on. This does not mean I don't respect your opinion. If we've reached a conclusion and I'm still talking, let me know."

"That was a very solid self-analysis, Rashelle," I said. "What are some of the actions you plan to take over the next twelve months in your development plan that would help you build a stronger and higher performing team?"

"I've thought of five I'd like to share, and I would ask the group to hold me accountable to these," she said. "I want to seek out resources to manage my time and projects more effectively; become more educated on processes I don't understand; create ways to become more engaged with my team; become more organized, and therefore more effective; and renew my motivation and passion for the things I do."

Rashelle spoke for twenty minutes, and the process was somewhat uncomfortable for her at times. As with most people—especially those in positions of authority—Rashelle understood she had some areas in need of improvement, but she didn't always find it easy admitting that to herself or her team. Rashelle and the team experienced several breakthroughs during her presentation.

After each individual finishes his or her presentation, I ask the team to contribute one piece of advice to give the presenter. Everyone always has an opinion on what another person can do better. The key for the presenter is avoiding the natural tendency to be defensive. The presenter can decide whether the advice is something he wants to implement or not, but at least he has to understand where the other person is coming from. I then summarize the assessment report's results and offer some thoughts on how the team can help the individual development process.

Rashelle's admission that her time management skills could use some work opened the door for constructive feedback. When people bring up something they want to improve about themselves, it gives the rest of the team permission to hold them accountable. It makes it acceptable for others to talk about it.

"Your tendency is to have a lot of projects going at the same time, Rashelle, but it's hard for you to actually complete them," Bobbie said. "My piece of advice would be to accept accountability from the leadership team for seeing those projects through to completion."

"That would be my suggestion, too," Kyle added. "The way things are now often leaves others to pick up the pieces."

"I know," Rashelle said, nodding in agreement. "It seems like I move onto whatever new idea pops into my head."

"That's great feedback," I said. "Let's make sure we work on that in your individual development plan."

An easel stands next to me with paper for writing notes. On the top I've written "Team Communication Plan," and my first entry now reads: "The team needs to hold Rashelle accountable."

"Rashelle's report shows she undervalues authority and currently is highly motivated by economic factors," I explained while the group scanned Rashelle's talent tracker. "She's wired to sell, but it's all about confidence for her. The only person that believes she can't sell on occasion is Rashelle, so you guys need to build her up in that regard. Rashelle wants to institute a process to sell before she'll get back out there, and she will have that by the time we complete the strategic planning process.

"Rashelle, your idea about needing coaching on time management is a great idea. You are wired to be a leader and to sell, and it comes down to your belief in that. Leaders get things done through other people. They wrap the warmth of their I (influence) around their D (dominance). Effective leaders *sell* their team members on what to do versus *telling* them what to do."

"I think it's my need for people to like me," Rashelle noted. "If people don't want what I'm selling, that works on my insecurities. It's somewhat of a personal affront to me if they don't want what I'm selling."

Rashelle was very effective in her role as the leadoff hitter for the assessment presentations. She enhanced her position as a leader with her team, coming across as a person you would want to follow. The team development process has set the stage for candid team discussions. Now let's see how the rest of the team responds with their presentations.

Kyle was next in the spotlight, and the operations manager's propensity for using a plethora of big words had the room holding its collective breath that his presentation would not be succinct. Kyle displays an impressive ability to self-analyze and dig to the root of his behavioral tendencies. He acknowledged that he's a perfectionist, but that he strives for balance. He described his tendency to take on challenges that push him out of his comfort zone. We spent some time discussing his tendency to adapt his natural style, and he concluded, "Short-term, I'm comfortable adapting, but five years from now if I'm still working this way, I'm going to be really crabby."

In theory, the type of behavioral adaption that Kyle is experiencing at work will eventually take a toll. Connecting Cultures hired Kyle for his natural style, which tended toward a common leadership style. It's okay for him to work outside his natural style for a period, as long as he understands it and is aware of it. Some people can adapt their styles significantly without it being a big deal, and Kyle may be one of those people. But in general, people feel more at home when they have a job that fits their natural style. We call that skill set—alignment.

In his operations role, the lack of systems and processes keep him mired in the day-to-day, slowing his response time. He needs systems to help him understand what's happening. Until he has them, it will be difficult for him to make faster decisions.

Kyle noted he believes others view him as a good speaker who uses verbal skills to his advantage in influencing others. However, he can appear condescending because of those skills, especially when you combine them with his high self-confidence. Kyle continued, "Provide me honest feedback, knowing I'm someone who seeks growth. If my message isn't being received, stop me so I can clarify."

In Kyle's case, his adapted style (analyzer) is on the opposite side of the behavior style wheel (fig. 7.2) from his natural style (promoter), which is unusual. He was increasing his attention to detail at work to handle all the day-to-day tasks he needed to focus on. Kyle indicated that he becomes more focused as pressure increases, which leads to the appearance of a lack of empathy and of being overly confident and even condescending.

Rashelle relies on emotion and gut feel, while Kyle shuts his emotions down. Finding that spot in the middle is where they need to head.

"What development actions will you take over the next twelve months as part of your development plan?" I asked.

"I need to become more direct and less wordy in my communications, and I want to increase my empathy by dedicating time to improve the quality of my relationships. I need to find balance between facts and emotion," Kyle responded. "I am also hearing that I need to push my direct reports a little harder, to be more direct and hold them accountable. I also want to lead by example and grow my personal accountability by striving to become more transparent in my actions and goals, because I believe this to be a staple of strong leadership. I also need to delegate more of the day-to-day tasks so I can get back to my natural style and the strengths it can bring to Connecting Cultures."

"Let's capture those items for your development plan," I said while writing Kyle's goals on the board.

Kyle's presentation built on Rashelle's in a positive manner. The team saw the organization's leadership reveal areas for ongoing individual development without resorting to a defensive mind-set. It is at this point the team realizes change will happen and this process is real. The stage has been set for them to come together and follow Rashelle and Kyle's lead.

Accordingly, Bobbie and Erin were revealing in their presentations. Bobbie became a bit emotional as she discussed her low sense of self and how surprised she was by the accuracy of her assessment results. She acknowledged that she feels less educated and less intelligent than the rest of the team. Rashelle and I reminded Bobbie of her strengths and of the critical role she had played and could continue to play in building the business. When Bobbie pushed to say that she was struggling to see her role in the growing and changing organization, Rashelle pushed back and encouraged her to take control rather than withdraw.

After discussing her strengths, I asked Bobbie about her growth opportunities, to which she replied, "I need to do a better job of establishing priorities and meeting deadlines," she said. "I think it would help me to journal my daily accomplishments, both professional and personal. Obviously, I have a tendency to underestimate my abilities and I need to be better about that, and I need to avoid being passive-aggressive when I'm resisting something." I reassured her and the team that one of the objectives of the process was to find the best fit for each person in terms of responsibilities. This would be particularly important for Bobbie going forward.

Erin's behavioral style of keeping her emotions in check and opinions under wraps provided an appropriate counterpoint for the next assessment presentation. Because she needs time to analyze a situation before she responds, understanding her communication style and how to most effectively communicate with her is critical to leveraging her value to the organization. Although Erin referred to her report notes often, she spoke as someone who had already internalized its findings. In a matter-of-fact tone, she discussed the motivations and limitations of her reserved communication style. She acknowledged that when pushed, she can become passive-aggressive or just shut down, which isn't productive.

Rashelle considered this and recognized that she needs to ask Erin what she's thinking more often and also acknowledge that Erin doesn't raise an issue unless it's important to her. "Your style has a tendency of being harder for other people to communicate with," I told her candidly. "It's not as apparent right away where you're standing on an issue; that's why it's more important for us to ask your opinion so we get to what you're thinking." Rashelle encouraged her to feel comfortable fully sharing her opinion, and that it would be valuable to the team if she did it more.

We headed into Eric's presentation with a bit of trepidation, knowing it might be a tough discussion. Eric's maximum score on the dominance scale foreshadowed an exceptionally direct approach to his assessment report. Trained as a military pilot, Eric can follow a checklist to the letter. He is not comfortable speaking extemporaneously, so he leaned heavily on his assessment report for his presentation. However, he quickly tired of reading the unflattering list of characteristics associated with his behavior style. "High ego, goal-oriented, . . . we can skip the rest of this," he said, sounding for all the world like a person hoping to avoid the gallows.

"I'm interested to hear what else it says," Rashelle said, not letting him off the hook.

Eric read directly from his report, and there was some solid discussion about his communication weaknesses, his aggressiveness, and the fact that he is uncomfortable when he doesn't understand how things operate, such as not understanding what other people in the company do. I encouraged

Eric; his honesty and recognition of his growth opportunities is a necessary first step in his development. "And as you can see Eric, you're not the only one with weaknesses in the room," I joked.

Bobbie shared that she had seen Eric adapt his behavior dramatically with his three daughters, so it was possible for him to do so. Rashelle shared that despite outward appearances, Eric is passionately motivated to learn. I jumped on the opportunity that statement represented. "Eric scores 9.4 on practical thinking," I commented. "So when it comes to a project, he can see the steps and resources needed to complete it. That's a gift. I suggest that Eric can bring more value to the organization through a project focus. He may enjoy working on his own more than in a strict team setting, because people moving more slowly than he does give him some frustration. IT clearly can be a competitive advantage for Connecting Cultures. The fact that we could have Eric as an IT expert allows for IT to become an area of strength for Connecting Cultures. Someone as smart as you, Eric, could be a tremendous asset if we can focus your energy in a productive direction. Do you agree?"

"Yes," he said. "Now let's find a place to put it to use."

I make mental and written notes about the participants as we come out of the behavioral assessment presentations. The Connecting Cultures team has such a range of individual styles and issues that there is no shortage of observations worth noting. The assessment presentation was a challenging exercise for Eric, but the discussions led to several breakthroughs that will likely end up adding a highly valuable member to the Connecting Cultures team. It's obvious to me that we need to find defined roles for Bobbie and Eric, and the company needs Erin to step up into more of a leadership role. There is some pain that comes with making the transition from a family-run business to a professionally run business, and that might be especially hard on Bobbie. Solving these issues is a result of the process.

THE MAKEUP OF THE TEAM

"Now let's talk about the overall makeup of the Connecting Cultures planning team," I said. "I often see some strong behavioral scores in the 80s and 90s when I conduct behavioral assessments, but to see three scores from the Connecting Cultures team at full throttle 100 is unusual. These extreme behavioral styles bring a variety of strengths and weaknesses to the table. High scores indicate pronounced strengths, but really high scores also tend to reveal impactful weaknesses in people's styles. The goal is to put people in a position to take advantage of those major strengths.

"One of the tools we use to help organizations and teams understand where they may have opportunities for growth is the Behavioral Style Team Wheel, shown on page 105. Ideally, teams will have balance around the wheel so they can leverage the various strengths of each behavioral style. The key to leveraging the information contained in the behavioral wheel is in understanding the needs and strengths of each individual," I stated. "That's why it's important to conduct the team development exercise."

Behavioral Style Team Wheel is important. Here are the reasons why-:

- ✔ It maps the natural and adapted style of each team member.

- ✔ It visually illustrates the behavioral balance of the team. A balanced management team has the natural styles of team members evenly distributed around the wheel.

- ✔ It identifies possible skill set voids on the team.

- ✔ It illustrates significant adaption of any team member.

- ✔ It helps team members understand and value each other's style and perspective.

- ✔ It allows the team to have healthy and ongoing discussions about their individual styles as well as how the team performs and works together.

"Individuals with high D (dominance) scores will show up in the Conductor, Persuader, and Implementor sectors," I explained. "Those with high I (influence) scores show up in the Persuader, Promoter, and Relater sectors; high S (steadiness) people show up in the Relater, Supporter, and Coordinator sectors; and those with high C (compliance) scores show up in the Coordinator, Analyzer, and Implementer sectors."

CONNECTING CULTURES BEHAVIORAL STYLE TEAM WHEEL

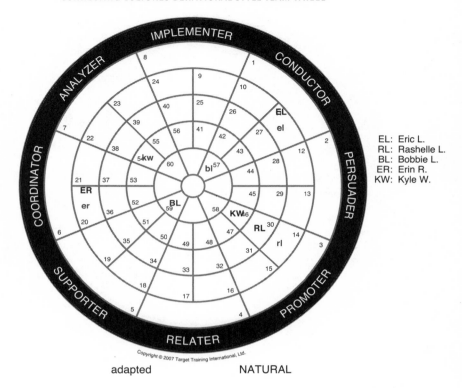

EL: Eric L.
RL: Rashelle L.
BL: Bobbie L.
ER: Erin R.
KW: Kyle W.

Copyright © 2007 Target Training International, Ltd.

adapted   NATURAL

The Connecting Cultures Behavioral Style Team Wheel reveals two individuals who have markedly different natural and adapted styles, likely causing a great deal of internal strife and stress. Kyle is a natural Promoter who becomes an Analyzer at work, while Bobbie is a natural Supporter who becomes a Conductor at work. Interestingly, no one falls in the Implementor, Persuader, or Relater categories.

"Each behavioral style brings a unique perspective to the team, which is extremely beneficial during the team decision-making process," I said. "It is important to note that any behavioral style can be successful in any functional position within the organization. However, significant adaption can take a lot of energy and may cause stress."

For sales teams, the distribution of natural styles will vary depending on the selling situation. For example, if all sales representatives sell the same type of product to the same type of customer under the same conditions,

CONNECTING CULTURES WORKPLACE MOTIVATORS TEAM WHEEL

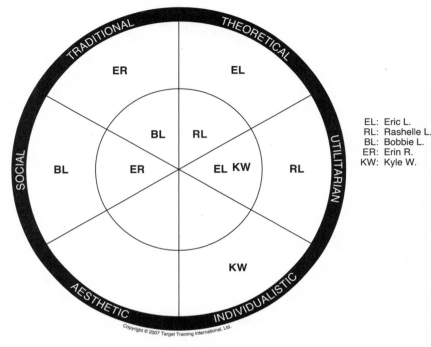

EL: Eric L.
RL: Rashelle L.
BL: Bobbie L.
ER: Erin R.
KW: Kyle W.

Outside ring = #1 motivator   Inside ring = #2 motivator

it would suggest that each individual will have similar natural styles. "Once the organization clearly defines the selling environment, it can identify the optimum behavioral style for each member of the sales team," I explained to the team.

The Workplace Motivators Team Wheel, shown above, is similar to the Behavioral Style Team Wheel in that it provides a visual depiction of where team members reside in relation to each other. This wheel illustrates the primary and secondary motivators for each team member, with the outside ring signifying an individual's primary motivator and the inside ring showing the secondary motivator. The Workplace Motivators Wheel shows what drives the actions and decisions of each team member at work. It gives the company the information to implement systems to ensure each team member remains motivated, which positively impacts job satisfaction and employee retention. The Connecting Cultures team has a wide dispersal in this illustration, reflecting their range of workplace motivators.

"It's common within a business setting to have several team members' primary motivator fall in the financially driven Utilitarian sector. However, only Rashelle has her primary motivator here; the rest of the planning team is spread around other sectors of the wheel. It's important to recognize your team's specific motivators and create systems that meet those motivators. For example, Eric is solidly in the Theoretical sector and has the motivation to learn. As a result, he needs a work environment that gives him the opportunity to learn. We can accomplish that through his development plan. Every team has a different motivator pattern."

"Is a wide dispersal like ours a good thing or a bad thing?" Bobbie asked.

"Having multiple motivators in play helps ensure the team views its opportunities from more than one perspective," I replied. "Knowing those differing motivators exist is the most important thing."

The team and each individual experienced several breakthroughs during the development exercise. The behavioral style presentations are a roller-coaster ride filled with highs and lows of emotion, but the results of the exercise change how the team interacts and performs together forever. The exercise also provides the foundation for the rest of the process. I try to prepare my clients, knowing the enthusiasm typically takes off as the excitement of formulating strategies within the "new" team builds to a crescendo. We typically have a highly energized team coming out of the team development session. I encouraged each planning team member to share his or her talent tracker with other members of the planning team and throughout the organization. As the collective knowledge level of behavioral science increases across your company, you will see an increase in the volume and effectiveness of communication.

"This was the most candid conversation our team has ever had," Rashelle said as we wrapped up the team development exercise. "Now we can have open dialogue about how to communicate and work more effectively together. I think we took some giant steps forward this morning."

"That was some great discussion and typical of what comes from the team development and assessment process," I said. "In the last couple of hours, you've become a stronger team, and I hope you can see that. Now that you're all in your underwear, so to speak, we can attack the real issues the company is facing together."

"That's what we're really excited to accomplish," Rashelle said. "I can't wait to see what we uncover next."

The Scoop

1. Which members of your planning team do you think will have the hardest time being open about their behavioral assessments and opportunities for growth? How will you optimize this opportunity?

2. How will you use information about the team makeup to ensure that the strategy development and execution process is candid and productive?

3. What are the strategies and techniques of the team communication plan that resulted from the behavioral style presentations?

Action Plans to Complete the Process

☐ Distribute to the team each member's talent tracker and his answers to the six behavioral presentation statements.

☐ Document the two to three top growth opportunities for each planning team member. These opportunities will be included in the individual development plans that will become part of the department plans.

☐ Finalize the team communication plan that resulted from the behavioral style presentations.

LOOKING IN THE MIRROR: INTERNAL ANALYSIS

The Connecting Cultures team had a relaxed vibe as they prepared to dive into the internal analysis of the company. The behavioral style presentations had successfully removed barriers that would have restricted the type of open conversation so crucial to a productive strategic planning process. The apprehension that filled the room at the start of our first meeting was gone. Team members were now figuratively "in their underwear," ready to tackle the strategic challenges facing their organization. Before a planning team can effectively tackle the strategy portion of the Stop Selling Vanilla Ice Cream process, you need to change the atmosphere from one in which people might be happy sitting on their hands to one in which people feel comfortable sharing their thoughts on where the organization should go. There should be no issues this team will not address candidly.

"We've focused on the talent and behavioral aspects of the process, and now we're in position to develop a proactive strategy," I said to the team. "As we go through this next portion of the process, we're looking for metaphorical lightbulbs to turn on as we uncover information about Connecting Cultures that will help us concentrate our efforts and develop our strategy going forward. As our strategy becomes more evident, those lightbulbs will burn brighter with energy, excitement, and focus."

"When you look in the mirror, inevitably you see things you like and things you want to change," I noted. "The combination of organizational strengths identified through the internal analysis, along with market trends and customer needs we'll identify later through an external analysis, produces the future competence that will set the company apart. You'll be selling mint chocolate chip ice cream rather than vanilla ice cream. In other words, based on your strengths and customer needs, what can you do better than anyone else that the markets in which you compete are demanding?

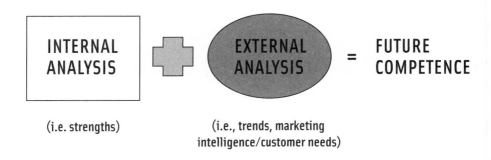

INTERNAL ANALYSIS   EXTERNAL ANALYSIS = FUTURE COMPETENCE

(i.e. strengths)   (i.e., trends, marketing
                          intelligence/customer needs)

"Conducting an internal analysis is a very healthy process, and it's important to come to an agreement on the points you identify as strengths and weaknesses," I continued. "Typically, a company will be able to eliminate half of its weaknesses in the first year after going through this process. This makes you less vulnerable to competitors because you don't have those blind spots anymore." The focus of the process is to build a competence based on your strengths, but eliminating or minimizing as many of your weaknesses as possible creates a stronger and less vulnerable organization.

Completing an internal analysis requires the team to:

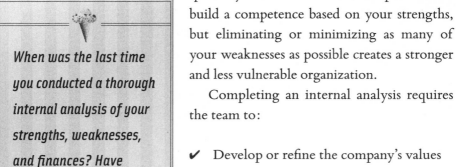

When was the last time you conducted a thorough internal analysis of your strengths, weaknesses, and finances? Have you ever?

✔ Develop or refine the company's values and beliefs statements

✔ Conduct a strengths analysis

✔ Conduct a weaknesses analysis

✔ Review the current financial analysis

These four steps create a wealth of knowledge and insight, and a strong foundation for the eventual discussions about your competence and strategies for moving forward.

COMPANY VALUES AND BELIEFS STATEMENTS

We began the internal analysis discussion with a look at Connecting Cultures' values and beliefs. The values of an organization are at the core of its existence. They define the code of conduct for the organization while it is executing the plan. Value statements detail how employees should interact with each other as well as with the external world. A company's values and beliefs statements shape the culture of the organization.

"It is the responsibility of every employee to make sure he or she carries out these values," I said. "If a person falters, then it's leadership's responsibility to ensure that the employee gets back into alignment with company values and beliefs. The outcome of the planning process in regard to values and beliefs is to develop action plans that align actual behaviors with defined values.

"If you picture a target with two rings around the bull's-eye, the inner circle—the bull's-eye—represents the core values and never changes. The inside ring represents an organization's core strategies, which seldom change. The outside ring represents tactical strategies, which often change. The Stop Selling Vanilla Ice Cream process begins with the bull's-eye and works outward from there."

The founder or owner of a business often defines the organization's core values when starting the company. As a result, the company values typically reflect the core values of the owner. It is in that person's best interest to define the company's values and beliefs early on in the life of the business to establish the guidelines and parameters for how employees will interact with internal and external customers. Without clear parameters, you ultimately leave the company's and owner's reputations to chance. I wrote SM Advisors' core values when I founded the company, and they are just as relevant today (see them at www.smadvisors.com).

Another approach is to create an internal cross-functional team of employees to define the company's core values. It often works well because the employees take ownership of the values. If the owner of the company is not involved in the planning process, I recommend that one team member take responsibility for gathering feedback from each of the planning team members and from any key leaders not on the planning team. Using that feedback, he or she should be able to construct a list of value statements to share with the team.

The right approach for each company depends on the company's current situation. Based on Rashelle's passion for her business and profession, I was confident her core values would be easy to identify. As part of her homework, I asked Rashelle to create the first draft of the company's values and share them with the planning team for input and agreement. She identified professionalism, communication, education, and integrity as the four core values of Connecting Cultures. I explained to Rashelle that, in my experience, the most effective approach is to define each core value and then include a simple statement detailing how to apply that value in the business. With that as the background, Rashelle prepared the following value statements to share with the team:

PROFESSIONALISM: We believe professionalism is the key to building partnerships with staff, customers, and community. Professionalism drives quality services, expertise, and policy and processes that support internal and external operations.

COMMUNICATION: We believe communication is the foundation of success. Communication connects leadership, interpreters, customers, and community. A connection between Connecting Cultures and its customers exists only when communication is strong. Direct communication to resolve issues and identify opportunities for growth is the future for Connecting Cultures.

EDUCATION: We believe education generates expertise and growth. Continuing education creates an ongoing competitive advantage. Education creates team members that bring increased value to Connecting Cultures.

INTEGRITY: We believe integrity brings trust and respect to the entire organization. It is important that staff and customers trust us to deliver on obligations. Transparency, honesty, consistency, and accountability are all parts of integrity and the value we see in it.

"Each of these in itself means little," Rashelle noted, "but taken together they create clarity on how all members of the company are going to conduct themselves in representing Connecting Cultures."

The planning team had an extensive conversation regarding the values and beliefs statements proposed for Connecting Cultures. Rashelle received input from the team on how to possibly improve the statements. Rashelle then accepted the action plan to finalize the company's value and beliefs statements and present them for final approval at the next planning meeting.

IDENTIFYING STRENGTHS

Next it was time to look in the mirror and identify the strengths of the organization, paying particular attention to whether or not those strengths go toward building a differentiation from the competition. In this strategic process, you aren't completing a strengths analysis just to say you did one. Knowing your strengths—especially your top strengths—lays the foundation for the development of your competence.

The first step in this brainstorming process involves reviewing strengths that team members identified during the interview phase. Oftentimes people find they want to add, delete, or change some of the strengths on that preliminary list after discussion with the team.

INTERNAL ANALYSIS CHECKLIST

The following checklist provides a list of possible strengths of the organization. Each planning team member should rate each item on a scale from 1 to 5, with 1 being a great strength and 5 being a great weakness. After each team member individually completes the internal analysis checklist, have an open discussion to finalize a list of the strengths and weaknesses of the company.

OPERATIONS/TECHNICAL CAPACITY

Operating systems _____
Efficiencies _____
Labor supply _____
Labor wage rates _____
Labor productivity _____
Raw material supply _____
Age of equipment _____
Quality control _____
On-time shipments _____
Downtime _____
Space for expansion _____
Plant location _____
Core of employees _____
Work environment _____
Technical knowledge _____
Vendor-managed inventory _____
Safety programs _____
Preventative maintenance _____
Level of automation _____
Material costs _____
Training programs _____
Technology _____
Labor organization _____
Attitude _____
Lot tracking _____
Turnover _____
Program effectiveness _____
Program interest/support _____
Product technology _____
New products _____
Patent position _____
R&D organization _____
Engineering design capabilities _____
Information technology _____
Other: _____

SALES DEVELOPMENT

Customer service _____
Reputation _____

Brand acceptance _____
Market share _____
Selling expense _____
Distribution facilities _____
Competitive pricing _____
Number of customers _____
Market information _____
Sales organization _____
Brokers _____
Contracts _____
Target customer database _____
Marketing plan _____
Sales reporting systems _____
Forecasting _____
Client driven _____
Other: _____

ORGANIZATIONAL

Ratio of admin to production _____
Strategic partnerships _____
Communications _____
Clear-cut responsibilities _____
Job descriptions _____
Employee manuals _____
Management information _____
Management turnover _____
Strategic plan _____
Company-wide vision _____
Team cohesiveness _____
Organizational structure _____
Decision making _____
Practice values and beliefs _____
Visionary thinking _____
Management reputation _____
Supportive attitude _____
Leadership _____
Debt-equity structure _____
Inventory turnover _____
Customer credit _____
Capital resources _____

Available cash flow	_____	Vendor discounts	_____
Performance vs. budget	_____	Overhead structure	_____
Return on investments	_____	Profit margins	_____
Cash flow	_____	Pro forma, future performance	_____
Ownership	_____	Problem identification	_____
Dividend history	_____	Sponsorships	_____
Bank agreement	_____	External funding	_____
Banking relationship	_____	Other:	_____
Financial reporting	_____		

Download the Internal Analysis Checklist template at www.stopsellingvanillaicecream.com.

I provide team members with an Internal Analysis Checklist that features an extensive inventory of potential strengths and weaknesses of an organization. Some of the items on the list may not pertain to your organization, but the list gets people thinking and serves an important purpose in this brainstorming exercise. We do not want to miss any strengths or weaknesses of the organization. The team should take a few minutes and give each member time to go through the list individually, rating each item on a scale of 1 to 5 by relative strength as compared to the competition, based on knowledge of the competition. That, of course, will be expanded when you do the external analysis of your market and competition.

"We're looking for real strengths here that will generate ideas for strategy development," I told the Connecting Cultures team, "and I'll challenge you to justify your opinions. It helps to ask, 'Are we better at X than our competition?' If the answer is yes, then it's a strength; if the answer is no, then it's not."

When the individual analyses are complete, it's time for the team to finalize its strengths. This is the easier part of the internal analysis, since talking about the positive traits an organization possesses is always a happier topic than discussing the areas in need of improvement.

As you talk through potential strengths of the company, add the items on which the team reaches at least a tentative consensus to a list organized into three categories: operations/technical, sales development, and organizational. I divide the strengths this way because it's helpful to see, from a big picture, where more or less of a company's strengths lie. Is it operationally strong but weak in sales? Is the organization sound, but operations are less than smooth? This big-picture perspective can help create a stronger strategic perspective for the team.

"Read what's listed in the strengths list and make sure you agree with each one," I told the team once they had discussed each member's insights. "Are there any that aren't strengths? Are there any we should move to a different column? Are there any that aren't clear? And finally, is there anything we need to add?" As we discussed each item, some were crossed off because they weren't real strengths compared to the competition, and some were refined and moved to different categories. Among the strengths the team kept on the list were knowledge of language services and interpreter training under operations/technical; the company's positive reputation and its strong relationships at multiple levels of client organizations under sales development; and the full-time professional interpreting staff and commitment to high quality under the organizational heading.

Have you asked for feedback from members of your organization on what the greatest strengths of the company are? How can you leverage those strengths?

The strengths analysis for Connecting Cultures showed a healthy collection of strengths under the organizational column, followed by operations/technical, and finally sales development. That's not a surprise, given how the team member interviews played out.

There was one obvious observation: sales development had the fewest strengths. It was a visual confirmation of what some members of the team already knew—Connecting Cultures' sales and marketing department is a significant growth opportunity.

"These are great strengths and we have a lot to build on here," I told the team. "Now let's decide which two or three of the primary strengths you just identified are the foundational strengths of the company."

The team quickly zeroed in on the operational strengths of knowledge of language services and interpreter training as the two areas that set Connecting Cultures apart from the competition.

"These are the foundational strengths of your organization," I pointed out. "These strengths could be what we'll build our competency around." I let that announcement sink in before moving on.

UNDERSTANDING WEAKNESSES

The next step in the internal analysis exercise is a discussion of perceived organizational weaknesses. Many times, team members are aware of these weaknesses but have never had a comfortable venue in which to bring them up. Collecting weaknesses during the interviews allows for candor and then honest dialogue while team members are in their "underwear."

The weaknesses analysis is typically one of the first steps in the process that directly benefits from the team development exercise. Due to the collaborative environment created through the exercise, teams are able to have the candid discussions needed for an effective internal analysis. The Connecting Cultures team was no different. They were ready to discuss the company's weaknesses openly.

"We conduct a weaknesses analysis because we want to minimize or eliminate as many of these as possible as a result of executing the strategic plan we're going to develop," I explained.

The team was energized by the strengths analysis and was ready to tackle the weaknesses of the organization. They followed the same process described above for identifying strengths to identify weaknesses.

The majority of Connecting Cultures' weaknesses came to light during the individual interviews earlier in the process. Some of the primary targets identified during the interviews included operational weaknesses, such as a lack of depth at key positions and few documented processes; and organizational weaknesses, such as poor company-wide communication, lack of accountability, and lack of a written plan.

"We saw that sales development had very few strengths in our last exercise, so it follows that we should concentrate on shoring up that part of our business," Rashelle said. "I can tell you that when I meet with potential customers, I feel like I'm going in with one arm tied behind my back."

"Go ahead and pursue that, Rashelle," I said. "Tell us what you mean by that."

"I would feel more comfortable if I had some sales tools to bring with me to these meetings," she explained. "I'm not sure exactly what I need; I just know I need something. We really don't have a sales process at all. I'm someone who feels better if I have a specific path to follow."

"I understand how she feels," Bobbie said. "I would like to explore getting back into more of a sales or account management role, but I would need a better understanding of details such as our pricing model in order to feel my own buy-in."

"Is it safe to describe the sales process in general as a weakness?" I asked the group.

"Absolutely," Kyle said. "It's something we hear from Rashelle all the time, and I don't blame her for feeling frustrated. We just haven't taken the time to do anything about it. As much as we want to avoid expenses, contracting some outside expertise to help us work through the challenges we have on the front end of our sales funnel would be a good investment."

"I think I could sell like crazy with a sales process in place and tools to help me at the point of sale," Rashelle said.

The team displayed clear unity on the issue of sales process improvement and brainstormed action plans to address the key weaknesses. They were in gear and ready to tackle the next challenge.

UNDERSTANDING THE FINANCIALS

"It is critical for the planning team to analyze the financials, because everything eventually flows through them," I explained. "We're looking for some lightbulbs to turn on. These revelations often form the foundation for future action plans that drive the organization forward." Profit is not a strategy, but the result of a great strategy, so having a clear understanding of your financial picture is essential. A lack of financial clarity is like driving your car with your lights off at night and hoping you don't hit anything.

If you don't have financial clarity in your organization, it's not hard to get. We recently hired an accounting firm for one of my clients and they did a complete costs analysis for less than $3,000. Every organization has to understand its financials, so if you don't feel prepared, ask an outside organization, such as your accountant, for help.

Kyle stood to lead this portion of the discussion, per his action plan to prepare a detailed financial analysis and observations on them. He displayed current and forecasted volume through a series of spreadsheets. The utilization summary report detailed the number of appointments, actual appointment hours by interpreter, and billable hours to the customer. His report also included discussions of revenue and expense lines this year versus the previous year; sales and gross margin by service line; and sales and gross margin by customer. It's important to look at financial data from multiple perspectives to generate insights into how to improve the bottom line.

As you review financials you want to ask, "Which products or services do customers seem to be willing to pay for now? Which have the highest demand? Are the numbers showing us there is a strength or competence our customers cannot get from anyone else?" Consequently, a gross margin analysis by product and/or service line is one of the more important components of a thorough financial analysis. Before you decide what you should be selling more of, you need to understand how much you're making on each of your current options. In many companies, the products or services with the highest gross margins are often due to a slight competence and differentiation already in place.

As I reviewed Connecting Cultures' financials, it became clear that their highest margin customers are those that value the consistency of their services. Connecting Cultures' model is unique in that their interpreters are full-time employees getting benefits, while the competition uses independent contractors off a list. That also means Connecting Cultures' rates are higher. The customers that had the highest gross margin for face-to-face interpreting had a significant quality program with measurements that tracked the efficiency of their caregivers. Health care companies that value superior level quality because of the consistency of a certified team of interpreters was a sign of a future competency in the making. Those companies could rationalize paying more because they were getting more in return. The lowest margin customers were those that did not have a comprehensive quality program to measure their return on the time of their caregivers. They were also the companies that always tried to negotiate the contract down when all of the expenses were going up. They didn't value Connecting Cultures' competence, and understanding that is important.

"Rashelle and I had a conversation several months ago about our financials and decided that if we do what we've always done, we'll get what we've always gotten," Kyle said. "Although we're operating as lean as we can, the level of profitability is just not there. We're focused on maximizing our opportunities with our interpreter staff, but it stresses our ability to grow and move forward because we focus so much on just getting through the day.

"We're three or four interpreters short of where we need to be," Kyle continued as Erin nodded in agreement. "We're making a profit, but not as much as we should be. When fully staffed, we don't operate at a profit anymore. There's no fat to trim from our existing operating structure." Personnel costs, such as the interpreting staff, comprise the vast majority of Connecting Cultures' expenses, making it difficult to add staff and remain profitable. This observation set the stage for a key measurement they would begin tracking, the breakeven analysis, which shows on average how much sales revenue is needed each month to break even.

The quality of the service that Connecting Cultures delivers is far above the competitors, and more and more health care companies are willing to pay for the business model Rashelle has put together. However, the financial analysis shows that they need to become much more efficient in delivering this model. In some cases, interpreters are only interpreting for half of their shifts or 50 percent of their time. Connecting Cultures needs to increase their utilization and more effectively deliver the service. This will come with documented processes, lean implementation, technology, and more volume and efficiencies.

The expectation is the Stop Selling Vanilla Ice Cream process will enable Connecting Cultures to make the leap from a company making a little money to one that's earning a significant return on investment. Because of the focus on strategy and talent, over 90 percent of clients make more money in their first year after going through this process. There is no reason to think Connecting Cultures won't be part of that 90 percent.

Kyle pointed out another financial observation. The majority of the revenue was coming from one service: face-to-face interpreting. "We are superior at face-to-face interpreting because of our training and certification program, but that also means that our costs are higher and our margins are squeezed. How come we use that unique program only on internal interpreters? Couldn't we create a new revenue stream by training and certifying the interpreters of a health care provider that wants to manage their own interpreting team? Right now we are only providing one service option in one price range. We need to leverage this foundational strength and increase our sales."

"If we offer more than just face-to-face interpreting and add a full line of services, the biggest challenge will be asking our customers to change fifteen years of perception of what this service is supposed to look like," Rashelle said. "How the industry has always done it, with hourly pricing. That's a change in perception that we need to develop."

"It makes me uncomfortable to see that the bulk of our business is dependent on the whims of our customers," Kyle said. "For us to really give ourselves a sense of confidence in our margins, we need to start telling our customers we do more than just face-to-face interpreting services. That way if they begin searching for alternative services, they'll come to us first. We need to mitigate the potential for a customer to do something differently than face-to-face interpreting. We need to increase those relationships and let them know we can be a full-service language-access solutions organization. It reinforces the value we're trying to provide in being a partner to our customers rather than just the company that will get you through until you get another strategy," Kyle said. "Our pricing needs to be such to warrant a premium when they request a face-to-face appointment."

"Let's table this discussion for now and come back to it when we discuss your competence and target markets in more detail," I interjected. "To wrap up the financial analysis, let's brainstorm any action plans related to the financial analysis."

"We've always kind of flown by the seat of our pants with regard to annual projections," Rashelle said. "This would be a good opportunity for us to get into the habit of creating an annual budget."

"That sounds like a good item for your action plan register," I commented. "A budget provides additional financial clarity and is the basis on which we judge the effectiveness of your strategy and plan. The plan is developed to achieve the budget. It would also increase the engagement level of your department heads in the planning process when we add department budgets."

"I would also like to research lean operation techniques, particularly for service companies," Kyle said.

> *Do you have financial clarity on your business or department? Do you operate with an annual budget? If not, why?*

"These ideas will add to the clarity we've already achieved with this financial analysis," Rashelle said. "I can't believe how many breakthroughs we had through this discussion."

"Now that we have a better understanding of the strengths of the organization and its financial performance, we can take the next step in the process and conduct the external analysis," I said to the team. "It's our version of looking out the window at the world around us. We need to determine what the external market even wants; it does us no good if our market doesn't want what we are offering."

The Scoop

1. What do you think are the top three strengths of your organization versus your competition?

2. What do you think are the top three weaknesses of your organization?

3. Please list and discuss four to six key insights or observations from the internal analysis.

Action Plans to Complete the Process

☐ Finalize the values and beliefs statements of the organization.

☐ Finalize the strengths, weaknesses, and financial analyses.

LOOKING OUT THE WINDOW: MARKET ANALYSIS

If an internal analysis is like looking in the mirror, an external analysis is the organizational equivalent of looking out the window. Rashelle, being the visionary that she is, was raring to go when we arrived at this portion of the first session. Her visionary mind could envision the future of the health care interpreting industry, and she was ready to explore the opportunities the marketplace would offer her company.

Conducting an external analysis requires you to identify trends and collect industry data that you need to determine future strategies and direction. It's critical to understand what your marketplace wants and doesn't want. You don't want to be selling Neapolitan ice cream if your market has no appetite for it.

Most of your market research needs can be identified in the interviews, based on answers to the question: What market research do we need to gather for the team to make informed strategic decisions? Once you have that list from the interviews, you can create action plans for the research each person will do. Most organizations, even large ones, don't consistently collect market research. So make a considerable effort up front to get as much research as you can. Then you can implement a market research gatekeeper to ensure that the company continues collecting market intelligence moving forward.

LEARN MORE ABOUT YOUR MARKET

Since you can't make strategic decisions in a vacuum, collecting market research and evaluating how it impacts your organization must be one of the early steps you take in identifying potential competence options. Market research helps you identify the strategic opportunities for the organization.

"Market research is one of the greatest struggles for an organization, because typically there is no one assigned to do it," I told the Connecting Cultures team as we got underway. "Every organization must challenge itself to collect as much market research and intelligence as possible prior to developing its strategy."

While collecting market research is a lot of work and it's tempting to ignore it, you can accomplish a lot without too much effort or expense. Market research companies can offer incredible insight, but it may be unrealistic to spend more money on research when you're already committing significant resources to planning. But you can rely on your team to step up and fill the role: they probably have the industry experience necessary to do their own market research without the need to hire an outside agency if you don't have the budget for it.

> *Does your organization value relevant market intelligence? What are you doing to stay abreast of current trends?*

"Many companies leverage information available from their industry associations, and a great deal of information is available online," I explained. "You just need to ensure the credibility of the source."

It's important to understand that market research and analysis are not one-time events. Through continuous market research, successful organizations adapt their competence and strategies to the changing marketplace.

This proactive approach enables companies not only to maintain their competitive advantage, but also to strengthen it.

You should use three primary questions to direct your market research efforts:

✔ What market research information do we need to collect and study to make the most informed strategic decisions?

✔ What trends are developing in the world, state, and industry right now?

✔ Based on the internal and external analysis, what are the strategic options for the organization?

For Connecting Cultures, I had compiled a series of research questions, action plans, and market trend ideas from information gleaned during the team member interviews. The objective is to provide a guide for external analysis efforts and facilitate better strategic discussion. It was on Rashelle's action plan to collect market research based on these lists and present it to the group. Some of the questions included:

✔ How many health care facilities have internal interpreting capabilities and how many are outsourcing that service?

✔ How might national health care reform change our business and the market?

✔ What accreditations are available from entities such as the American Translators Association (ATA)?

The action plans included:

✔ Obtain census information and school district data on the growth of ethnic groups in the area to see whether Connecting Cultures should be planning to add languages.

✔ Obtain census data to estimate the growth of each ethnic group in the markets in which Connecting Cultures currently does business or is considering as new markets.

✔ Create a geographic map of health care accounts.

In addition, the team had identified during the interviews some specific trends in the marketplace that might impact Connecting Cultures' strategy development:

✔ A general movement toward certification for health care interpreters is growing.

✔ The National Council on Interpreting and Health Care (NCIHC) is identifying what qualifies as providing good interpreting skills.

✔ National forums for health care language consulting are becoming more prevalent. (Rashelle is beginning to speak nationally on the subject.)

✔ Some federal health care reform plans would provide insurance coverage to the populations that Connecting Cultures serves.

✔ Community diversity is growing, and thus the need for language services continues to increase.

✔ Customer focus on fiscal responsibility offers an opportunity for Connecting Cultures to market its full-service approach to interpreting services, creating a partner to help customers manage this critical demand on their business.

Kyle responded to the information. "It would appear that many of the high-level trends would provide a lot of opportunities for Connecting Cultures. The question is which opportunity has the greatest upside. I look forward to digging into these numbers and figuring that out."

"Remember what I said about lightbulbs turning on in your head when you combine your internal analysis with information compiled during the external analysis?" I asked the group. "Ideas and options will emerge during this stage that might frame your future competence."

"Those lightbulbs have started turning on for me already," Rashelle said, eager to dive into her presentation. She came armed with enough information to get the ball rolling. "In preparing for this session, one of the things I did was collect demographic information from some of the larger school districts," she said. "It shows a significant influx of Spanish-speaking people into the area, particularly from Mexico. The Hmong and other southeast Asian populations also continue to grow in many of our target markets." Rashelle's presentation included demographic data on various population centers in counties throughout northeastern Wisconsin, along with some information on major metropolitan areas such as Milwaukee, Madison, and Minneapolis.

"The number that's the most staggering to me is that school enrollment for Spanish-speaking students statewide was 31,000 a few years ago, and now it's 73,000," Kyle commented. "30,500 of them are limited English proficient. So not only is the population increasing significantly, the percentage of students considered 'limited English proficient' went up, too. Households aren't doing a lot to increase their English proficiency, which creates more opportunities for us."

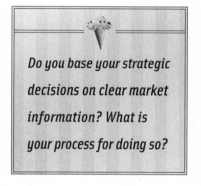

Do you base your strategic decisions on clear market information? What is your process for doing so?

"This information will help us target specific health care providers who are already seeing an increase in demand for interpreting services," Erin noted. "This data will reinforce their understanding of why they should consider doing business with us."

ESTABLISH A MARKET RESEARCH GATEKEEPER

The type of information Connecting Cultures had gathered is the same type of information you'll want to have at your disposal regularly, not just one time. Establishing a market research gatekeeper is a step to consider in organizing the flood of information collected by team members.

The gatekeeper's task is to collect and organize all of the market research that team members gather throughout the year, including articles from trade journals, personal observations of the marketplace, updated census and other demographic data, articles from major news organizations, and customer surveys and feedback. The gatekeeper's duties include:

- ✔ Collection of market research data from all company associates

- ✔ Organizing the information into appropriate categories

✔ Determining which information is time-sensitive and which can wait until the annual planning process

✔ Preparing a summary for presentation to the planning team at the start of each annual planning process

"Your team is typical in that collectively you have decades of experience in your industry," I told the team. "That experience, in itself, is market research. But you still need to challenge your thinking by collecting additional information. You can hire an outside market research firm or conduct your own research, but most teams choose to pull together as much market research as they can on their own and install a process to continue collecting information throughout the year.

"You can't rationalize spending significant dollars to hire a market research firm, yet you also can't afford to make strategic decisions in a vacuum. We need to make sure the developing external trends support your competence and vision. Make the best decisions you can, and then as you execute your plan, the information you collect will help you hone your strategy as you go to market. Will you have as much information as you'd like? Probably not, but you will have enough to take appropriate action.

"If you establish a market research gatekeeper, every year when you go through the planning process you'll have a file folder filled with this kind of information."

"I can take that role," Rashelle said.

"You can take it?" Bobbie asked, with an eyebrow raised in doubt.

Several at the table sported a wry smile or even chuckled as they tried to picture Rashelle being organized enough to tackle an ongoing research assignment of this size.

"That's like asking Eric to slow down his pace," I pointed out with a laugh. "It can be done, but it's not a natural trait in the same way that organization isn't one of your strong suits, Rashelle."

"Fine," Rashelle said, recognizing the reality of her skill set. "I just thought I'd offer it up."

"I'll take it," said Kyle, realizing this task fell directly into his area of strength. The behavioral assessments were already having a positive impact on the Connecting Cultures team dynamics.

"This is a great first step today with the market intelligence to maintain and increase your differentiation," I said. "You'll find that over time you're going to get really good at it. Your competition hasn't set a high bar, so we need to make the gap between what you offer and what they offer as big as possible. Continuous market research allows your organization to adjust its strategy.

"Now that we have completed the internal and external analyses, we should have the information we need to develop the future competence of Connecting Cultures."

The Scoop

1. What market research do you need in order to make good strategic decisions?

2. What questions or trends do you need to answer or explore in your market research efforts?

3. Who is the best person in your organization to tackle an initial market research project?

4. Who is the best person in your organization to be a market research gatekeeper?

Action Plans to Complete the Process

☐ Finalize action plans for any additional market research your company wants to gather for the next planning meeting.

☐ Implement the market research gatekeeper process.

10

THE PROCESS TO CREATE
A REAL DIFFERENTIATION

"We're in the homestretch," I told the team. "We're in position to move forward and develop your future competence. This is one of the most important steps in the Stop Selling Vanilla Ice Cream process. You've got some powerful information in your hands from the analysis of Connecting Cultures' strengths and weaknesses, financials, and the market. Now we'll use that information to develop your future competence, or what I call your mint chocolate chip ice cream."

Possessing a competence and delivering on it consistently bring a number of benefits in addition to creating a point of differentiation. Think of how many customers will choose to do business with you because they cannot obtain the same level of product or service from any other company. The greater the level of differentiation through your competence, the larger your margins can be. Plus, it becomes more and more difficult for your competition to catch up and duplicate your competency, because you keep getting better at it every year through an annual plan.

Another unique step of the Stop Selling Vanilla Ice Cream process is that it provides an opportunity for all members of the planning team to present their recommended strategy for the company moving forward. Few employees get that opportunity, so when they get the chance they usually take advantage of it. "As a planning team, we will review the process to define your competence and target markets, and I will provide you the templates to complete it," I told the Connecting Cultures team. "Then we will break the planning team into smaller homework teams that will develop and present their strategy recommendation back to the planning team at the next meeting. After all the strategy recommendations have been presented, we will come to agreement on the future competence and strategy of Connecting Cultures. It is a simple and exhilarating process. So let's review the process to define your future competence and the specific action plans to complete your homework."

UNDERSTANDING COMPETENCE

"Your competence is defined as the singular strength or combination of strengths that you do better and will do better than anyone else in the geographic markets in which you compete," I explained. "Your target markets are those that value your competence the most. Because they value your competence, they will give you more business and are often willing to pay more for it. They choose to do business with you because they cannot get what you provide at the same level from anyone else. We'll work to strengthen your competence by building your organization around it, creating the best mint chocolate chip ice cream in the marketplace."

"I guess I'm having trouble wrapping my mind around the concept of why customers would pay more for what we do," Eric said. "I can see it happening in the short-term, but not so much in the long-term."

"Let me offer you an example," I said. "Herb Kohler, president and chairman of the Kohler Company, accomplished this when he turned a small Wisconsin town an hour from here into one of the most famous golf destinations in the world."

Kohler enlisted the talents of one of the top golf course designers, Pete Dye, to build a world-class golf course down the road from the Kohler Company factory. That original course was so successful that Kohler commissioned Dye to build a second one, and then two more courses several miles north of the village of Kohler on the shores of Lake Michigan.

Kohler's pride and joy is the Straits Course at Whistling Straits, located on that lakeside property. The Straits Course consistently ranks among the best courses in the United States and has hosted the PGA Championship on two occasions, and will host other prominent competitions in the near future. Whistling Straits provides a golf experience unlike any other in North America. Its high sand dunes and approximately one thousand sand traps are a rare sight this side of the Atlantic. The Straits does not allow golf carts; instead, knowledgeable caddies tote your bag around the windswept links.

Predictably, greens fees at the Straits are not for the faint of heart. In 2012—two years after the PGA Championship paid a visit—golfers could expect to pony up $350 to play eighteen holes, plus $60 for the required caddy and a recommended gratuity of $35. As a comparison, you could play one of the top municipally owned courses in the United States an hour away for $31 on a weekday, less than 9 percent of the total cost at the Straits.

If you're wondering whether Whistling Straits provides enough differentiation to validate those prices, just try getting a tee time there and see how difficult it is to find an open spot. Why does Kohler charge such premium rates for its top course? Because it can. People are falling all over each other to pay it. The Straits, like other Kohler businesses, predicates its success on providing quality so high that the competition can't match it. The company comes right out and announces on its website home page that high quality is its overarching competence with the slogan, "A single level of quality regardless of price." It's genius.

"Whistling Straits illustrates the power that tangible differentiation can have on the margins that top organizations can command for their products and services," I said to the team. "The stronger your competence, the less impact a down economy will have on your organization. The golf industry as a whole suffered mightily through the economic recession that began late in 2007, yet Whistling Straits was able to increase its fees consistently without experiencing a drop in play."

"I get it," Eric said. "I just haven't made the connection yet to what we do. Will we be able to charge a premium like that?"

"Well, maybe not that large," I said with a chuckle. "But there's no reason your company can't differentiate itself from the competition to the point where your customers won't want to live without your services. You can create customer loyalty that enables you to retain business and attract additional business even though you charge a premium for what you do. As a consumer, you choose to do business with companies every day because of something they provide that you can't get anywhere else. You shop at certain stores and go to certain restaurants because they have a competence that's unique to that business. You pay more for certain products or services because you want them. So why would you not apply that same concept to your business?

"I have clients who know exactly how much more they can charge over the competition because of their competence," I said. "One client knew they could get 2 to 3 percent more for their competence, and that added up to millions of dollars over the years. The larger the differentiation from your competition, the higher your margin can be—like the Kohler example. Companies with a clear competence know it, and they can hold out to get the price and margin they want and deserve."

"Can profit be our competence?" Kyle asked.

"Profit is not a strategy," I answered. "Profit is the result of executing a great strategy. Profit tells us how well our strategy is working, but we need to develop a competence for which your customers will willingly pay and give you more business."

"Wouldn't we be better off with two or three competencies?" Erin asked.

"That would be the organizational equivalent of having multiple personalities," I said. "Each company or business unit has a unique personality based on one competence that dominates all other elements. Drifting from one competence to another is a sign of poor strategy and a lack of discipline. Also, in order to be the best at your competence, you need to focus all of your company or divisional resources on that differentiation. When I find a company

> *Is there a company in your market that successfully charges a premium for its goods or services? What competence allows it to do so?*

with two or more competencies, we create separate divisions within the company around each competence so there can be focus and accountability."

"Our people and the relationships we have with our customers are a point of differentiation for us," Rashelle said. "Can we consider that when we work on our competence?"

"That's a question I hear often and it's a good one," I replied. "The first question I ask business leaders is why their customers do business with them, and the most common answer is relationships. But no, relationships do not qualify as a competence. Strong relationships are a result of your competence. Relationships have significant value and can be a competitive advantage, but relationships in and of themselves cannot be your competence because they are not sustainable in the long-term. People change positions within the organization or simply move on. As a matter of fact, many large retailers have a policy that requires buyers to change positions every few years so external salespeople can't build too close of a personal relationship with them and gain an advantage."

If a sale truly exists because of a relationship, it opens the door to a worst-case scenario in which an employee leaves your organization and takes his or her customers. You never want to become people dependent, because you can't control that. What you *can* control is the differentiation your organization delivers. Your competence may be masquerading as a relationship, but it likely is something deeper and more tangible than that.

Over time, you'll want the primary reason your customers buy from you to be something your company provides rather than something one employee provides. Building a strategy that centers on the strengths of your organization will eliminate any chance of your differentiation walking out the door. A competence should be something all aspects of your organization continually strengthen and deliver and that creates a clear differentiation between your organization and your competitors.

START WITH STRATEGIC OPPORTUNITIES

With a clear grasp of the nature of competence in hand, the team was ready to take some of the insights gathered from the internal and external analyses and discuss strategic opportunities.

"I've come to the conclusion that we need to do a better job of asking our customers what type of services they want from us—face-to-face interpreting services, telephonic services, or a combination of both," Rashelle said. "They're used to being told what our hourly rate is, and that's it. Now it needs to be about giving them an opportunity to make a choice based on their own organization's needs. A-la-carte billing would be a welcome change for them."

Rashelle is convinced Connecting Cultures needs to create additional streams of revenue beyond the current focus on face-to-face interpreting services. She wants her company to expand into additional metropolitan areas, delve into providing continuing education services, and perhaps even introduce telephonic interpreting services as ways to expand its reach and meet client demand.

"We're not looking to provide wide-ranging telephonic interpreting services like some of our national competitors," she said. "I realize this may sound contradictory, but I do think providing telephonic service on a limited basis may be where some of our opportunity lies. It would create a point of differentiation for Connecting Cultures if we give our customers the opportunity to create a mix of services that fits their needs."

From a facilitator's perspective, the challenge in working with visionaries is finding the line between letting them run and sensing when to pull back on the reins. You never want to dampen visionaries' enthusiasm by throwing water on their ideas; they just may need reminding that some intermediate steps have to take place before the big picture comes into focus. But I didn't need to play that role in this discussion. The team development exercise was paying huge dividends. The team was holding nothing back; all team members engaged in some of the most passionate and productive debate this company had ever had. Kyle was the one who questioned Rashelle on her short-term ideas.

"It would take a considerable amount of time to develop any telephonic capabilities," Kyle pointed out. "What are your thoughts about creating additional revenue in the near term?"

"Creating a dynamic pricing plan is going to bring the most near-term value to the organization," Rashelle replied. "Changing our pricing model to per-minute usage would eliminate the customer paying for unutilized time. Instead, they would pay a premium to have us available face-to-face. Adding telephonic services would cut down on our travel time and enable us to handle more cases than we do now. And adding training and continuing education services would create a revenue stream from those organizations that decide to handle their interpreting services internally."

After more discussion that leveraged information from their internal and external analyses, the team brainstormed strategic options the homework teams could consider when completing their action plans. The strategic options brainstormed included the following:

✔ Become the best at providing face-to-face interpreting

✔ Become the best Spanish-interpreting company

✔ Expand revenue streams by adding training services for organizations with internal interpreters

✔ Adjust the pricing model away from the pay-by-the-hour model.

"These are important insights to take into account as you work with your homework teams to develop your competence," I said.

"We know our local market and we've been here for ten years," said Rashelle. "The question is: How are we going after it? We have to define our go-to-market strategy."

COMPETENCE RECOMMENDATIONS

"Defining the competence is the most challenging part of the process, in part because you're new to the concept and you will have to make some tough decisions regarding your strategy," I said to the team. "So our next step is to break the planning team up into smaller homework teams. Each homework team will create its own strategy recommendation on the future competence and strategy of Connecting Cultures. You'll need to be prepared to present your strategy recommendations at the next team meeting."

> *Which homework team recommendation will be the foundation for your company's future competence and strategy? Will it be your team? Why?*

Homework teams are a unique aspect to the Stop Selling Vanilla Ice Cream process.

This is an opportunity to pair team members who might not interact a great deal during the normal course of business. It's also an ideal setting for someone like Erin to step forward or someone like Eric to be forward thinking. One of the things I love about team homework assignments is it forces more people to work on the strategic planning process. Most companies have only a few people working "on" the business—if at all—while the rest are working "in" the business. After this process, those ratios typically reverse.

The intriguing possibilities of what strategic ideas might come out of Connecting Cultures' mix of behavioral styles immediately reenergizes the group. The homework team concept creates a bit of a competitive environment—each team would like their brainchild to become the chosen direction for the company.

A lot of the "why" component and rationale behind the strategies generated by the homework teams will come from the internal and external analyses. The process provides tools and templates for all of the methodologies, but one of the most important tools we provide is the Competence Hierarchy chart, shown below. This tool begins with the stated competence at the top, supported by primary and secondary target markets that would value and pay for that competence. It is a powerful visual that lets

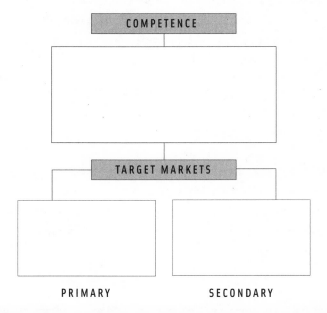

COMPETENCE HIERARCHY

COMPETENCE

TARGET MARKETS

PRIMARY　　　　　SECONDARY

the other members of the planning team quickly see a team's recommended strategy. It forces homework teams to provide some rationale in support of their stated competence for the organization. "Creating the future competence hierarchy of Connecting Cultures is our ultimate objective," I said.

In recognition of the heavy influence that the Spanish language has on Connecting Cultures' business, we organized the teams and named them with Spanish numbers: Team Uno—Eric and Erin; Team Dos—Kyle and Bobbie; Team Tres—Rashelle. The action plans for each homework team were as follows:

- ☐ Review the plan completed to date (strategic challenges, internal analysis, external analysis, etc.) and make sure you are in agreement with it. Be prepared to discuss any changes at the next session.

- ☐ Using the competence process and templates provided, develop the future competence hierarchy for your company and your rationale to support it. Will it differentiate your organization well into the future?

- ☐ Based on the future competence you recommended, identify your target markets and how they should be prioritized. Identifying who values your competence the most determines your target markets.

- ☐ Based on the competence hierarchy you recommended, document key aspects of your future strategy that we need to discuss (i.e., services delivered as part of the competence, strengths the organization needs to develop to deliver the competence, etc.).

- ☐ Brainstorm action plans the organization needs to complete in the near future to implement and/or strengthen the competence and strategy you have recommended.

By the time they get to this point in the process, most organizations have some sense of what their competence should be or at least what their competence options are. I have seen some companies define their competence in ten minutes, while others can take hours or days. It is the single most important strategic question you will ever answer for your business, so stick with it. Persevere!

Companies continue to implement and strengthen their competence over years, so try to establish a foundation for your future competence for the next year. Taking your strategy to market is an educational process in which the most successful organizations continue to adjust their competence hierarchy based on what they learn, like sharpening the tip of a pencil. Remember, strengthening your competence is an evolution that takes place over years, not a revolution that happens overnight.

"The following step-by-step process is to assist the homework teams in developing and presenting the future competence and strategy of your company," I said. The process is simple to follow and acts as a guide for your homework. The templates referenced in the process below are available at www.stopsellingvanillaicecream.com.

1. Review and discuss the internal analysis of the organization.

   ☐ **Strengths**—Ask your team what strengths can be the foundational strengths of your competence. What single strength or combination of strengths can you do better than anyone else in the markets you compete? Do you have to work on creating foundational strengths to support the competence you want to deliver?

   ☐ **Weaknesses**—What weaknesses do you need to eliminate or minimize to enhance your foundational strengths and deliver your strategy? What action plans would help you do that?

   ☐ **Financial analysis**—Which of your products or services have the highest demand (growth) and margin? Which products or services do customers seem to be willing to pay for now? Why do your customers do business with you? Are the numbers showing that there is a strength or competence your customers cannot get from anyone else?

2. Review and discuss the external analysis and market research

summary. What are the emerging trends that could create an opportunity in the markets in which you compete? Is there a need you are filling in the marketplace right now that you can expand on? What are the growing segments in your market (for example, the baby boomer population)?

3. Review the strategic opportunities list and brainstorm and list additional possible competence options for your organization.

4. Discuss how you think your top competitors are trying to differentiate themselves. Is there a void in the marketplace? Can you outperform one of your competitors on the competence it appears to have selected?

5. Complete your first draft of the future competence and use it to build the competence hierarchy using the template. Remember that your competence is what your organization will provide better than anyone else in the markets in which you compete. How is the organization going to differentiate itself moving forward or in the future? Some teams find it helpful to determine what their current competence or competitive advantage is. Why do your current customers choose you over the competition? Consider taking some customers to lunch and asking that question. Can you build on a possible current competitive advantage, or do you need to go in a different direction?

6. Provide your rationale as to why you chose this competence, for example, because of a certain strength or a void in the marketplace. Why is this competence going to separate your organization from your competition? One method to determine whether you like the competence structure you have chosen is to consider what the company will look like in two to three years based on pursuing your chosen competence. If you don't like what the company might look like, develop another competence until you have created a future that is attractive to you and that will match the needs of the marketplace.

7. Now that you have completed the first draft of your competence, you need to define the target markets of the company. These are the

companies or consumers that will value your future competence the most and will be willing to pay you for it. After you have identified your target markets, prioritize them by identifying them as primary and secondary. Your primary target market should or will value your competence the most. Consider the following when developing your target markets:

☐ Do you have a current type or group of customers that values a strength or unique offering your company provides? What types of customers have the highest margins?

☐ A well-defined target market is a finite group of people or companies. This is important so you can develop a marketing plan to go right at your target markets. Usually the most target markets on which a company or division can focus is two to three.

8. Now that you have completed your competence hierarchy by defining your competence and target markets, discuss other aspects of the strategy on which you need to gain agreement. What other strategic issues does the planning team need to discuss that may have been raised in the interviews or discussions to this point?

9. Brainstorm and list all the strategies and action plans from your discussions that the organization needs to complete during the next year in order to implement, strengthen, and deliver your competence.

"Each team will present their competence hierarchy and strategy recommendation at the start of the next session," I explained. "This is where you really want to expand your thinking and evaluate all strategic options. The presentations will be very interactive as each group tries to sell the planning team on their strategy. Once each team has presented their recommendation, we will have several strategy recommendations on the table that we can start discussing."

ACTION PLANS FOR PHASE 3			
PROJECT DESCRIPTION	Owner	Due Date	Date Completed
To prepare for the next session, in your teams (Team Uno: Eric and Erin; Team Dos: Kyle and Bobbie; Team Tres: Rashelle) please do the following:			
1. Review plan completed to date and make sure you are in agreement with it. Be prepared to discuss any changes at the next session.	All Teams		
2. Using the defined process and templates, develop the future competence hierarchy for your company and the rationale to support it. Will it differentiate Connecting Cultures well into the future?	All Teams		
3. Based on the future competence you recommended, identify your target markets and how they should be prioritized. Your target markets are determined by who values your competence the most.	All Teams		
4. Based on the competence hierarchy you recommended, document other key aspects of your future strategy the team needs to discuss (i.e., services delivered as part of your competence, strengths the organization needs to develop to deliver your competence, etc.).	All Teams		
5. Brainstorm action plans the organization needs to complete in the near future to implement the competence and strategy you recommended; record these action plans in the brainstorming template.	All Teams		

PLANNING PROCESS			
Planning Meeting		9/9/XX	
Planning Meeting		9/29/XX	

One of my advisor responsibilities will be to bring the planning team back together around a differentiated strategy. We will have had our fun thinking outside the box, but in the next team meeting it will be time to consider all the strategic options on the table and hash out why a selected target customer is going to buy from Connecting Cultures rather than the competition.

"That's more homework than I had when I was in school," Eric said. "You're really putting us to work."

"The stakes are high and require a matching effort. The benefits of clearly defining, strengthening, and delivering a competence to a target market that values it will drive significant growth in sales and profitability. As we say at SM Advisors, 'Those who plan, profit!'"

Rashelle, wanting to maintain the momentum from the team development exercise, quickly vocalized a note of encouragement. "I would ask going forward that we remember everyone's communication styles," she said.

"It will be up to you to come back and say, 'This is what we think the company should do and this should be our strategy,'" I told them. "The future competence and strategy definition can be somewhat overwhelming the first time, but once we start executing the plan, you will understand it more every day as Connecting Cultures begins to realize the benefits of having a clear differentiation."

It was exciting to see the lightbulbs turning on as the planning team prepared to embark on the process of crafting the future course of Connecting Cultures. The newly assigned homework teams already were checking schedules and making plans to connect as we prepared to wrap up. I felt confident we had created clarity around the process and built enthusiasm for moving forward.

"I can't wait to hear the ideas everyone comes back with," Rashelle said. "I'm excited that all of us get the chance to contribute to this effort. We've got a great team with a lot of talent, and I'm confident we'll have a winning strategy at the end of this process."

"Take advantage of this opportunity," I urged everyone in the room. "This is a big moment for the company and for each of you individually. You're about to play a part in writing the strategy of this company. You're at the doorstep of something big. Now it's just a matter of getting it on paper, agreeing to it, and positioning the organization to deliver it. It's time for Connecting Cultures to define its mint chocolate chip ice cream."

The Scoop

1. What are the competence options and strategic opportunities the homework teams should consider in developing their recommendation on future competence and strategy of the organization?

2. Which planning team members would you pair up into homework teams to present their recommended competence and strategy? Why? How would those pairings build stronger internal relationships and a stronger planning team?

3. Is there anything else you need to do to effectively prepare the homework teams to develop their strategy recommendations?

Action Plans to Complete the Process

☐ Provide the updated plan to this point to each planning team member, including the internal and external analyses.

☐ Provide the process, action plans, and templates to each homework team to develop their competence and strategy recommendation (templates available at www.stopsellingvanillaicecream.com).

☐ Set date and time of your next planning meeting when each homework team will present their strategy recommendation.

STRATEGY DEVELOPMENT

DEFINING YOUR COMPETENCE AND STRATEGY

Today would be a big day for the Connecting Cultures team: they would define their competence, setting the company on a clear path to differentiation. Some good-natured trash talking among the team members was a positive sign that they felt loose and ready to work. Each homework team boasted they had the future competence and strategy of the company all figured out. This semicompetitive atmosphere is healthy and serves as a catalyst to building a stronger team. In fact, watching teams come together like this is one of the most enjoyable parts of the Stop Selling Vanilla Ice Cream process.

"I have what I jokingly refer to as a strategic illness," I said to get the discussion underway. "When I go into a company, I try to figure out if its employees know what the company's competence is—or if they even have one. If they do, then it will be tough to negotiate with them on price. If they don't, I'll try to negotiate, and usually I'm successful.

"Today, we'll define your competence: what you offer that will help you avoid competing on price. It is the critical first part of your strategy development. Without a clear understanding of why your customers should

> *Do you think most of the people in your organization understand how the organization is trying to differentiate itself? Do they put it in to practice in their daily internal and external interactions?*

value you over your competitors, you can't define your direction and you can't make smart decisions about the future of the company. As you discuss your competence, the decisions surrounding your competence develop into your strategy."

Defining your competence and how you are going to differentiate your company is the single most important strategic decision you will make as a planning team. Why is a customer going to do business with you versus one of your competitors? How could there be a more important decision than that? It varies by company, but the process to define your competence can be a roller coaster of emotions. However, once it starts coming into focus it creates momentum. The ultimate measure is when you begin to see growth in your top and bottom line.

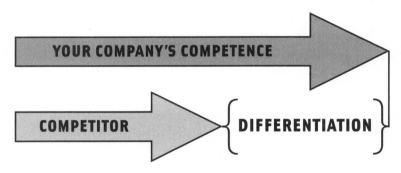

FOCUS THE TEAM

"I want to emphasize the point of your being very strategic in your thinking today," I said to open the session. "Your focus should be on where you want to be two or three years from now as an organization and the strategies to get there. The expectation should be that you will go from a company making little money to one that's getting a significant return on its investment."

As is the case at the beginning of each session, we start by going through the action plan register, which documents the action plans from the previous session. This creates the most effective form of accountability, and that's accountability to the team. No one wants to announce she has failed to complete her assignments and let the team down. This first step in implementing a culture of accountability begins here at the planning team level and eventually filters throughout the organization as leaders implement it within their respective department teams. Granted, sometimes action plans aren't complete until the wee hours of the morning on the day of the meeting, but it's meaningful that team members make the effort to get them done.

"I would like to follow through on one of my action plan items and update you on the work I've been doing on our values and beliefs statements," Rashelle said. "My previous version was too wordy. I wanted to bring the four key values—professionalism, communication, education, and integrity—into focus for a greater cross section of the organization. Here are the revised statements."

> **We value *professionalism* because it fosters a relationship of respect in all settings.**
>
> **We value *communication* because it is the bridge to understanding.**
>
> **We value *education* because it builds a stronger future.**
>
> **We value *integrity* because it guides our decisions.**

"I feel we have some internal struggles with respect and communication," Rashelle said. "Some of our people thought that while we were working on the foundation, we lost sight of them as people, that we only started this company to make money and that we cared only about the customer. In reality, one of the main reasons we started it was to provide employment for people like me—interpreters who wanted full-time positions with benefits. It was to make a living doing what we love to do. We didn't communicate that well. And there's a level of professionalism we want to see given to each other and to our customers. Health care interpreting is not just telling people about their health; it might mean telling them life or death information. For me, that means I won't shoot from the hip. If everyone knows this is what we expect, we'll have a fantastic working environment. And it's all based on those four values. We become a stronger and more reputable business because of these values."

Rashelle suggested action plans to "live" the values: Connecting Cultures would post the values and beliefs on the office walls and website and make them part of the orientation process for new employees. I captured those action plans and added them to the sixty or so already on the list, reminding the team of the importance of verbalizing the insights and action plans that pop into their head as we work our way through the process. It is extremely important to document all the action plans as we proceed through the process: at the end of the process we will use them to build the department plans.

"It's important that these values and beliefs are presented for everyone to see," I said. "One of the action plans I would suggest is determining how to communicate and use these values. This is an awesome start, and it provides us the opportunity to provide more role clarity for our team in executing the plan." The team agreed with the values and beliefs statements Rashelle presented and accepted responsibility to see them carried out.

COMPETENCE AND STRATEGY

It was time to dive into the meat of the session: defining the future competence and strategy of the organization. "The process of hashing out a competence that we can illustrate through a brand strategy with tangible benefits for the customer is crucial to ensuring your ability to stand out from the crowd," I said to begin the discussion. "As consumers, we pay more for certain things every day because we know we cannot get them anywhere else. That's what we want to identify for Connecting Cultures."

This typically is the most challenging meeting of the process because it requires you to think 100 percent strategically for a long period of time, and most people are not used to thinking that way, especially for that length of time. The requirement to make decisions that will impact the future of the company often generates some anxiety. At the same time, the process is very exciting because you will be working together to design the future of your company. This creates a special bond between the company owners, leaders, and each team member.

Every organization is different when it comes to the speed with which it is able to define its future strategy. Discussions aimed at identifying the company's competence can take anywhere from a few minutes to a full day or more, depending on how clear their differentiation is from the competition. Every organization is different, so sticking to a proven process is critical to achieving success.

Organizations usually figure out their core strategy, how to remove those four to six large rocks in the water, in the first year. It's difficult to figure everything out all in one year, much less execute it. The theory is if you try to do everything at once, you'll get nothing done. After the first year, the strategy is refined. You will build on your strategy in the second year and beyond, sharpening it over time. Organizations will continue to learn and apply polish to the strategy as they take it to market. The marketplace has a way of teaching you a few lessons, some of them a little harsh. The process of defining and refining your strategy is an evolution, not a revolution, eventually resulting in a razor-sharp competitive focus. But the first step in that process is to define your competence.

I sensed the team was chomping at the bit to present their homework assignments. Fulfilling her behavioral style to a "T," Rashelle confirmed their readiness by jumping in first. "I can't wait to hear what everyone has prepared," Rashelle said. "This is the session I've been waiting for."

"Great," I continued. "Here are some ground rules for the homework team presentations. First, each team must present not only their competence hierarchy and strategy recommendation but also the rationale behind them, recommendations on other aspects of the strategy that will need to be discussed by the planning team, and action items that need to be completed to deliver and strengthen the competence. You must explain why this competence and strategy will work. If you aren't presenting, listen carefully and please hold your questions to the end of each presentation so the team can lay out its entire recommendation; then challenge their thoughts with questions that will help sort out the strategy. We will see numerous lightbulbs turning on during these discussions until we have total clarity and agreement on our future competence."

One of the objectives of this methodology is to stretch those creative minds and get as many ideas on the table as possible. The more creative ideas the better. Then it is the advisor's responsibility to lead the team through the process of synthesizing all the ideas down into one future competence and strategy. By having all members of the team get their chance to present their ideas, it creates buy-in for the ultimate strategy that comes out of the session.

This session can be a struggle for those who aren't used to thinking strategically. The members of the planning team can go through periods of enthusiasm and self-confidence, and anxiety and self-doubt, which is why the earlier sessions are so important. The strategy development session provides an opportunity for individuals to step up and become leaders; many get the chance to consider, develop, and present on strategy for the first time. The cream will rise during this step. I encouraged Rashelle, as the organization's leader, to pay attention to which of her team members would take advantage of the opportunity.

Strategy discussions often are intense, and it's common to see teams drift apart somewhat during the course of the session before coming back together to zero in on the shared prize. They are in the process of making the most important decision, and members of the team will stand up for their ideas and be heard. Healthy conflict is the backbone of a high-performance team. If the conflict is on the topic at hand, I let them go. If it turns into something personal or tangential, I'll jump in and get them back on track. It is important to remind the team to rely on what they learned about how to communicate and work together more effectively. Relying on the conflict management and emotional intelligence techniques they learned is what eventually helps them come back together as a team and hash out the competence.

"Remember, we're looking for a competence that is the singular strength or a combination of strengths that sets Connecting Cultures apart," I said. "Your competence will drive human resource and financial allocation, structure, compensation, skill sets, and systems and processes. It will serve as a filter for new customers and acquisition opportunities. The outcome of this discussion is huge, because once we define your competence we will build everything else in the organization around it."

First up was Team Uno, comprised of Eric and Erin. Eric can be an out-in-front presence when he feels a comfort level with the subject matter, while Erin is more comfortable in the background than taking the lead. I was curious to see how this presentation, in particular, would play out. From the projector, the team's competence hierarchy, shown below, lit up the front wall of the conference room for the entire planning team to view. Team Uno's competence hierarchy featured the following competence statement: Measurably superior language access solutions supported by an unrivaled training process. Their prioritized target market was shown as the director of quality/risk management at health care facilities in current geographic service markets. (Note: We'll discuss the target markets in the next chapter.)

"Essentially, what we came up with for our competence is—" Eric began, and then paused. "I don't really know where to start."

Somewhat surprisingly, Erin took immediate control of the situation. "In trying to work on our competence, we ended up looking at the services we offer and backtracked from there," she said. "I'm not sure we have anything ground shaking, but our objective is to show we're not just an interpreting service. As we considered the foundations, the strength of our

ERIC AND ERIN'S COMPETENCE HIERARCHY

COMPETENCE

SERVICE-DRIVEN
Measurably superior language access solutions
supported by an unrivaled training process

TARGET MARKET

Director of quality/risk
management at health care
facilities in our current
geographic markets

PRIMARY

training and certification process stood out as an expertise we could build on. We looked at our services and what we're good at, and what we want to continue delivering." Erin spoke very quickly and with authority, holding her hands in front of her and using occasional hand gestures, while Eric stood close to the wall and kept his eyes on the screen.

"So you're talking about a total language solution," I clarified, "not just interpreting services."

"Right," Erin replied.

She then offered up commentary about the state of Connecting Cultures' competition: many competitors display deficiencies and fall short of what Connecting Cultures can do already or could do in the not-too-distant future.

"We have the potential to offer courses for interpreters to help them prepare for certification," Erin continued. "We're doing that internally already."

"We have to make the market aware of our training and support capabilities," Eric interrupted, suddenly engaged in the discussion.

"We have the skills and knowledge to provide these services as part of our competence already," Erin added. "There's work to be done, but we're ready to start taking that on."

Erin wrapped up Team Uno's presentation by noting that their action plans show a high need for additional internal training. Other action plans included fully documenting the training and certification process, and developing sales and marketing tools to sell the training process to health care facilities in the markets in which they are currently offering services.

"And of course, I have no bias toward our training," she said facetiously. Erin had created the majority of Connecting Cultures training processes.

When asked where Connecting Cultures stands on a scale of 1 to 10 in terms of its ability to provide this competence and strategy now, Eric responded with a 6 and Erin with a 5.

"Some things we're ready to do now, but we have a lot of work to do on others," Erin said. Erin proceeded to list seven action plans that she and Eric had brainstormed during their homework discussions.

"What we need to do first is shore up things internally," Rashelle stated. "That way we can become process dependent and not dependent on us individually."

The other teams offered applause as Eric and Erin wrapped up their presentation and took their seats, yielding the floor to the Team Dos pairing of Bobbie and Kyle. This duo also held the possibility of a one-sided presentation. As Bobbie and Kyle approached the front of the room, Bobbie fulfilled a key characteristic of her team player behavioral style and let Kyle take the lead—which he did, also holding true to his style.

Their competence hierarchy was displayed on the screen, with a competence presented as "We provide customized language access plan design and execution." Team Dos's presentation listed health care providers as the primary target market, with secondary markets in community-based groups such as law enforcement and other government departments. The team also listed a third-level market focusing on independent health care interpreters, specializing in consulting services and continuing education.

"We have ten years of experience in delivering far beyond what our competitors deliver," Kyle said. "That affords us the ability to provide an appropriately skilled interpreter to our customers' facility for whatever their needs might be. In contrast to our competitors, what we do well is provide something that's more consistent and transparent. We take

KYLE AND BOBBIE'S COMPETENCE HIERARCHY

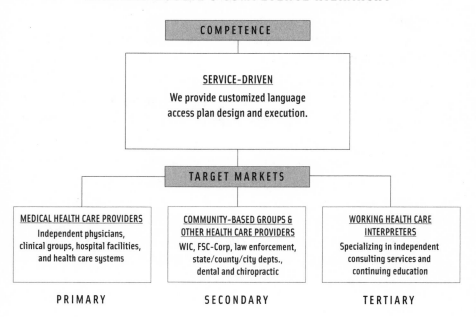

advantage of that by asking our customers about their needs and designing a plan to address those needs. We can offer blended service offerings created to meet customer needs and demands, compliant with state and federal regulations. We can develop a curriculum to help health care interpreters advance their learning.

"Also, Rashelle's expertise is something we don't do a good enough job of marketing. She differentiates us," said Kyle.

"Keep in mind that an individual—even Rashelle—can't be your competence," I stated. "However, Rashelle has the expertise to design a consulting or training process that we could build into a proprietary methodology that can be part of your competence. You could also build on Rashelle's strength as an industry visionary by implementing a thought leadership marketing strategy. Rashelle has plenty of content to become the thought leader in the industry through public speaking, blogging, and other social media. Again, your competence cannot be delivered by one person, but individuals, especially those with an outgoing behavioral style like Rashelle's, can effectively communicate and illustrate your competence to your target markets and industry associations. A thought leadership strategy is one of the most effective methods to educate your target markets on your expertise while simultaneously creating leads to dramatically increase your sales and profit."

Kyle gave a knowing nod and then quickly continued his thought. "Our execution of our face-to-face interpreting comes from having a clearly defined interpreter certification process. Each interpreter is at different stages of the training process, which is unlike any in the industry," he said. "Interpreter credentialing is something that Bobbie has dreamed of for a long time." The team had an extended discussion of how Connecting Cultures could play a key role in formalizing the credentialing process in the industry. Their foundational strength in their interpreter training process could focus on preparing health care interpreters across the industry for certification. Kyle listed six additional action plans he and Bobbie brainstormed while they completed their homework.

The room gave Bobbie and Kyle a round of applause for their recommendations and insight.

Rashelle jumped right into her presentation. She seemed like a coach preparing to spark her team with a pregame pep talk. "This assignment got me thinking about where we are and where we need to go," she began. "It forced me to think at a new strategic level. What we do really well is deliver face-to-face interpreting services, because we've developed training and management techniques that are unmatched. The things we do differently and do well are what are going to allow us to break into new markets."

Rashelle proudly read her competence recommendation to the planning team: "We provide comprehensive interpreter acquisition, training, development, and management that delivers professional language service options to the health care industry."

Rashelle's visionary strengths and her high D behavior style allowed her to describe her vision of how Connecting Cultures could craft a customizable service offering of individual products that would put control of the sales situation in the customer's hands. "That way health care organizations can buy our educational and training services even if they don't plan to use the face-to-face interpreting service line. We can tell clients, 'If you want to take your interpreting internal, let us give you the

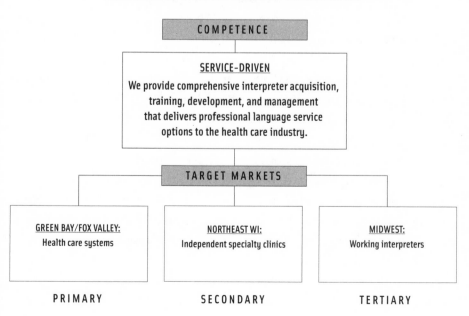

RASHELLE'S COMPETENCE HIERARCHY

COMPETENCE

SERVICE-DRIVEN
We provide comprehensive interpreter acquisition, training, development, and management that delivers professional language service options to the health care industry.

TARGET MARKETS

GREEN BAY/FOX VALLEY:
Health care systems

NORTHEAST WI:
Independent specialty clinics

MIDWEST:
Working interpreters

PRIMARY   SECONDARY   TERTIARY

blueprint to do it.' It's an opportunity for revenue and potential access to continuing education classes for their working interpreters. What makes us different? I think what we do exceptionally well is the development and management of the interpreting service, whether Connecting Cultures is delivering it or the customer is. It all goes back to the concept of our foundational strength.

"We could create licensed products of our training and certification process, essentially developing an interpreting consulting service while we are also strengthening our face-to-face interpreting services," Rashelle continued.

As the advisor, one of my key responsibilities is to consistently ask questions to facilitate discussion and agreement. The question is an advisor's most effective tool. As a visionary, Rashelle needed to be challenged to ensure her strategy was obtainable and not entirely out of reach. Many of the most successful entrepreneurs I work with admit that one of their greatest weaknesses is their lack of attention span. Around our office, we jokingly call this Entrepreneurial Distraction Disorder, or EDD. EDD doesn't necessarily have to be a weakness, however. Managed properly, it can be an incredible gift that brings significant value to the organization. An entrepreneur's active mind is what gives him or her the ability to generate the ideas that businesses are built on. The key is putting a plan in place to take advantage of this gift.

"Rashelle," I said, "does Connecting Cultures have the resources of time and money to become the best at the consulting and training side of the business while improving upon the superior service it provides in face-to-face interpreting?"

"I think we have to find them," Rashelle responded, adding that she sees the company's delivery of face-to-face interpreting at a 7 in terms of differentiation, and the development of licensed products and consulting service in the early stages at a 4. "We have the wherewithal to provide a unique service offering to the health care market. We just need to execute this plan to make that happen. Our competence is in reach."

"Team Uno and Team Dos talked about increasing your service line offering, and now you've added the products piece," I noted. "A service competence is about doing things that provide the best service; a products competence is something totally different."

"I think we can develop a good product but sell it in conjunction with services," Rashelle continued. "There's an opportunity to take a product-driven competence, but that's not the correct path in my opinion. We would focus 100 percent on strengthening our training process."

"So the products would help you deliver the language services?" I asked.

"Yes," Rashelle replied, as ideas flowed. "Books, CDs, DVDs, we could sell them all. But the products are just a means or a vehicle to deliver our service-driven competence of interpreter training and certification."

"We have lists and lists of these products and projects on our server, but they just sit," Kyle commented. "We're not marketing them."

"We have a service line that needs products to support it," Erin chimed in.

"I don't have a client in my database that's pursuing a dual path of a service- and product-driven competence. It is extremely difficult to be the best at both," I stated. "From my experience, the greatest level of success comes when you choose one or the other. When you choose a competence, you allocate all of your resources to it. My last company had a service-driven competence, but we made food products. Our differentiating factor was our ability to change over a manufacturing line immediately and run a different product that the client had requested. So we allocated our resources to having a second set of equipment on standby, with plenty of trained mechanics on staff to continuously strive to minimize change-over time and downtime. If we had been product-driven, we would have invested our resources in research and development talent to create new product formulations. Do you see how if we had chosen to deliver both service and product competences, it would have been difficult to afford to allocate the resources to be the best at both our services and our products in the markets in which we were competing?"

"I do," Rashelle responded. "I see our competence as being service-driven."

"Then your products can be a means to deliver your competence but not the competence itself," I explained.

"With our current strategy, our only target markets are the health care organizations that outsource their interpreting needs," Rashelle said. "This new competence I am recommending enables us to provide incredible value to all health care organizations. We're successful because of what we've developed to support and train our own staff. Over time it turned into one of our foundational strengths that we now need to leverage. We need to have continuing education internally, but there is also a market for that externally. We have figured it out, and we're the ones that do it better than anyone else in our markets. We need to package it and share it, because we know how to do it."

Kyle added, "And this strategy gives us the opportunity to adapt our service offering and foster the relationship with our customers so we can still have some revenue stream, and it creates the relationship to retain that customer if they decide to bring interpreting under their roof."

By now some lightbulbs were going on in my head, too. Shifting into documenting and authoring mode and considering all the team recommendations and discussions, I offered up the following as a possible competence statement for Connecting Cultures:

"The recognized thought leader in providing measurably superior complete language solutions, from consulting to interpreting, to the health care industry."

The planning team exchanged some agreeable looks around the table as they quickly absorbed the statement.

"This would enable Connecting Cultures to position itself as a strategic partner and valued advisor, regardless of the economy," I added. "As the economy ebbs and flows, the health care industry goes back and forth between outsourcing their interpreting needs and handling this perceived expense internally. When times are tough, organizations are more likely to eliminate the external service—insourcing it rather than outsourcing it. Adding a consulting piece and/or telephonic capabilities would better position the company as a partner to health care organizations. You could also create a competitive advantage with technology solutions to more effectively deliver language solutions. You need to develop an IT plan that starts to separate you. The way you deliver these services would also become a competitive advantage. You should be delivering incredible technology solutions."

"One of our major clinic customers wants us to do video interpreting already," Rashelle said.

In wrapping up the competence analysis, the team members noted that all three of the competence options were similar in that Connecting Cultures should expand its service offerings from where they are today.

In addition to providing face-to-face interpreting services, the company should provide consulting services to companies that have their own interpreters. There was quick agreement that Connecting Cultures is capable of providing a full breadth of interpreting services better than anyone else in the markets in which they compete.

"Remember that one of the key findings to come out of the internal analysis was that your current competence of delivering just interpreting services has helped you build a solid organization," I said. "However, the current business model is producing below-average financial performance in that the cost to deliver such high-quality interpreting services is generating minimal margins. And you are not effectively communicating the tangible value of your superior face-to-face interpreting; as a result, you are not getting compensated for it and have to negotiate on price."

Discussion then turned to developing a preliminary list of services the company would provide once it reached the ability to deliver its full competence. Services that made the list included consulting, interpreter training, face-to-face interpreting as well as telephonic and video interpreting services, and licensed products such as a training curriculum for corporate customers.

After some additional discussion, the team arrived at a working version of a competence statement:

> **"We provide comprehensive interpreter hiring, training, development, and management that allow us to deliver customized language service options to the health care industry."**

"How close are you to being able to deliver on this competence right now?" I asked the group.

"Probably about a 5," Rashelle admitted. "But executing this plan will move us toward a 10."

"The greatest benefit of this competence to your customers is the ability for Connecting Cultures to customize interpreting services to meet the exact needs of the organization," I said. "Unlike the competition, which offers only one option of complete interpreting services, you can provide a unique, customized solution. It's apparent from our market research

CONNECTING CULTURES FINAL COMPETENCE HIERARCHY

discussions that the health care industry has been conditioned to consider only two methods of interpreting: outside agencies or their own staff. However, Connecting Cultures will provide several levels and types of service across the interpreting continuum. As a result, your competence emerges as a new approach to a long-term challenge for the health care industry."

The energy in the room was almost palpable. The team discussed the fact that the organization will need to prioritize and complete several major initiatives to put itself in position to deliver on such a differentiating competence. We brainstormed several action plans to complete these initiatives.

"At least now we have an idea of where we're headed," Rashelle said. "This will definitely differentiate us from our competition. As long as we stay focused on developing, strengthening, and delivering our new competence, we'll make progress toward our goal instead of spinning our wheels."

"Once we finalize our competence," Erin said, "what types of things will we have to do to strengthen it over time?"

"We'll build your organization around your competence to support and strengthen it," I said. "That includes assets such as strategic partnerships, an efficient organizational structure, employee compensation, applicable skill sets for each position, established systems and processes, and human and financial resource allocation. The competitive competence analysis, which is on Rashelle's action plan, will help us identify what competence your competitors are trying to deliver, and to what level our competence will differentiate against those competitors."

"How do we figure out whom, exactly, our target market is?" Kyle asked.

"Perfect timing with that question, Kyle," I said. "That's why identifying your target markets is the next step in the Stop Selling Vanilla Ice Cream process. Your ideal target markets are those who value your competence the most and will be willing to pay for it and give you more business because of it."

The Scoop

1. Once implemented, will your newly defined competence effectively differentiate your organization in the markets in which you compete?

2. To what level (on a scale of 1 to 10) do you currently deliver on that competence? (1 = vanilla ice cream and 10 = deliver competence and have clear differentiation)

3. What other decisions do you have to make regarding your competence and strategy?

Action Plans to Complete the Process

☐ Have all homework teams present their competence and strategy recommendations to the team.

☐ Finalize the future competence of your organization.

☐ Document all brainstormed action plans.

☐ Document any other strategic decisions made by the team.

IDENTIFYING YOUR TARGET MARKETS

The energy and excitement generated by the interactive team competence presentations and decisions carried over into the next step in the Stop Selling Vanilla Ice Cream process: identification of target markets.

"Now that you have defined how you're going to differentiate your company, we need to define who is going to value your competence the most," I said to the team. "The temptation is to target every organization that would remotely have a need for your services, but what we want to do at this point is identify which organizations or types of organizations value your competence so much that they will be willing to give you more business and pay a premium for it."

Truly successful organizations push beyond generalities and hone in on specific target markets. This enables them to effectively craft their message and appeal directly to the decision makers within companies or demographic groups that will want their brand of mint chocolate chip ice cream. For example, the upper-tier auto manufacturers focus solely on quality, features, and benefits in their advertisements. That's their version of mint chocolate chip ice cream. Seldom do they even mention a price, unless it's in the fine print. You'll find more ads from these companies during television programs and in publications that cater to their target market of affluent professionals. Your goal now is to define your target market and develop messages that will appeal to customers looking for your specific type of mint chocolate chip ice cream.

With a differentiating competence now in hand, the Connecting Cultures team was in position to better define who, exactly, will value their competence the most and be willing to pay for it. "The reason we discuss target markets in more detail after discussing competence is that many of our clients discover they need to reevaluate their target markets after establishing their competence," I explained. "What you considered to be your target market previously may or may not be your target market going forward. Some of your current customers may not value your competence, and as a result, they won't be willing to pay for it. But that's okay. Maybe they're happy with vanilla ice cream and will leave to search for the best price, or perhaps they want a different flavor than the mint chocolate chip you plan to offer."

"It doesn't matter whether or not we have strong relationships with our current customers?" Bobbie asked.

"Relationships always matter," I replied, "but remember that relationships cannot be your competence. Your competence must be something delivered by your company, not one person. Remember, your competence is why your customers will choose you over your competition. A strong competence leads to a clear differentiation for your organization, because without it, your product or service becomes a commodity too often tied to price. We want your customers to ask for— even demand—your brand of mint chocolate chip ice cream. It's a fundamental aspect of business that you can't be all things to all people. If you are, then by definition you're selling vanilla ice cream. Your competence has to be the specific thing you do better than anyone else in the markets you compete."

> *Does your company have a clearly defined target market or customer? How is that information communicated internally? How is it communicated externally?*

"Steve," Rashelle interjected, "can you give us some things we should consider as we set about identifying our target markets?"

"Absolutely," I said. "There are several factors to keep in mind during a discussion of potential target markets. The most important are to be specific in your definitions, to use current customers as a basis of analysis, and to focus and prioritize. If you do those things, you'll have clearly defined target markets that are aligned with your competence."

BE SPECIFIC

Limit your target to a finite group of organizations or people. It is far more effective, especially for a small to midsize company in the business-to-business market, to create a marketing plan that targets a few hundred companies (or consumers) rather than several thousand. This enables you to implement a hypermarketing plan that uses customized tools for targeting each company within the target market. By removing the inefficiencies inherent with casting too large of a net, this philosphy will dramatically increase your closing rates. "For example," I said, "if you're targeting a specific multispecialty clinic or medical center, all of your sales and marketing tools can feature that organization's logo or the specific name of the decision maker."

LOOK AT CURRENT CUSTOMERS

Chances are some of your current customers already value your competence, assuming you are delivering it at any level of differentiation. Conduct a customer gross margin analysis and look at which of your customers have the best margins. One of your target markets might be right there. You will need to reevaluate your customers based on your new reality, since oftentimes determining the companies *not* in your target market is the toughest decision. Some of your current customers may not value your competence or may fall outside your new definition of a target market. Not every entity will value your competence equally, and on occasion you might have to walk away from a company that does not value it enough to pay for it.

FOCUS AND PRIORITIZE

Inevitably, you will be tempted to sell to as many target markets as possible. Resist this urge to avoid diluting your marketing efforts and minimizing their impact. Since it can take years to fully penetrate just one target market, you will stretch your resources too thin if you reach for too many markets. In addition, you certainly won't be effective with the organizations that value your competence the most. Instead of trying to cast a net over the entire ocean, you'll find you can increase your sales by focusing resources on the primary and secondary target markets that are most likely to value your competence the most.

"Think about how much effort it will take for a team as small as ours to adequately cover our primary target market, much less several secondary target markets," Kyle noted.

"Precisely," I added. "Targeting a specific group of companies requires a sales and marketing plan that includes action plans to build a database with accurate contact information, develop an appropriate marketing plan and supporting sales tools, execute that plan, and make the actual sales calls," I said. "If you stay disciplined to your plan, it could take years to get through your primary target markets before you even scratch the surface on the markets far down your list.

"I've seen companies in their first year of the Stop Selling Vanilla Ice Cream process want to go after five or six target markets. That tendency is understandable because of the massive momentum generated by the process, but once they get to the second year of planning, they see the rationale for focusing on three target markets or less. Ask yourself, 'If we had just one dollar to spend on our target markets, how would we spend it?' You want to focus your resources on the target markets that value your competence, are willing to give you more business, and will pay a little more for it. A good rule of thumb is allocating 70 to 80 percent of your sales and marketing resources toward your primary target markets and the remainder toward your secondary markets."

Remain dedicated to pursuing business within your target markets, even if you secure business from outside your target market during the early stages of your strategy execution. "This trend typically decreases as your strategy starts working and sales increase within your target markets," I explained. "The business from outside your target markets often ends up being at a lower margin and operationally inefficient, because you're not set up to service them."

"I don't know if we're in a position to turn away business at this point," Rashelle stated. "If an organization from outside our target market requests our services, we'll want to take it, won't we?"

"In the early stages of your strategic life cycle, you may find yourself making price concessions to keep or obtain business," I replied. "However, as you build a customer base within your target markets, many companies make a strategic decision to walk away from customers who do not value the competence enough to pay for it. Again, though, that's okay! You can raise prices on non–target market accounts to bring their margins into line or until they leave. When you get to decision points like this, I recommend bringing the leadership team together to talk through your strategy."

"What if a company outside our target market approaches us?" Rashelle continued. "Are you saying we should tell them 'no'?"

"Possibly," I replied. "What you're describing is what we call reactive sales and marketing versus the proactive sales and marketing efforts you can control through your strategy. Proactive is when we spend dollars or dedicate resources toward pursuing our primary and secondary target markets. Reactive is when companies approach us to do business. You will have to make a strategic decision about whether or not to take on reactive sales opportunities from outside your target markets. Keep in mind that companies outside your target markets tend to require more of your resources to service."

I had a front row seat to a perfect example of what can happen when a company takes on business outside its target market. Prior to founding SM Advisors, I was a minority owner and leadership team member for a dry food contract manufacturing company called EnzoPac. Our product offering featured blending and packaging dry food products that contained a considerable amount of sugar or flour, and we specialized in high-speed packaging of cocoa, gelatin, and pancake mix. Our competence was completing high-speed changeovers to a new product. Branded companies value that ability to cost-effectively manage inventories—or palletized cash, as we affectionately called it. Our target market was the top 100 branded food companies in the United States. We implemented a great strategy with a talented team, and successfully grew the business from $5 million to $30 million in annual sales in five years.

A national cheese company located only ten miles from our plant asked if we would blend a cellulose product for its shredded cheese products. It was just a blending job and did not use any of our competence and packaging expertise, nor did it use any flour or sugar. It was outside of our wheelhouse—beyond our target market and competence—and our leadership team knew it. However, we wanted to help our local friends and didn't want to turn away business, so we accepted the job.

In short, it was a complete disaster. We were not equipped to handle this type of product, and it showed. Whenever we blended this product, it looked like a snowstorm had hit the blending department. There was white dust everywhere. Members of the operations team would let me hear about it whenever I walked into this winter wonderland of a plant floor.

It wasn't long before every member of our team realized this product clearly fell outside of our strategy, and our financial performance on that product proved it. It was a tough decision, but the correct decision was to walk away from this business. The lesson learned was that we had a clearly defined strategy and competence, and we needed to stick to it in order to succeed.

"As we execute the strategy, we want to be very conscious of the response we get from different target markets," I said. "In most cases we can predict who will value your competence, but on occasion a new target market may surface that values your competence but for slightly different reasons than what you might have expected. Your sales force needs to become the eyes and ears of the organization in the marketplace. Remember, the greatest teacher of strategy is the marketplace, and if a certain type of customer keeps coming back for more business, you may need to

> *Have you ever turned away a customer because you thought that they weren't the right fit for your services or products? That they didn't value your competence?*

reevaluate your target markets. Strategy is an evolution, not a revolution. Listening to what your target markets are saying about your competence and strategy will help you fine-tune the strategy as you move forward.

"From my experience with SM Advisors, I have seen that when a target market really comes to value the competence of an organization, those customers begin offering additional work outside of your competence. In essence, they say, 'You've solved one problem for us, now here is another we'd like you to fix.' When that happens, I love to observe what action my clients take. Do they take the additional business—like we did at Enzo-Pac—and risk disappointing the customer and losing the initial business that falls within the competence? Or do they strategically inform the customer that this opportunity falls outside of their competence and they want to focus on continuing their superior performance with what they do best? In most cases, saying 'no' strengthens the relationship and reinforces your competence and its value in the eyes of your customer."

DEFINING YOUR TARGET MARKETS

"Wow," Rashelle said, sitting back in her chair. "I never realized there could be such a thing as business you shouldn't take. I've always focused on getting every piece of business we can find. But now that I think about it, we would completely drain the margin out of our business if we took on a customer that required a lot of travel. But I'm convinced we need to expand into the larger metropolitan markets of Wisconsin, such as Milwaukee."

"That's something that will require more discussion," I said. "But before we go down that path, let's discuss the process to define your target markets and then review what each homework team presented as their target market recommendations."

The process to define your target markets has a few high-level steps:

First, review your competence to ensure it is fresh in your mind. Then you want to define your primary target market: those consumers or companies that will value your competence the most. How many potential target customers are within that target market? To answer that question it is helpful to discuss your geographic target market. Once your geographic target market is defined you can determine the approximate number of companies in your primary target market. Is that number large and would it take you years to penetrate, or can you pursue a secondary target market while devoting a majority of your time to your primary? These are the types of questions the advisor can ask when the team is debating target markets. The amount of time needed to finalize your target markets will vary by organization. We often see that it typically takes longer to define your competence than your target markets; however, I have worked with companies that really struggle to focus their efforts on a specific target. So identifying the target markets can take longer.

The homework teams presented recommendations for Connecting Cultures' target markets as part of their strategy presentation.

Team Uno's primary target market was the director of quality/risk management at health care facilities in the geographic markets they currently service. Their rationalization was now that Connecting Cultures is offering more than just face-to-face interpreting, there are several new potential customers.

Team Dos had outlined a series of markets. Their primary was health care providers, independent physicians, clinical groups, hospital facilities, and health care systems. Their secondary was community-based groups and other service providers, such as WIC; FSC-Corp; law enforcement; state, county, and city departments; and dental and chiropractic providers. Their tertiary market was working health care interpreters (by offering independent consulting services and continuing education). Team Dos had aggressive plans for their target markets, and many in the room wondered whether Connecting Cultures had the resources to effectively and proactively go after this many target markets. The discussions were heating up.

Rashelle—Team Tres—had similar target markets, though. Her primary was health care systems, her secondary was independent specialty clinics, and her tertiary was working interpreters.

After significant discussion, the planning team came to a consensus concerning the types of organizations that Connecting Cultures should pursue. Larger health care organizations with multiple facilities stood out as ideal candidates for the company's brand of mint chocolate chip ice cream. Their competence would allow health care providers with multiple facilities to receive a customized interpreting solution for each facility, based on the market dynamics. A large trauma facility might need the superior face-to-face interpreting expertise Connecting Cultures can bring, while other facilities may like to have their own internal staff. Or even better, Connecting Cultures could partner with the health care provider by providing a blend of services. This gives the health care provider total control to develop a program that fits their exact needs by facility. They would value a consulting approach in which Connecting Cultures could help them implement consistent, quality interpreting services across their multiple facilities, which is a real challenge.

These organizations typically have sophisticated efficiency and metric systems, so they understand that a better trained and more experienced interpreter will enable their health care providers to be more efficient. Paying a little bit more for a superior qualified interpreter (be it internal or external) will enable physicians and care providers to see more patients in a day. Measuring caregiver productivity is a key driver in larger multi-facility health care organizations.

Secondary target markets would include larger independent specialty clinics and rehabilitation facilities, some with single locations but preferably with multiple locations. These more sophisticated organizations would value Connecting Cultures' competence for many of the same reasons the primary target market would.

DEFINING YOUR GEOGRAPHIC TARGET MARKET

Now that the planning team had defined its primary and secondary target markets, it launched into a discussion of geographic target markets. Since the company's competence is service-driven, having the resources in place to effectively market and deliver those services is a key consideration. The team concluded it should continue to increase market share in its current service areas of Green Bay and the Fox Valley, just to the south. The newly defined competence enables Connecting Cultures to target all large health care providers with multiple facilities in their geographic markets versus just the companies that outsourced their interpreting. The team agreed to take advantage of that new opportunity before expanding into new markets.

Their proactive sales and marketing efforts would be focused on their target markets in the current service areas. The team discussed the fact that the consulting and training service line of the new competence is not limited by geographic constraints because it doesn't require on-site interpreters. However, the team agreed that when they entered new geographic markets they would need to provide all service lines, including face-to-face interpreters, because that is the true value of their competence to their target market—their mix of services that large health care providers can customize to specific interpreting needs.

The team agreed to hold off exploring other secondary geographic target markets that extend down the Lake Michigan shore to Sheboygan, Milwaukee, and Racine, and over into western and central Wisconsin.

"But my hope is that we will be ready to pursue new geographical markets in the second year of the process," Rashelle said, "so I suggest we develop metrics that will help us determine when that move is appropriate. Because I think it needs to be sooner than later."

"Connecting Cultures will need to take an educational sales approach with its primary and secondary target markets," I said. "We need to illustrate to your target markets that they can now customize their interpreting services to meet their exact needs. It's no longer a cookie-cutter approach with only two choices, outsourcing or taking interpreting services internal. This educational approach will take patience, but it will be a very effective sales process.

"Do we have agreement on this competence hierarchy?" I asked the team. "If not, please suggest any alternatives."

"I think it makes sense," Bobbie said.

"It does for me, too," added Rashelle.

"In the past, we would target only health care organizations that used third-party interpreting companies," Kyle stated. "With our new competence and service offering, we can now target all health care organizations, from those with an internal interpreting staff to those who use outside

CONNECTING CULTURES FINAL COMPETENCE HIERARCHY

COMPETENCE

We provide comprehensive interpreter hiring, training, development, and management that allow us to deliver customized language service options to the health care industry.

TARGET MARKETS

Health Care Systems

Multiple Location
Health Care Providers
(large clinics/practices)

PRIMARY   SECONDARY

agencies. This opens up all health care systems in our geographic target markets as prospective new customers."

"Your proactive sales and marketing efforts will focus on the primary and secondary target markets," I added, "and you will evaluate new business opportunities outside of the identified target markets on a case-by-case basis. Now that we have defined your mint chocolate chip ice cream and the target markets who value it, let's look at your competitors to ensure we can clearly differentiate Connecting Cultures in the markets you compete."

The Scoop

1. Which current customers do you think value your services or products the most? Do they value the future competence you've defined?

2. Are your target markets geographically limited, limited by industry, or limited by business type or model?

3. What percentage of your proactive sales and marketing efforts should you spend on your primary and your secondary target markets?

4. What percentage of your current customers fall within those definitions of your primary and secondary target markets?

5. What is your strategy for those customers that fall outside those target markets?

Action Plans to Complete the Process

☐ Document your primary and secondary target markets.

☐ Document your geographic target market.

☐ Document any other strategic decisions you make.

COMPETITIVE COMPETENCE ANALYSIS TO VERIFY DIFFERENTIATION

"Now that you have completed the first draft of your competence and target markets, you need to make sure it will clearly differentiate your company in the markets in which you compete," I told the Connecting Cultures team. "However, before you can finalize your competence and strategy, you need to analyze the services and competencies your competition is offering. Completing a competitive competence analysis enables you to compare your new competence against the apparent competences of your primary competitors."

A competence only benefits your organization if it helps you stand out from the crowd; otherwise, it's just another version of vanilla ice cream and too likely to become a price-driven commodity. Your organization has to be different from anything else out there, or you're simply not there yet.

"Strategy is an evolution, not a revolution," I reminded the planning team. "If we determine Connecting Cultures' competence is different from those displayed by your competitors, then the green light is on and it's full steam ahead. On the other hand, if your competence is similar to that of the competition, then it's back to the drawing board. As Vince Lombardi said, 'There is no room for second place.' A second place strategy is not a strategy."

From an SM Advisors perspective, there are two types of competitive analysis: First is the competitive competence analysis methodology I'll describe here, which focuses on evaluating how your competitors are trying to differentiate themselves and how your newly defined competence compares to your competition. Second is a comprehensive competitive analysis that captures each competitor's strengths, weaknesses, and apparent competence/strategy, and then develops any counterstrategies. It is much more thorough and may include counterstrategies for specific competitors. For example, if a competitor is trying to differentiate itself with a larger product or service offering, you could also consider a larger offering to minimize their level of differentiation.

"Most organizations going through their first strategic planning process have so much work they need to do internally that time spent on what the competition is doing is not worth the effort or the distraction," I told the team. "In other words, as a company you are in no position to compete with the competition because you have to get your Strategy and Talent in place first."

This is like building a ship to go to war. In the first year, we need to have the right strategy, equipment, and people in place before we leave the harbor. The focus needs to be on getting the ship and crew prepared for the competitive battle. By the second year, we have the fundamentals in place and are ready to leave the harbor. We can then implement a thorough competitive analysis that includes counterstrategies to take on the competition. However, it's still helpful to take a look at the perceived competence and differentiation of your competitors in the marketplace and the degree to which your organization matches up. Are they selling vanilla ice cream or mint chocolate chip? This information is useful regardless of how deeply we delve into analyzing the competition at this stage.

"I've found that it's probably a better use of your time in the first year to focus on your own organization rather than worry too much about countering a competitor's strategy," I said. "So my recommendation is we complete only the basic competitive competence analysis in the first year, and then in the second year and beyond we complete a comprehensive competitive analysis. Once your competence is in place, we can develop counterstrategies to minimize your top competitor's competence."

The competitive competence analysis examines your perception of how your competitors are trying to differentiate themselves. And once you have completed the competitive competence analysis, you can insert your future competence and compare it against the perceived competence of your competitors to test its viability as a truly differentiating factor.

ASSESSING YOUR COMPETITION

At this early stage, a snapshot of the marketplace should provide sufficient information to determine whether your future competence has the potential to be unique or not. In addition to first-hand knowledge, you can gain some insight into how competitors are differentiating themselves by looking at their websites and sales collateral.

COMPETITIVE COMPETENCE ANALYSIS		
INDUSTRY:		
Competitor	Apparent Competence/ Positioning Statement	Team's Perception of Whether the Competitor Is Delivering Its Competence to the Market
Insights and Conclusions:		

You should be able to answer several questions while completing a competitive competence analysis:

✔ Who are your primary competitors in the markets where you compete?

✔ What is the perceived competence of each competitor? How are they trying to differentiate from you and others?

✔ Based on their competence, to what level does each company differentiate itself on a scale of 1 to 10? (A rating of 1 means they are selling vanilla ice cream, while 10 means they have a clear differentiation. They're selling their form of mint chocolate chip ice cream.)

✔ Are any of these competitors delivering or trying to deliver a competence similar to that of your company?

✔ If yes, can you tangibly prove that you will deliver it better?

Does your company regularly assess the competition and how they are trying to differentiate themselves? How does it do so? What actions are taken based on what you learn?

If you find out that your competence is similar to that of the competition, then you need to go back to the drawing board until you define a competence that you can deliver better than anyone else in the markets where you compete. Gain team consensus about whether you can create a real differentiation for your company after you implement your competence and execute your plan.

Completing a competitive competence analysis report was on Rashelle's action plan list for this session, and she organized her notes as the group settled in to listen.

"As you listen to Rashelle's competitive competence analysis," I said, "think about whether you will be different from the competition if you go forward with your strategy recommendation."

Rashelle took the floor and delivered an overview of Connecting Cultures' primary competitors, including the services each provides and a look at their primary customers. The relatively small field of competitors runs the gamut from the oldest and best-known provider in Wisconsin to a national provider we'll refer to as Company A. As Rashelle discussed each competitor, we viewed its website on the screen. If you can't determine a company's strategy from its website, the company most likely lacks one.

"One of our regional competitors is a challenge because of its state-wide coverage," Rashelle began. "They compete on price, but their service offerings are limited to interpreting and translating. Another company carries a similar model but is recognized within the market for training interpreters. For the most part, the services are the same for those providers.

"The main national provider, Company A, is the only one of our competitors with an actual positioning statement, and they deliver services well. They started as a local face-to-face interpreting agency and have expanded to provide national service telephonically. They have standards and values of professionalism, and they deliver on interpreter development. They have regional account reps with high levels of contact and customer service. They offer more than 180 different languages through telephonic service. Even some of our current customers have some contact with them because of that language availability."

REFINING YOUR COMPETENCE

"One of the most important decisions you can make as an organization is what not to be," I said. "Connecting Cultures' ability to provide service options customizable to your customers' needs qualifies as a differentiating competence, because no one else is offering anything like it. However, telephonic capabilities in one form or another probably will need to play a role."

Rashelle interjected, "Where we stand out is that our standards of interpreter qualifications are higher, and we're more hands-on with our interpreter staff. We have interpreter management expertise that Company A does not, but we must prove that differentiation to compete in a broader market. We're not going to have 180 languages, because we can't control the quality. We're not trying to be that provider, but we might be able to coordinate the plan for our customers to use services like it.

"I don't believe we would be delivering what we stand for if we just did telephonic, the way that Company A does," Rashelle continued. "However, in places where the customer wants us to handle the interpreting, we can provide services telephonically. Companies that don't want to deal with agencies want to do it all telephonically."

"What is the Achilles' heel of being all-telephonic?" I asked.

"I think it's the quality control," Rashelle replied. "Video conferencing is the best of both worlds. At this point, people in the health care industry don't know what this could look like. They don't know what else is out there other than face-to-face or telephonic."

"When it's a face-to-face appointment, we do all the work," Bobbie noted. "But if it's telephonic, the health care providers are the ones who have to initiate the contact, and it freaks some people out."

It was good to see multiple members of the Connecting Cultures team participating in the discussion, buying into the benefits of brainstorming and making this more of a team effort than would be possible in a typical executive-only exercise. Contributions by Bobbie and Eric showed they remained engaged in the process and were eager to contribute. I wouldn't have offered strong odds of that transformation happening a few weeks ago, but I've seen where the Stop Selling Vanilla Ice Cream process helps people reconnect to the organization.

"The telephonic industry is its own industry and its own beast," Rashelle said, sounding as though she was backing away from a telephonic-dominated business model. "I'm not looking to take over the telephonic industry."

"Earlier today we came to an agreement on your competence that read: 'We provide comprehensive interpreter hiring, training, development, and management that allow us to deliver customized language service options to the health care industry.' Do you still like this?"

"Yes, I think that's perfect," Rashelle replied as the rest of the planning team nodded in agreement.

"Now that we have reviewed each competitor," I asked, "if you deliver on your competence, will it differentiate you?"

"Yes, it will," Rashelle answered. "We would be the only provider to offer those language service options."

The energy emitting from the group was growing to a fever pitch. Team members sat on the edge of their chairs, heads nodded in agreement, and ideas flowed freely around the table.

"Customization or minute-based pricing," Rashelle said to her imaginary customer contact. "Ultimately, it's your choice."

"In contrast to everyone else," Kyle added.

"Who are selling vanilla ice cream!" Bobbie said to conclude the thought.

"How we communicate that to our customers is our challenge," Rashelle concluded.

Now even Eric couldn't help himself from jumping into the debate. "At first I was dragging my feet on the telephonic stuff," he said. "Now I think this needs to be included in our service offerings. We've got to offer that after what I just saw."

"I'm excited!" Rashelle blurted out to her smiling teammates, as if that emotion wasn't already readily apparent.

By the end of the brainstorming session, we had compiled action plans filling two pages. A brainstorming session aimed at strengthening your competence against what's known or perceived about the state of the competition typically generates a lengthy list of action plans. It's important to capture those action plans and assign the department plans that will include them. But avoid spending time discussing the action plans in any detail at this point. The focus of the exercise is to come up with a list of ways to increase the degree of differentiation and implement your strategy.

"It seems like we have a lot of things to fix internally," Rashelle said.

"We have made great progress, and as we complete these next steps it will only increase your level of differentiation," I replied. "We have determined your competence is different from those displayed by your competitors, and it's apparent the market opportunity available to Connecting Cultures is significant. We have the opportunity to create an entirely new mind-set in the industry that we can deliver through a very profitable business model. Now let's make your competence tangible to your current and potential customers."

The Scoop

1. Based on its competence, to what level does each competitor differentiate itself on a scale of 1 to 10? (1 = vanilla ice cream and 10 = a clear differentiation or mint chocolate chip ice cream.

2. Are any of these competitors delivering or trying to deliver a competence similar to the strategy you've defined?

3. Will delivering your competence clearly differentiate your company in the markets in which you compete? If not, how would you change your competence?

Action Plans to Complete the Process

☐ Finalize the competitive competence analysis.

☐ Finalize the competence hierarchy of your organization.

COMMUNICATING YOUR COMPETENCE
TO INCREASE SALES AND PROFIT

Many teams who go through the Stop Selling Vanilla Ice Cream process for the first time find that one of the hardest parts is identifying the tangible benefits of their organization's competence to their customers. They've been so busy working in the business—completing their daily tasks—that they've never stepped back long enough to view their competence from the standpoint of their customers. Or they have not had a process to do so. What is it specifically about your competence that customers would value and would make them want to do business with you? Once that question is answered, building sales is simply a matter of communicating the answer.

With the first fundamental of the Stop Selling Vanilla Ice Cream process in place, the Connecting Cultures planning team was ready to capitalize on its momentum and focus on the next fundamental of communicating the tangible value of its competence to current and potential customers to increase sales and profit. The process would lead them from a well-defined competence to the development of the necessary tools to drive new sales growth: measured benefits to make the value of the competence tangible to customers and prospects, competence-aligned brand strategy and mission, and effective sales and marketing tools.

MAKE YOUR COMPETENCE TANGIBLE

"Is your competence always obvious to the customer?" Rashelle asked.

"It should be," I replied. "You have to reinforce your competence at every touch point your company has with a customer. That includes branding, business reviews, e-mail signatures, and your mission statement, to name a few. For example, at SM Advisors, we end e-mails and voicemail greetings with the statement, 'Have a profitable day.' Profit is the result of our competence for our customers. You have to look for ways to make your competence tangible to current customers and, more important, prospects. Rarely will your customers comprehend the total value your competence delivers to their organization unless you tangibly illustrate it to them through consistent business reviews.

"You must be able to measure and illustrate the value that your product or service brings to your customers, otherwise it doesn't matter if it is actually valuable or not," I told the team. "It's even more important to make services tangible than products, because it's hard for your customers to visualize value with a service. SM Advisors works with a lot of service organizations, and one of the biggest opportunities for most of them is proving the value of their competence. Your customers need more than just your word to justify giving you their business, much less paying a premium for it. The only way to accomplish your revenue goal is to make the value of your services tangible to your customers.

"And yet, in our experience, fewer than 7 percent of all companies do this. Which means you have an opportunity to differentiate yourself from every blowhard that comes through the door, claiming its product or service is the best without any evidence to back it up. Even if you are delivering on your competence, you still have to prove it."

It is important to understand the difference between a competence and the benefits that competence provides. For example, Connecting Cultures' competence of "providing comprehensive interpreter hiring, training, development, and management that allows us to deliver customized language service options to the health care industry" generates a number of benefits for clinics, such as higher kept-appointment percentages and shorter appointment times. It enables health care providers to see more patients in a day and ultimately generates more revenue for the customer. Those are benefits that Connecting Cultures might be able to measure in partnership with their customers.

SM Advisors provides a tangible measurement of what we do by illustrating that more than 90 percent of our clients increase their sales and/or profitability in their first year after developing and executing strategic and tactical plans with us. Our competence—strategy and talent delivered through the Stop Selling Vanilla Ice Cream process—generates that performance. Business owners can relate to a statistic like this, and it brings us credibility compared to planning firms that don't illustrate their competence.

> *Have you clearly defined and measured the benefits your customer receives from your competence?*

"You've got to convince customers to re-evaluate their interpreting model and prove to them that there are new ways to do old things," I said. "Connecting Cultures needs to become the educator and thought leader of the interpreting industry. It's imperative that you educate customers on the different options available to them and how each would benefit their organization. Identify the pluses and minuses of each and make it customizable to a customer's situation. Your ability to quantify those benefits will be the key component in creating a partnership relationship and helping the sale occur at different levels of the customer's organization."

Going back to the golf example, the Kohler Company can show its customers that in 2011, *Golf Digest* ranked Whistling Straits as the third-best public golf course in the United States. *Golf Magazine* ranked Kohler's American Club as the number one golf resort in the country in 2012 and ranked Whistling Straits as the best public golf course in Wisconsin. Kohler doesn't have to say it has the best courses and best overall golf resort that money can buy; the leading golf magazines are saying it. Third-party statistics can be even more powerful than those you generate and market on your own.

The most difficult step in this process is developing and implementing a measurement system across the entire organization that captures the value of your competence at each customer touch point. Begin by identifying two or three longstanding customers who can help you sharpen the process by providing candid feedback. Track those measurements with these top customers and gradually expand it across your customer base. You want to make every effort to prove the tangible value of your competence with measurements that you can collect regarding the value you are delivering the customer. However, you can also ask your customer to provide additional information that will help you calculate the value you deliver. I find that if you explain why you need the information, most customers are willing to work with you and want to know the information as well. This will improve your process while creating a venue for the customer to gain a greater understanding of the significant value you deliver to their organization.

"Unfortunately, the people who use our services aren't the people who buy our services," Rashelle said. "The clinic administrators and purchasing teams make the buying decisions, not the doctors. So we have to find a way to measure value for those decision makers. We're a service they don't want to pay for, and in some cases, one they don't understand."

"This group looks at the services you provide as simply an expense, right?" I asked.

"Yes."

"Then our job is to maximize the value the clinic receives out of that expense," I continued. "If their physicians are able to see more patients in a day because your interpreters show up on time and help the appointment go smoothly, then we need to be able to measure that. Even though you charge more per hour, your net cost is actually less because of all the other value you're delivering."

"They're paying us a premium for our competence," Rashelle responded, "which is a customized language access solution that optimizes the performance of the health care providers and ultimately the organization. Our health care provider customers are more efficient and make more money because we help them optimize their language access services. The health care provider is able to see more patients in a day, which results in higher profits for them."

"Then we need to measure these interactions with the user and show the tangible value to the buyer," I suggested.

"How can we do that?" Rashelle asked.

"Simple. Survey the user," I replied.

"The primary complaints I hear about our competitors are that their interpreters are often late or unprofessional and display an inability to do the job," Rashelle said. "And patient no-shows and late arrivals are a big problem for the clinics. It's lost opportunity and costs them a lot of money. If we can make our performance transparent to the buyers, we should be able to use that as a point of differentiation. And if our consistency is of value to them, they will be willing to pay for it."

"Can you measure calls and arrival times?" I asked. "Let's start there if that's the biggest complaint about your competitors. Your point about making your performance transparent to the buyers is huge. So how do we do that?"

"By offering up our utilization report," Rashelle said.

Kyle could barely contain himself as ideas popped into his head. "We get paid more to consistently do the job the other agencies don't do," he said. "We could help our customers better understand the level to which we excel by developing metrics around what exceptional service needs to look like and providing statistics related to that. For instance, we're the only agency that makes a phone call to remind the patient about her appointment. The no-show ratios typically are higher with this population because of the intimidation factor. The clinics are paying us to reduce that figure. They can't bill the patient if the patient doesn't show up."

"We also need to highlight our ability to respond to same-day requests," Erin interjected. "That makes up 30 percent of our volume and is another differentiating factor."

"Your performance will become transparent through business reviews, metrics, and utilization reports," I added. "Testimonials from the internal users would also help. If you can prove exceptional performance, that can be powerful. You really need to make this a priority, and you'll want to put this type of information on your sales materials."

Once the Connecting Cultures planning team understood how to make their competence tangible, we generated a lengthy list of measurements and action plans. I informed the team that measuring the tangible value of their competence is a companywide responsibility, but making their competence tangible usually is the responsibility of the sales and marketing department, so these action plans would become a part of the new business development department plan. Rashelle smiled when she heard that. She could already see the benefits this would offer to the sales process.

BRAND STRATEGY THAT COMMUNICATES COMPETENCE

A skill set–aligned sales force is an essential asset for a growth-oriented company, and implementing an effective brand strategy is a key aspect to supporting their efforts. Salespeople can have a tendency to come and go, making it risky to depend on them for the long-term health of your organization. You never want to become people-dependent; rather, you want your organization anchored in the more stable position of being process-dependent and strategy-dependent. The good news is your brand strategy serves as the top sales producer in your organization, and that producer won't be going anywhere.

Conversely, an ineffective brand strategy can be the primary cause of an underperforming sales force. One of the benefits of the Stop Selling Vanilla Ice Cream process is that it helps organizations define what they want their brand strategy to communicate. Creating brand clarity is critical to success in an increasingly crowded marketplace. Experts estimate as many as 40,000 brands cross our path each day, so you can see the importance that effectively communicating your message has in helping you rise above the crowd.

"Now that you have defined your competence and are working toward making it tangible, we must wrap the entire organization around it, including your brand strategy," I explained to the team. "Your brand strategy contains three components that, combined, must clearly and effectively communicate your competence and/or the benefits of your competence to your target markets. The first component is the brand name of your organization, the second is your logo, and the third is your positioning statement."

THE POSITIONING OF YOUR BRAND

Leads to

Competence

Brand Strategy
Selling Tools
Marketing Campaigns
All Customer Touch Points

"I understand the brand and logo, but what is a positioning statement?" Bobbie asked. "Is it like a slogan?"

"The positioning statement, as the name implies, positions your competence in the minds of your target markets, while a slogan communicates something other than your competence. The challenge is having the positioning statement accurately reflect your competence. When we brainstorm ideas for your positioning statement, keep in mind that there's a danger in promoting a competence you don't or can't deliver. It diminishes your organization's credibility and casts you in a negative light. And that mixed message of promoting something you can't deliver is hard to recover from. Consider United Airlines' slogan, 'Fly the Friendly Skies.' Yet in 2009 and 2010, United received the lowest score for the airline industry in the American Customer Satisfaction Index (www.theacsi.org). United's slogan communicates something other than its competence.

"When you look at other companies' branding," I continued, "consider how their strategy tells you something about their competence. For example, the Home Depot used 'You can do it. We can help' as its positioning statement for many years. It was effective because of its base in the fundamentals of its competence—the company's ability to help do-it-yourselfers.

The company changed its positioning statement in 2009—during the height of the recession—to be more price-driven: 'More saving. More doing.' In my opinion, this version isn't as effective because it strays from the company's competence and seems like a low-cost producer strategy.

"One of my personal favorites is John Deere, which markets high-quality, dependable equipment under the positioning statement 'Nothing Runs Like a Deere.' It's a great play on words that reinforces the dependability of the company's products. Deere's logo, featuring the silhouette of a running white-tailed deer, also is instantly recognizable. Complemented by its familiar green and yellow color scheme, it effectively puts all three components of John Deere's brand strategy to work.

"I call it a *home run* when an organization's brand strategy clearly communicates the competence and the benefits of that competence."

"What I like about the companies you just mentioned, Steve, is they don't need any additional explanation—their brand is their number one sales producer," Rashelle said. "One of our challenges right now is we have to explain the tangible value we deliver to our target markets through conversation or sales materials."

"That's exactly the point of spending time on brand strategy and why it's part of the process," I said. "The most effective brand strategies are easy to understand because they clearly communicate the competence of the organization. If a salesperson has to be present to explain your brand, your brand strategy isn't working hard enough for you. It puts your sales force in a challenging position right from the start as they prospect with potential customers. An effective brand strategy opens the door for your sales organization. And it doesn't hurt when the brand strategy is easy to remember and has a catchy hook."

SM Advisors is not a branding agency, but we understand how essential it is to have a brand strategy that communicates the company's competence and the benefits of that competence. Who better to define that than your planning team? In our experience, an organization's planning team is able to use the process to successfully determine what they want their brand strategy to say. We brainstorm with the planning team to generate a pool of ideas and work toward making decisions on each component. If we can't arrive at decisions, we'll create action plans to finalize the brand strategy.

The majority of the organizations we work with are able to implement an effective brand strategy on their own, while others develop action plans and invest in expert help to make that happen. If we decide the organization could benefit from a new logo, for example, that's an area in which we'll enlist expert help.

The process for brand strategy development begins with a review of where you are currently with each of the three components.

Your Company Name

"First, let's talk about your brand, or your company name," I said. "When your target markets hear or see your brand strategy, they should immediately think of your competence."

Sometimes it's difficult for organizations to part ways with existing names, logos, and positioning statements, even if they're ineffective. If a company's name contributes little or nothing toward brand clarity, the planning team needs to consider whether the amount of equity they have in their name is sufficient to retain it or not. If they come to the conclusion that their name doesn't hold a significant amount of brand equity, then this examination could present an opportunity to change it.

"So tell me: Is the Connecting Cultures brand working for you and generating brand clarity?"

"I think it does work," Rashelle said cautiously. "But I do think we need to communicate the benefits to our target markets better than we are. I'm attached to our name because I worked hard to come up with it during the formation of the business. I think it conveys what we do. Our interpreters are 'connecting cultures' so our customers don't have to."

"I think 'Connecting Cultures' has brand equity in our market," Bobbie added. "The name may not be perfect, but it's more memorable than 'Whatever Interpreting Services,' and there are a lot of those types of names out there."

"I agree with you, but I wanted to hear your thoughts on the matter first," I said. "'Connecting Cultures' is more effective than 'Rashelle and Associates.' It's an example of why I'm not a big fan of people naming companies after themselves. You waste one of the three ways available to communicate your competence with your brand strategy. If your company name isn't working because you named it after yourself, the logo and positioning statement have to work that much harder to carry the load."

With the amount of brand equity the name has and the value it brings to their brand strategy, the rest of the planning team agreed that Connecting Cultures should remain as the company name.

Your Logo

"The second leg of the brand strategy stool is the logo," I continued. "At SM Advisors, our name only tells part of our story. We turned the 'M' into a line graph to represent profit growth and added the phrase 'Strategic Management' to clarify what the 'SM' stands for and further differentiate our position in the market. What are your thoughts about Connecting Cultures' logo? Are you satisfied with it?"

"I like our current logo," Rashelle said. "The globe tells our target markets that we deal in a global industry. When you combine our brand, Connecting Cultures, with the logo, it communicates that we connect cultures from around the world. But how are we doing that? We know what our company name and logo means, but this probably isn't as obvious to the potential customers in our marketplace as we would like it to be. Should we spend more time on our logo, or do you think we can more effectively communicate our competence through an impactful positioning statement?"

"I like our logo, too," Kyle stated, "but it is missing something."

As teams work through this process, they have to acknowledge that sometimes not every component of the brand is going to offer the same level of clarity about the competence. What is most important is that the three combined offer brand clarity. "If everybody likes the logo, you can add brand clarity through the positioning statement," I offered.

"Let's try that," Kyle said.

Your Positioning Statement

"We need to make your brand strategy obvious to your target markets," I said. "Too often I see companies out-think themselves and get too creative. The result diminishes the effect of the brand strategy because it's too hard to figure out. The challenge of coming up with a positioning statement that communicates the organization's competence in a clever way can be a challenge, but it's one most planning teams want to take on because it's a fun part of the plan development process."

The Connecting Cultures planning team members were enthusiastic as they began brainstorming phrases that might be appropriate to pair with their logo and brand name.

"How about, 'So You Don't Have To,'" Rashelle offered. "We connect cultures so our clients don't have to. Or 'Opening Your Door to the World.' That introduces the global aspect."

"But those statements still don't say what we do," Bobbie commented. "If we use something like, 'Making Communication Easy,' that kind of says what we do."

"Yes, but it still doesn't tell our target markets that interpreting is the part of communication we provide," Erin noted. "If we used 'Interpreting for the Health Care Industry,' that would say what we do."

"I call that a literal positioning statement," I noted. "It says exactly what you do. The problem is there's no memorable hook to grab your target market's attention. The good news is that it's a good place to start, because you've identified what you want to communicate. Defining the literal positioning statement is a great first step in coming up with a final positioning statement. The next step is working on the spin to create a statement that hits the sweet spot and sticks in your target market's memory. Erin, your suggestion may not be that far off. We just need to find the hook in your literal statement."

"Our company deals in language services for health care clients, which is more comprehensive than just 'interpreting,'" Bobbie said. "Maybe we could consider 'Our Language Is Health Care.'"

That suggestion sent a bolt of energy surging through the team.

"Ooo, that's good!" Eric said, and everybody else in the room voiced their approval.

"I love it," Rashelle stated. "It says what we do and speaks directly to our primary target market of health care organizations. It even has a great hook!"

The more the team discussed its brand strategy, the more their level of excitement grew.

"Do you think we can improve on any of the three components?" I asked.

"I think we've got it," said Rashelle, and others nodded. "But I think it's worth sleeping on and making sure that we're comfortable with it in the morning." The team quickly developed action plans to finalize their brand strategy, but the enthusiasm that stems from a creative and effective brand strategy was already driving the team. I knew that soon they would begin seeing employees across the organization wearing the brand with pride on jackets and shirts.

ALIGNING MISSION WITH COMPETENCE

One simple question—What does your company do? — can turn the most innocent of interactions into an uncomfortable moment if you and your employees are not prepared with a good answer. Do you have a specific script committed to memory that you can easily access when asked that question? More important, does your response effectively communicate your competence—your mint chocolate chip ice cream—in a way your listener will retain after the interaction is complete?

"It's important to spend some time crafting a mission statement that communicates your strategy," I explained to the planning team. "Having a competence that separates you from your competitors is less impactful if your employees don't know how to consistently communicate it."

> Do you have a mission statement? If so, does it communicate your differentiation in the market?

"What's the difference between what we should include in a mission statement and our competence?" Bobbie asked. "Aren't they the same thing?"

"They're usually pretty close," I replied. "An effective mission statement and elevator speech are simplified versions of your competence, constructed in a way that makes them easily understood and meaningful for their intended audience. The mission statement is the number one tool for communicating your strategy to stakeholders, including employees, vendors, customers, and target markets. Other than your values, the mission statement is the only document you share outside the organization. The rest of your strategy should remain confidential and be shared only internally or with strategic partners."

Your mission statement should communicate your competence and differentiation to your target markets. It must clearly describe the competence of the organization with the goal of educating and motivating your target markets to do business with you. The mission statement should be a written, visible description of your competence, but it should be concise enough to have a strong impact.

"How often have you seen a mission statement that's so fluffy, so verbose, that it's not even clear what industry the company is in, much less what it's good at?" I asked the team. I received a few nods in response. "People's attention spans are only so long, so your mission statement needs to capture their attention long before their eyes glaze over. The most effective mission statements are only one or two sentences in length. I favor one-sentence mission statements that people can remember."

The verbiage should be present tense to convey the notion that you're accomplishing this mission right now, such as, "Our mission is" or "We deliver." The first sentence of the mission statement should describe your organization's competence and the benefits that competence holds for your customers. The second sentence, if needed, describes how or where you concentrate your focus.

A spirited discussion ensued as team members reviewed their competence to help them begin writing the company's mission statement. The simplest approach is to copy and paste your competence into the mission statement template (available at www.stopsellingvanillaicecream.com) and then edit it with the team. It usually takes five to ten minutes to write an effective mission statement with this approach. Simple, but effective.

The Connecting Cultures team debated the most effective focus for the statement, and the word "create" seemed to be a popular choice for the statement's verb. "That's a relatively weak word," I said. "A lot of people create things, but not many execute or accomplish them. I'd like to see you use the word 'execute' or 'accomplish' as the verb, because that's really what matters. A great plan by itself doesn't get you anywhere."

That suggestion seemed to provide enough forward motion to propel the team toward finalizing its mission statement. After a little more discussion, they had crafted a clear description of the company's competence in its new mssion statement:

> **Our mission is to provide the health care industry with customizable options for language access plans. We accomplish this through our comprehensive interpreter hiring, training, and management processes that create a unique solution for every health care organization. Our language is health care!**

The team felt it was important to add the second sentence here. Many organizations shorten or refine their mission statements in the second year as their competence and vision come into clearer focus. Also, putting your positioning statement at the end of the mission is a nice finishing touch.

"We'll need to record some action plans to ensure this mission statement is posted around the organization as well as on your website," I said. "Think of the mission statement as a sales tool to hook your own employees as well as your external target markets."

"So then what's the difference between the mission statement and the elevator speech?" Eric asked.

"The elevator speech is the mission statement in layman's terms," I responded. "It's shorter than the mission statement, easier to remember, and used when a non–target market contact asks what your company does. It's an icebreaker, yet it still communicates your competence. Let's see if we can boil down your mission statement into an effective elevator speech."

"How about something like this: We provide interpreting programs for the health care industry," Kyle offered.

"I can remember that," Eric deadpanned.

"I think that's perfect," Rashelle said. "Without getting into too much detail, that statement says exactly what we do and who our target market is."

"Every employee in your organization should be able to recite this brief elevator speech, regardless of their job duties," I said. "Understand that all of your associates are in sales, whether they are directly involved in sales or account management or not. At some point, someone will ask them what their company does, and they should have a consistent answer for that question. It could be at a family reunion, a church function, or a school event. You never know who you might run into during the course of your day."

COMMUNICATING YOUR COMPETENCE THROUGH SALES AND MARKETING

Companies that grow by only 2 to 3 percent annually oftentimes do not effectively communicate the tangible value of their competence through their sales and marketing tools. Their growth is coming from current customers. They're not able to grow any faster than that because they're not landing any new business. Many organizations struggle to land new business because potential customers have never experienced their competence and are unwilling to pay for a value they don't understand. In addition, their current customers rarely comprehend the total value their competence delivers.

It is your responsibility to prove the tangible value of your competence to current and prospective customers. You can't just hope they figure it out by chance.

One reason many organizations struggle with sales and marketing is that they do not have a strategy. A strategy creates the foundation for a focused sales and marketing plan by providing your organization with the content it needs to write the plan. Your organization now has your competence (the sales message), its tangible value to your customers, your new brand strategy, a mission statement, and other critical information needed to develop

> *Has your organization struggled to develop an effective sales and marketing plan? Is it because you lack a strategy?*

your sales and marketing plan. With a strategy now in place for Connecting Cultures, the task of writing the plan and creating effective sales and marketing tools had become a lot easier.

For prospective customers, package your information into a presentation format that illustrates the tangible value you deliver to other customers, or the estimated value your competence would bring to your target customer. Your objective is to prove that the total value they would receive from your organization is greater than the value any of your competitors can provide, especially any low-price competitors. You must show that the total value you deliver goes beyond a low price.

"Without communicating the difference of your competence, you run the risk of losing customers to a competitor who may simply deliver vanilla ice cream rather than the mint chocolate chip you are providing," I said to the team. "Are your sales tools communicating the tangible value of your competence? If not, you're setting up your sales force to sell vanilla ice cream."

"See, I told you I'm not a good salesperson," Rashelle said almost triumphantly. "Now I know why. I need better tools to be able to sell."

"You're partially right," I said. "I've seen too many competent salespeople fail at companies where the sales process and negotiations focus on price. The leadership team hasn't developed a strategy that effectively paves the way for sales success. Some salespeople are so talented they can sell ice to Eskimos, but in order to have your entire sales team functioning at the highest level, strategy must come first. If you have all of these fundamentals in place and the sales team still isn't producing, then you probably don't have the right talent. However, a clearly defined strategy paired with a skill set–aligned sales team armed with effective selling tools and a targeted marketing machine out in front of them will generate a significant increase in sales every time. The Stop Selling Vanilla Ice Cream process helps ensure that you have both process and skills through its focus on strategy and talent."

Competence-aligned sales materials can also be useful when you aren't selling to the final decision maker. These materials can give the buyer ammunition to sell your company internally to the decision makers, making the salesperson's job easier. Sharing the tangible value of your competence across your customer's company is the best way to solidify a long-term partnership. A change in a buyer will not jeopardize the business because others within the organization will understand the tangible value your company delivers to them.

Another effective sales tool for sharing the value of your competence to numerous people across the customer's company is business reviews. Annual business reviews with current customers provide an opportunity to illustrate the tangible value you provide. It's important to make the effort to have all levels and departments within the customer's organization have representation at the reviews, or at a minimum, review the metrics. This is your opportunity to help the decision makers understand the tangible value you deliver. It's also the easiest place to obtain new business and referrals and to ward off competitive threats.

"Oftentimes when a customer realizes the tangible value you deliver to their company, they will give you other opportunities for business, especially in areas where another vendor is underperforming," I said to the team, emphasizing that selling is a process that everybody is involved in. "As long as you've proven the ability to keep one problem from cluttering their desk, they're more likely to see if you can solve another problem for them as well, even if it falls outside of your competence."

The Connecting Cultures team began brainstorming ideas they could implement to make the value from their service-driven competence tangible to current and potential customers. It's important to brainstorm ideas and record them throughout the process so you have an inventory of ideas ready to act upon when you arrive at the department planning stage.

"The administrators are the ones who make the purchasing decisions and give us most of the negative feedback," Rashelle said. "So my job will be to communicate how our company is performing and how we make their jobs easier."

"Since your administrative contacts view interpreting as an expense," I said, "we need to help them view it as a value-added service for their patients and a way to increase their daily revenue. This is a way for them to build their business. It's about helping the customer meet their needs, so your message needs to be more about value creation than cost containment."

The planning team had made incredible progress toward clearly differentiating Connecting Cultures from its competitors and determining how they would communicate that difference to its customers. The foundation for a growth-oriented sales and marketing plan was now in place. They were close to having a fully defined strategy, and the final step of developing their strategic vision would complete the strategy development process.

The Scoop

1. On a scale of 1 to 10 (1 = vanilla ice cream and 10 = mint chocolate chip ice cream), how well do you think your current brand strategy communicates your competence and the benefits of your competence to your target markets?

2. What would you change about your brand strategy to make it more effective in communicating your competence or the benefits of your competence?

3. Do your sales and marketing materials communicate the tangible value of your competence to your target markets? How can you improve them?

Action Plans to Complete the Process

☐ Define the tangible (and intangible) value of your competence to your target markets.

☐ Define measurements that will capture the tangible value your competence delivers to your target markets.

☐ Define the first three customers for which you want to implement the process to make your competence tangible.

☐ Define your brand strategy or any actions to complete your brand strategy.

☐ Define your mission statement.

☐ Define your elevator speech.

☐ Brainstorm action plans to improve your sales and marketing tools.

☐ Brainstorm action plans to develop your business review process and identify three friendly customers to help you pilot it.

CREATING CLARITY THROUGH A STRATEGIC VISION

One of the leadership team's primary responsibilities is creating a detailed vision for the organization that all employees can understand and shoot for. Without that vision, it's too easy for personal variables to play a role in day-to-day decisions across the organization. Achieving the vision will take less time when all the daily decisions in your company are made with the vision as the target.

"The vision serves several purposes for an organization," I said to the Connecting Cultures team. "It contributes to strategy development by helping leadership specify what the organization needs in the future and why. It also serves as a rallying point for the rest of the employees, instilling a level of excitement and anticipation. People enjoy the pride they feel in working for a successful organization. The vision unifies the organization, and you can feel the positive momentum building from everyone being on the same page."

"What is the best way to create the vision and make sure it doesn't just collect dust?" Kyle asked.

"The process of creating your vision starts with your competence," I replied. "Your competence is at the core of your vision. Within the vision's time frame, your goal is to become the best at your competence in the markets in which you compete."

"This is the part that gets me excited," Rashelle said. "I realize we have a lot of work to do in the near term to bring Connecting Cultures up to where it needs to be, but once we do that, I have all sorts of ideas about what we should look like in the future."

"That's exactly the attitude we need from the planning team for this discussion," I said. "The vision serves as a tool for the leadership team to strategically allocate resources. Companies without a solid vision often struggle to realize a good return on investment from their resources, because they're not pointed toward a specific target."

"I'm embarrassed that we haven't put together a vision prior to this," Rashelle said. "It was always just ideas in my mind that I shared only with a few people."

"Don't beat yourself up about it," I said. "You're not alone. In fact, it astonishes me how few companies take the act of creating a vision seriously. They don't have the rudder and navigation system necessary to move their ship toward its destination. And then they wonder why they sail in circles, never really making any significant progress. It's been proven that people who have personal goals achieve a higher level of success than those who don't, so why wouldn't that same principle hold true for a business? The answer is it does. You want your organization moving every day toward accomplishing your vision and making it a reality."

A compelling and clear vision has subjective and objective components to it. The subjective components of your vision include how you want your internal culture to be described by your employees and what you want your customers to be saying about you when you achieve your vision. The objective components of your vision include the market and scope of the products and services that will be offered in the vision time frame, and the strategic measurements and financial factors.

SPECIFIC, MEASURABLE, AND ATTAINABLE

A common mistake many organizations make is failing to make their visions specific enough. Flowery words that lack details are not as effective as specific targets that together act as an organizational bull's-eye. Companies are comprised of people, and people need a finish line to know if they've won the race.

"Your vision needs to be a clear picture of what you want to achieve, because if you aim at nothing, you'll hit it every time," I said. "A clear vision generates more horsepower for the engine that drives your company forward, enabling employees to make everyday decisions that move the organization in the right direction."

Crafting a specific vision also helps remove emotion and knee-jerk reactions from the equation, and we all know that entrepreneurship and company ownership is a roller coaster of stress, joy, and excitement. Personal variables should not impact company decisions. Instead, decisions should depend on whether or not the proposed action moves the company toward its vision.

"Many companies fall short of the ideal with their vision by creating a single vision statement versus a vivid, objective picture of where they want to be," I continued. "For example, saying you will be the best in your industry is way too vague. How motivating is a vision if you don't know when you have achieved it? Without a specific target and accompanying measurements to gauge your progress, you won't know if you're moving closer to your goal. We need to identify the measurable goals that will help you achieve your vision."

"I know Rashelle would like to achieve everything tomorrow, but that's not realistic," Bobbie said. "How far into the future should we look in developing our vision?"

"That's a good question, Bobbie, and the simple answer is that it depends on what stage of development your company is in and the overall dynamics of your industry," I replied. "Your status as a young company or as a more established company has a direct bearing on how much change you can expect to achieve in the stated time frame. Your vision should capture the ideal within the spectrum of believability."

Does your organization have a clearly defined and communicated strategic vision? If not, how are resource allocation and other decisions made?

"That's where I struggle," Rashelle said. "Sometimes I forget that what I want for Connecting Cultures isn't necessarily going to happen overnight."

"From our market research, we saw that your industry is ripe for rapid change because of changes in technology, and that may impact the time frame for your vision," I said. "For example, an Internet company might have a vision that reaches only a year or two ahead because of rapid technology advancement, while a consumer products company may have a five-year vision. Typically, most companies use a three-year vision."

"I think that's appropriate for us," Rashelle said.

A true vision is like a painting created by an artist, where each brushstroke has meaning and strengthens the overall emotional attachment to the final result. To develop a powerful vision, you can use the vision template shown here (available from www.stopsellingvanillaicecream.com). It's important that the vision you develop has buy-in from the entire leadership team. You will need everyone to agree on all aspects of the vision, including what new products, markets, and geographic territories you're going to pursue within the vision time frame.

BUSINESS PLAN
VISION
[DATE]

By the date listed, we will make our vision a reality in these key areas:

COMPETENCE:

INTERNAL OPERATIONS (CULTURE):
How do we want the culture of our organization to be described by the end of our vision?

EXTERNAL (CUSTOMER) PERCEPTIONS:
What do we want our customers saying about us by the end of our vision?

FUTURE PRODUCT/SERVICE SCOPE:
What will our future product or service scope look like by the end of our vision?

FUTURE TARGET MARKET SCOPE:
What target markets will we be targeting? Will they change?

FUTURE GEOGRAPHIC MARKET SCOPE:
What geographic markets will we be servicing? Will they change?

MEASUREMENT (see Measurement Matrix)

A VISION FOR YOUR CULTURE

"How do you want your employees to describe the organization's culture in the future?" I asked. "What types of things do you want your culture to demonstrate by the end of the vision? What are your greatest frustrations with the current culture of the organization that you would like to see changed? How do we make Connecting Cultures a better working environment? These types of questions should be answered in the vision. Creating a healthy internal culture is an important step in reaching your vision."

"We need to be the employer of choice for the interpreting community," Rashelle said. "That means we need to give employees the tools they need to succeed. We have to offer a safe and positive work environment with open channels of communication and where we value our people as individuals. I want them to see us as professional, innovative, and family-oriented."

"Do any of those viewpoints exist right now?" I asked.

"Only to some extent," Erin interjected. "I think many of the interpreting staff view communication with the leadership level as limited, and they don't believe they're truly valued as individuals."

"It's imperative that members of each department feel they are part of the whole," I said. "The existence of an 'us vs. them' attitude can destroy an organization's ability to achieve its vision."

The team wrapped up the discussion of the future culture of Connecting Cultures, which included the following attributes: open communication, giving employees tools to succeed, being the employer-of-choice, and being family-oriented.

EXTERNAL PERCEPTION

"What do you want your customers to say about Connecting Cultures in the future?" I asked, to help the team consider the external perceptions aspect of their vision.

"It would help our sales efforts if we were seen as the experts in language access for the health care industry," Bobbie answered. "We need to be viewed as easy to work with and a critical business partner for our customers' success. From the leadership team to our interpreters, we want to be proactive, cordial, reliable, and compassionate. We also should be seen as having high integrity and excellent problem-solving abilities.

Does your organization have a system for gathering feedback about customer perceptions of your company? How effective is it?

"We need to know how our customers perceive us," Bobbie continued. "Right now it's just an opinion we have about their perception of us."

"Absent any survey results at this point, how do you think your customers perceive Connecting Cultures?" I asked.

"Dependable and capable," Erin stated.

"Especially in comparison to some of our competitors," Rashelle added.

"They provide customized language access options that are the best for our business," Eric added.

"No one provides us the service offerings that Connecting Cultures does," said Bobbie.

"That's a good place to start," I said. "Customer surveys will turn those estimates into solid research and provide a starting point for your future relationship-building efforts."

"Can we use those customer surveys to measure things like how professional and compassionate our interpreters are, or how easy we are to work with as a company?" Bobbie asked.

"Absolutely you can," I answered. "Those surveys will become part of your ongoing effort to make your competence tangible. You'll want to use these results on sales calls with potential customers, as well as for internal tracking purposes. Conducting a survey right now will also establish a baseline of where you are today in the eyes of your customer. After completing the first year of the plan, you can resurvey your customers to see what progress you have made."

The team discussed and agreed on several descriptors they wanted their customers to be saying about Connecting Cultures by the end of the vision time frame, and we discussed the need to make sure they have the action plans in place to make those statements a reality. Some of the descriptors included experts in language access in health care, critical business partner, problem solvers, reliable and consistent, and compassionate.

MARKET AND SCOPE

An important component of your vision is identifying what your scope of services and your target markets will look like once you've achieved it.

"Right now, we earn all of our revenue from language services," Rashelle noted to begin the conversation. "Like we talked about earlier, at some point we may have products to sell. I'm thinking of things like video interpreting, telephonic services, reference tools packaged as separate products, written translations, and training programs."

"As you put together your three-year vision, you'll need to determine which of those products and services will become reality at different points in that time frame," I said. "Rashelle, I'm guessing you'd like to add all of them sooner than later."

"Yup," she replied with a smile. "But I know that's not realistic. I could see having them all in place by the end of the three-year time frame, though."

"If you think that's realistic, then you should include that in your vision," I said. "Along those same lines, your vision should identify which markets Connecting Cultures might serve in the future. What types of organizations do you see as potential future users of your products and services, and what factors could change the location or type of those markets?"

"At least in the near term, I can see us servicing entire health care systems and clinics with multiple provider locations," Kyle answered.

Rashelle's visionary tendencies again took hold as she suggested future large-scale expansion of Connecting Cultures' footprint.

"For our interpreting business, I would like to see us pursue additional customers in Green Bay, and then go down the Lake Michigan shoreline to Manitowoc and Sheboygan, and on south to Milwaukee," Rashelle stated. "Depending on margins and demand for telephonic and video services, the potential is there to expand into surrounding states such as Minnesota, Illinois, and Iowa."

"That's a big jump in coverage," I said. "Many of our clients find the greatest benefit from running as much business as possible across existing assets before adding branch locations and incurring significant capital investment."

"I know," Rashelle said, "but that's my vision. I just need to figure out how much of that is reasonable to expect during the next three years."

The team hashed out what they thought was realistic to achieve by the end of their vision. They agreed Connecting Cultures would pursue business in Green Bay, Sheboygan/Manitowoc, and Milwaukee.

FINANCIAL VISION THROUGH STRATEGIC MEASUREMENT

The next step in the creation of your vision involves developing and maintaining a tool called a measurement matrix. The matrix provides an objective view of your progress by tracking the results needed to achieve your plan. This is a key aspect of moving toward your vision, because you have to be able to measure whether you're moving in the right direction.

Establishing goals for each of the metrics requires that you tie the targets to your budget and performance numbers. The measurement matrix monitors these metrics and tells you if the plan is working. The first year's targets tie directly to your budget, while pro forma numbers—which are more of an estimate—link to the three-year vision. If you see the plan is not working, you can and need to take action.

BUSINESS PLAN Measurement Matrix						
	HISTORY			GOALS		
MEASUREMENT	20XX	20XX	20XX	20XX	20XX	20XX

"How do we use the metrics to track our progress?" Rashelle asked.

"I usually suggest identifying four to six strategic company measurements that you can review on a monthly basis," I said. "The lead financial person is the owner of the matrix and responsible for completing it by adding the history and recommended goals for each measurement that are finalized by the planning team. The owner of the matrix also presents the updated measurements at the plan execution review meetings. Measurements that are on track and color coded in green illustrate which aspects of the plan are working, while measurements that are falling short of the objective are color coded in red and highlight areas in need of focus or adjustment. Let's get started by identifying which key company measurements you should include in Connecting Cultures' measurement matrix."

"We certainly need to keep a close eye on our internal operations," Kyle suggested. "For me, that refers to the productivity of our interpreting and translating staff. The key measurements within that are percentage of payroll spent generating revenue and the amount of time lost to nonbillable travel time."

"I think tracking productivity is a great strategic measurement, Kyle," I said, "but travel time is more of a department-oriented statistic. It is important to separate strategic measurements from departmental measurements. For example, tracking the sales closing rate would be a great statistic for the sales department to follow, but it's not a strategic measurement because it doesn't apply to the entire organization. Department-specific measurements will be captured in the department plans."

Make sure the strategic measurements are specific to what you are trying to accomplish in the strategy. If you are making a major shift in your strategy, it is important to have measurements that will help you monitor that shift. For example, Connecting Cultures' strategy was to increase sales in specific geographic target markets, so sales in geographic target markets is an appropriate strategic measurement.

"We need to track sales, and not just in gross numbers." Kyle sat forward in his chair and his speech picked up speed as he grasped the concept. "We should break out sales by geographic territory and delivery method, and we need to determine if we're devoting resources in the most efficient places."

"We should look at sales by language, too," Erin added. "We know Spanish is our largest group and Hmong is next, but I sense we'll be asked to provide more Somali services going forward, and we need to have a handle on that."

"I'd like to add a section on the human resources side, too," Rashelle said. "It's very important that we track and improve our retention rate for interpreters, so we need to promote a dynamic, family-oriented work environment."

The planning team quickly settled on a list of strategic measurements that would illustrate Connecting Cultures' ability to reach its vision.

COMMUNICATING THE VISION

"Once we finalize Connecting Cultures' vision, we need to make arrangements to communicate it to the entire organization," I said. "This will ensure your organization makes daily decisions based on achieving the vision, as opposed to letting personal variables dictate actions. You'll find that you will achieve the vision sooner when everyone is pulling on the rope in the same direction."

Business Plan
Vision
December 31, 20XX

By 12/31/20XX, Connecting Cultures, Inc., will make our vision a reality in these key areas:

COMPETENCE:

We provide comprehensive interpreter hiring, training, development, and management that allow us to deliver customized language service options to the health care industry.

INTERNAL OPERATIONS (CULTURE):

- Open communication
- Safe & positive work environment
- Innovative
- Give employees tools to succeed
- Employer-of-choice

- Proactive
- Value the individual
- Professional
- Dynamic
- Family-oriented

EXTERNAL (CUSTOMER) PERCEPTIONS:

- Experts in language access in health care
- Easy to use/work with
- Critical business partner
- Proactive
- Cordial

- High integrity
- Professional
- Problem solvers
- Reliable/consistent
- Compassionate

FUTURE PRODUCT/SERVICE SCOPE:

- Video interpreting
- Face-to-face interpreting
- Consulting/training

- Phone interpreting
- Products (reference tools)
- Translations

FUTURE TARGET MARKET SCOPE:

- Health care systems and multiple locations/multiple providers clinics

FUTURE GEOGRAPHIC MARKET SCOPE:
- For interpreting, we will pursue business in Green Bay, Sheboygan/ Manitowoc, & Milwaukee
- Telephonic & video: Depending on margins and demand, potential here to expand into more rural markets, possibly regional (MN, IL, IA)
- Regional/national for consulting, training, and reference materials

MEASUREMENT:
- Dollar sales by service line
- Sales percentage by geographic territory
- Sales percentage by delivery method (i.e., in person, phone, video, translations, consulting)
- Sales by language
- Interpreter productivity
- Net income
- Gross margin percentage

The team developed several action plans to communicate the vision across the organization. The first was presenting the entire business plan to the company, and that would be followed by working in teams on departmental plans to support the vision.

ANNUAL PLANNING TO ACHIEVE YOUR VISION

Performing annual plan updates is the most effective way for an organization to methodically move toward its vision. The annual reviews create a platform by which the planning team can take stock of progress made during the previous year, and develop action plans and goals for the next that help the company go on a run of success. For example, a vision with a three-year time horizon would begin with a first-year business plan and the subsequent execution of that plan. At the end of the first year, the team would review progress made and develop action plans to execute the second-year business plan. It would repeat that process entering the third year, with the organization ideally achieving the ultimate vision at the end of that year.

For example, we went on a five-year run at EnzoPac during the time I served on the leadership team. We established a three-year vision that started with a first-year business plan. We executed that plan, then created a second-year business plan and executed that, etc. We achieved our vision at the end of the third year, and then reset a new vision. We grew from a $5 million company to a $30 million company in less than five years. By the time we achieved the second vision, we were in position to sell the business.

The annual plan review process enables leadership to make adjustments to the business plan or even tweak the vision itself. It's helpful to turn your vision into questions, filters to identify any adjustments needed, such as: "Does your organization have good communication?" and "Is the strategy working?" Once the organization achieves its vision, the process to go on another run starts all over again.

As I explained this planning process to the Connecting Cultures team, I could see their excitement about the vision and the regular progress toward it growing.

"I think we did a great job today," Rashelle said. "It's really cool to see our focus refined. This is something we've wanted to do for years, and we're finally at a point where we're able to follow through and execute on it."

"We've completed a great deal of groundwork, and now it's about developing the action plans we need to implement the strategy," I said. "When we achieve this vision, will you consider your efforts a success?"

"There's no way we can't!" Bobbie said.

The Scoop

1. What factors in your industry or your company might affect the time line for your vision?

2. What is your vision for the culture of your organization? How far are you from that vision?

3. How do you want your customers to describe your company when the vision is accomplished?

4. Have you surveyed your customers to determine what is their perception of you as a company? What kinds of questions do you ask them (or would you ask them if you have never surveyed them)?

5. What products or services do you think your company should be offering by the end of the vision time frame?

6. How might your target markets change within the vision, in terms of industry, company type, or geography?

Action Plans to Complete the Process

☐ Define the length of your vision (2 years, 3 years, 5 years).

☐ Define the subjective and objective components of your vision using the template.

☐ Develop action plans to effectively communicate your vision to all employees.

PREPARING TO TURN STRATEGY INTO ACTION

"I can't wait to begin putting all this work into practice," Rashelle said as we wrapped up our discussion of vision and began to prepare for the next stage of the process. "It seems like we've come so far already."

"You have, and I'd like to commend you on that progress," I said. "The process will help you really hit the ground running after we put the final pieces in place. You defined your mint chocolate chip ice cream—your competence. You identified those who will value your competence, and how you can make it tangible for current and prospective customers. You determined that your competence will clearly differentiate Connecting Cultures from its competitors. You nailed down your brand strategy and mission statement. And you looked into the future to create a vision of what your company will look like in three years. You've come together as a true team to develop a clear vision for your organization's future."

"This is the highest level of agreement and cohesiveness we've ever experienced," Rashelle said.

"I can't believe what we've accomplished," Bobbie said. "It's more than we've done in the history of Connecting Cultures."

"Nothing brings a team together like candid and honest discussions about the future direction of an organization," I said. "I would encourage you to stay in your metaphorical underwear so you can continue having candid and professional dialogue. It is important that you hold each other accountable and not revert back to your original state.

"Now all that's left is putting your strategy into action. Phase 4 of the Stop Selling Vanilla Ice Cream process focuses on steps the organization needs to take in order to effectively implement the strategy you've worked so hard to develop. I can tell you're really looking forward to finally putting the plan into action.

THE TRANSITIONAL ISSUES TO DELIVER YOUR COMPETENCE AND ACHIEVE YOUR VISION

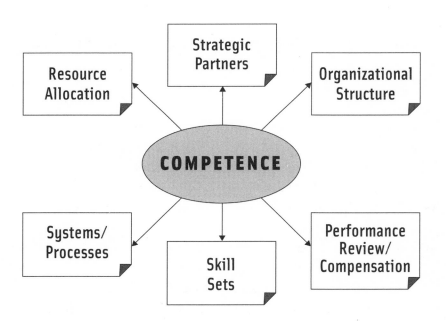

"Before we can begin executing, though, we need to focus on resolving transitional issues (see above), those issues that will help the organization transition from its present state defined in the internal analysis to the desired future state defined in the vision. We'll also identify goals for the next year, establish a plan execution program, and launch the department planning process."

"We are so ready to take the next steps and move this company forward," Rashelle replied.

"I'm sure you are, and I'm excited for you," I said. "Before we adjourn for the day, let's discuss how to prepare to tackle the next steps and establish the homework that needs to be done. Before the next meeting, I'd like each of you to review the current plan and bring to the meeting any components of the plan that might need more refinement. In your homework teams, you'll design the functional organizational structure that will help you achieve your vision, identify skill set voids, address sys-

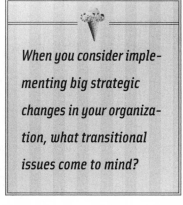

When you consider implementing big strategic changes in your organization, what transitional issues come to mind?

tems and processes that need to be developed or improved, and establish the company goals for the next twelve months.

DESIGNING THE FUNCTIONAL ORGANIZATIONAL STRUCTURE

The first homework assignment is to design the functional organizational structure needed to achieve your vision and strengthen your competence.

"The first step in creating an effective organizational structure is a clean sheet of paper," I said. "The goal is to develop the functional organizational structure needed to achieve your vision and strengthen your competence. You'll need to include all necessary functions on this chart, whether they currently exist or not. Keep in mind this may or may not match up with current roles and responsibilities. We're looking for the optimum structure that needs to be in place by the time you achieve your vision."

A functional organizational chart begins with the leader position and works downward from there. While building the functional organizational structure, you should not discuss or assign any names to positions within the structure. It is important that you follow the process. All you want to do is identify responsibilities and functions. Once the structure is complete, between planning meetings you'll work on job descriptions and identifying the necessary skill sets to accomplish those jobs. You'll create clear accountability for each position, with efficient and clear lines of authority and communication. These are some of the strongest benefits of starting fresh. Remember: the functional organizational structure is designed around the talent you need, not around the talent you have. But much of the talent you require is likely in the organization already and will be developed through your Talent Management System.

"But some of our people need to be in certain positions," Rashelle said. "Can't we just put their names in the boxes where they belong?"

"No," I quickly replied. "I have found from doing hundreds of organizational structures that the best approach is designing the functional structure needed to achieve your vision. Don't think about any of your current employees while completing the structure. You want to eliminate all bias in developing the structure that will help you achieve your vision. I realize that's easier said than done, but we've found the process works best if you stay focused on functional roles at this point."

> *How did your current organizational structure evolve? Do you think it's effective?*

Most organizations begin implementing parts of, if not all of, the functional organizational structure right away. The timetable of the transition to the new structure varies from organization to organization. Some may maintain their current structure for some time before they feel they can or need to make changes, while others implement their new functional organizational structure immediately to experience the benefits it offers. It all depends on where the company is.

Once a team completes its functional organizational structure, SM Advisors works with them to identify the job descriptions and job benchmarks for each position. Ownership and/or leadership then can place specific individuals in each role of the organizational structure based on the necessary skill set match. We consider the education, experience, and behavioral assessments of each person in evaluating existing skill sets, and place people with the right skill set matches in the appropriate positions within the organizational structure. We will discuss in more detail how to implement the functional structure into your company in the next chapter.

IDENTIFYING SKILL SET VOIDS

"The process of developing a functional organizational structure has the added result of highlighting any skill set voids and sets the stage for action plans to fill those voids," I explained. "For the next session, I would ask the homework teams to review the list of skill set voids we identified in the interviews and be prepared to discuss the ones we need to fill to achieve the vision, particularly given the functional organization you develop. During this discussion focus on talking about only possible skill set voids and do not use specific people or names."

Skill set misalignment—along with not having an organizational competence—is typically one of the main reasons a company underperforms. The positive impact that proper talent in the most effective positions can have on solid strategy can't be overstated. It's the fuel that powers the organization's engine.

IMPROVING SYSTEMS AND PROCESSES

"The next assignment for the homework teams is identifying the systems and processes needed to achieve the vision. This is an important component for the first year's success because you need to ensure that you consistently deliver your competence throughout the organization. You accomplish this by consistently executing documented processes in every department. What's even more exciting is that as you grow, the systems enable you to handle significantly more business with your current assets and team. You'll find you're able to get more done with less and increase your bottom line."

"That's something we could use right now," Kyle commented.

"Well, that will happen," I responded. "You'll see fairly quickly how much more efficient you can be when you have systems and processes in place to handle your most common organizational tasks."

ANNUAL GOALS

"The last assignment for the homework teams is developing a list of three to five organizational goals for the next twelve months," I said. "What are the major goals you want to accomplish that will take you one step closer to achieving your vision?"

When creating goals, nothing is simpler or more effective than the tried-and-true SMART approach introduced in 1981 by George Doran, Arthur Miller, and James Cunningham. You may have heard about this goal-setting technique before, but it bears repeating, and I'll explain it in more depth in chapter 18. In our variation of the model, SMART stands for:

✔ **Specific:** be able to answer who, what, where, when, and why questions about the goal

✔ **Measurable:** identify concrete criteria for gauging progress

✔ **Agreed-upon:** in a team setting, gain consensus regarding the appropriateness of the goal and any incremental steps to achieve it

✔ **Realistic:** you must believe the goal is possible in order to make it happen

✔ **Timely:** ground the goal in a time frame

"If you have three years to accomplish your vision," I said, "what are the most important goals you need to accomplish in the next year to take the first step? Try to identify some attainable goals to take a small bite out of this elephant. As you work through this goal-setting exercise, you'll want to brainstorm action plans to attain each goal."

"How far out should we be looking?" Bobbie asked.

"Our planning time frame for goals is twelve months," I answered. "Keep in mind that enjoying some early successes will help the organization gain momentum and build some confidence.

ACTION PLAN REGISTER TO PREPARE FOR PHASE 4			
PROJECT DESCRIPTION	Owner	Due Date	Date Completed
To prepare for the next session, in the teams (Team Uno: Eric and Erin; Team Dos: Kyle and Bobbie; Team Tres: Rashelle) please do the following:			
1. Review the plan completed to date and bring any corrections or items to discuss further to the next session	Teams		
2. Review the competence hierarchy, competitive competence analysis, mission statement, and vision and prepare your thoughts to finalize	Teams		
3. Complete the following transitional issues; for each, please list what is needed to strengthen your competence and achieve your vision by 12/31/XX	Teams		
a) Using the template provided, develop the future functional organizational structure (do not include names) that will be needed to achieve your vision and be prepared to present it to the team			
b) Identify key skill set voids that need to be addressed to achieve your vision (do not include names)			
c) Identify systems/processes that are needed to achieve your vision			
4. Using the enclosed goals from the interviews, develop three to five company goals for the next year	Teams		
5. Brainstorm a list of action plans for each goal that need to be completed in the coming year	Teams		

"Be prepared to present your recommendations on the functional organizational structure—with no names—at the next meeting," I said, "and prepare notes covering the rest of the action plans on the register so you're ready to discuss them."

"I can't wait to get done with these homework assignments," Eric said with a wry smirk. "It's bad enough I have to help my daughters with their math homework; now I have my own homework, too."

"I think these homework assignments are great," Rashelle jumped in. "This is exactly what we needed to grow closer as a leadership team and build the kind of company we want. We're gaining organizational clarity like we've never had before."

There was palpable excitement as the team packed up. Everyone was on board, and as they left the conference room they began talking about how they would make their vision a reality.

The Scoop

1. Does each homework team understand how to create a functional organizational structure?

2. Are there any other transitional issues that need to be addressed by the planning team at the next meeting that may have come up in the interviews or a previous session?

Action Plans to Complete the Process

☐ Ensure each homework team has clarity on their action plans for the next meeting.

☐ Distribute the templates the teams need to accomplish their homework assignments. See www.stopsellingvanillaicecream.com.

STRATEGY IMPLEMENTATION

17

DEVELOPING THE STRUCTURE AND SKILLS TO EXECUTE THE STRATEGY

Phase 4 of the Stop Selling Vanilla Ice Cream process focuses on preparing the organization to implement the strategy the team has developed. While the tactical thinking required typically is easier for planning teams than the strategic thinking of the previous phase, that doesn't mean there's any less work to be done. On the contrary, this is where the team hashes out the details of how the organization will operate on a daily basis. This is where they make their mint chocolate chip ice cream come to life!

The team's vibe was loose and ready to work when the members arrived in the conference room. As usual, we reviewed the action plan register and agenda to set everyone's minds on the tasks at hand, and the team's sense of excitement let me know they were ready to jump right in.

"I'd like to thank all of you for your hard work, because this was an incredible thought process," Rashelle said to open the session. "But we still have some work ahead of us."

"The best part is that we now know what you have to do," I said. "Now we know where to focus your resources. Today we'll work on the transitional issues you'll need to overcome as you move from the current organizational profile as defined in the internal analysis to the new strategic vision. Here's the fundamental question: What do you need to do to strengthen your competence and achieve your vision? Once we fully answer that question, I'm confident this coming year will be a breakthrough for this organization."

There are some fundamentals you have to put into place as you accelerate the organizational transformation process. This chapter and the next couple will define those factors. Then it's just a matter of getting them done. The first year of implementing the strategy is the most challenging because you are working "in" the business at the same level as you are also working "on" the business. However, the collective effort of having multiple team members working on the business accelerates the success of the organization. Working in the business becomes easier as the action plans to work on the business start getting checked off. It is an awesome feeling when everyone can sense that you finally are heading in the right direction. Things become progressively easier the second year and thereafter.

Following the action plans and templates provided, the homework teams had brainstormed thoughts on several transitional issues in the weeks since our last meeting. With all the homework teams coming prepared for discussions, the planning team was ready for productive dialogue on the following topics:

- ✔ Developing an optimal functional organizational structure

- ✔ Addressing skill set voids in the organizational structure

- ✔ Identifying systems and processes to implement, including a performance-based compensation system and a communication system

- ✔ Establishing an annual business planning calendar

- ✔ Any other significant transitional issues that could be identified by the advisor or a planning team member that came out of the preplanning interviews or planning meetings. There are typically one to two transitional issues that are very specific to each organization.

Once you address these issues, you'll be ready to tackle annual goals and departmental plans.

CREATING A FUNCTIONAL ORGANIZATION

The first item up for discussion was the new Connecting Cultures functional organizational structure. Like many companies, Connecting Cultures' current organizational structure evolved without much thought to a specific plan. From our experience, most organizational structures take shape in pieces through individual decisions over the course of several years, so Connecting Cultures wasn't alone in that respect. Now, however, as part of this process, the leadership team was ready to invest the time and resources in developing and implementing the optimum organizational structure to effectively deliver their competence, achieve their vision, and execute the strategy.

"Remember, we're talking only about functions at this point; we're not talking about a specific person assigned to those functions," I said. "We're designing this functional organizational structure based on what you need to have in place to achieve your three-year vision."

The homework teams came prepared to present their recommended functional organizational structures. Team Dos went first this time, with Kyle doing the presenting, followed by Erin leading the Team Uno presentation, and Rashelle, staying true to her behavioral style and visionary roots, presenting last while referencing her handwritten sheet of notes.

After each homework team presented their recommended functional organizational structure, I worked with them to fill in a blank functional organizational chart (see template at www.stopsellingvanillaicecream.com). Some of the team's suggestions were no-brainers, while others generated considerable debate. We started the discussion at the highest level of the organization, talking about each functional position, and working down through the entire structure and taking ideas from each of the homework teams.

The top of the organizational chart took shape quickly, with the shareholders listed above the company leader function. I asked the teams to identify the primary departmental leadership positions that would report to the company leader, and through discussion they agreed that new business development, operations, interpreter development, and administration were the most appropriate functions for that level of the chart.

"Those positions, along with the company leader, typically make up the leadership team," I said.

However, like many businesses, the Connecting Cultures planning team struggled to determine how to handle the support functions like IT and human resources. They asked questions like, Are these support positions full-time employees or should we outsource them? Do these support positions report in to the company leader? The answers to these questions depend on many variables, including your strategy. For example, if technology is a key vehicle in delivering your competence and strategy, should the IT position report to the company leader and sit on the leadership team? With the challenge many organizations are facing in finding and retaining talent, the human resources function can be a valuable member of the leadership team and may need to report to the leader. After significant discussion, the Connecting Cultures team agreed to have the IT, HR, data analyst, and accounting functions report into a lead administration function. The team was in agreement that a cohesive administrative team could provide high-level support services to the organization and its departments.

After significant discussion about the administrative function, the team turned to identifying the rest of the roles that would report to the leadership team positions.

"Right now we have the customer service managers at the different sites reporting into the operations manager," Erin pointed out. "I think it would make sense to have scheduling, account management, and customer service report directly to operations."

"I would agree," Rashelle said.

The theory behind an organizational structure is that if you are going to hold a position accountable for a specific responsibility, then you have to give that position all the resources to deliver on that responsibility. For example, if you are going to hold the operations manager accountable for delivery of the interpreting services, then the structure needs to

FUTURE FUNCTIONAL ORGANIZATIONAL STRUCTURE
TO ACHIEVE THREE-YEAR VISION

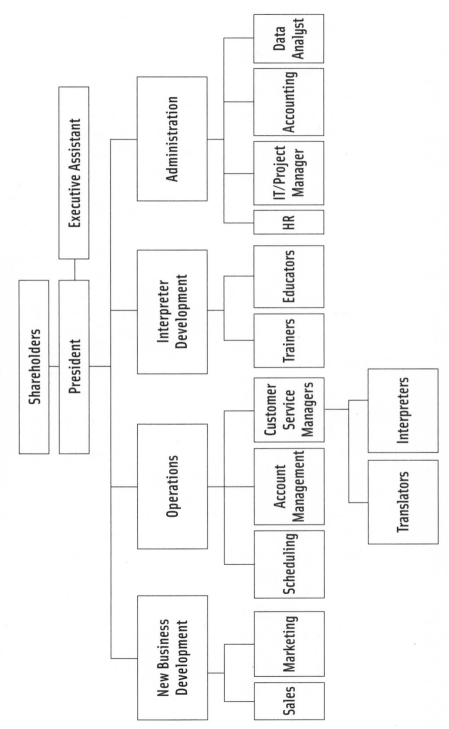

give that person responsibility for all of the functions necessary to deliver on that service. The scheduling function is a great example of a position that the operations manager needs in his or her department to fulfill the responsibility of delivery of timely interpreting services to ensure customer satisfaction.

After finalizing the administrative and operational department structure, the team completed the functional organizational structure, shown on page 231, by designing the new business development and interpreter development departments.

"I am really excited about the functional organizational structure we designed," Kyle stated. "Once it's implemented, it will create clear lines of communication and accountability."

"Those are two of the greatest benefits of a clear and functional organizational structure," I responded, "and now Connecting Cultures is about to experience those benefits. And what's the next step in making sure these changes take place?" I asked, prodding the team to complete the thought.

"Make it an action plan item!" they responded in unison.

"Speaking of action plans," Rashelle said, "now that we have completed the functional organizational structure, what are our next steps?"

"Your role as the company leader will be to meet with each planning team member individually prior to the next meeting and talk about where they can bring the greatest value to the company and themselves," I explained. When meeting with each member of the planning team, the leader should have a candid discussion and accomplish the following:

- ✔ Review their behavioral assessments with them. Talk about the strengths of their style and where those strengths bring the greatest value to the company. The objective of these discussions is to create skill set alignment, matching the natural talents of the individual with the requirements of the position. Skill set alignment also leads to job satisfaction and retention because the position satisfies the workplace motivators of the individual.

- ✔ The leader should work to understand the career goals and aspirations of the individual.

✔ If the individual currently is a department leader, the owner/leader should talk to the individual about the structure of his or her department.

After meeting with all the planning team members, the leader needs to complete the organizational structure by filling in specific names. It's not unusual in smaller companies for one person to have his name in several boxes. In the case of Connecting Cultures, the head of administration may also serve as the accounting manager. Also, in almost every company we've worked with, we see boxes left blank or people left over that do not fit in a particular box. That's when the owner/leader has to make a decision about those individuals:

✔ Keep them and accept a less-than-optimum solution for a particular function.

✔ Increase their performance to an acceptable level through individual coaching and development.

✔ Professionally exit the individual from the organization. We find that people are happier when they move on and find a position that better fits their style.

Oftentimes when an individual is aware they're not a good fit for their current position, they approach their leader to discuss options, such as an individual development plan or a change in responsibilities. The ultimate goal is to help employees find a position within the organization that we refer to

> *How does your company assess and consider skill set alignment when placing people in positions, particularly leadership positions?*

as "home," where the position matches the person's natural skill set. It's where people are happiest and bring the most value to the organization and themselves. The behavioral assessments help accomplish this task. You know you've found a home when you wake up in the morning and feel that you have a career and not just a job. You love what you do.

We try to find homes for as many existing personnel as possible while identifying potential skill set voids. Additional training for existing employees, new hires, and even outsourcing specific functions are all options when it comes to filling those skill set voids. If we determine a particular skill set void will require outsourcing or a new hire, it makes sense to benchmark the job to determine what the optimum performer in the position looks like in terms of education, experience, behavioral style, etc. We then compare all candidates to the benchmark and hire the person with the best fit. The benchmarking process makes writing the job description very easy.

Rashelle's action plan was captured in the register as the team completed a productive discussion on the organizational structure needed to deliver their competence and achieve their vision.

"Once we determine the look of your new organizational structure," I said, "you will need to stay disciplined to it. Many organizations struggle with this, especially for the shareholders and owners who are used to jumping around the organizational chart. This creates chaos. It's imperative that the shareholders and owners respect the structure and deal with issues through the appropriate channels, such as at a consistent shareholders meeting. As a shareholder, you have a responsibility to interact with all of your employees, but if an employee comes to you looking for advice regarding a departmental issue outside of your functional area, you need to ask that employee to go back to his or her immediate supervisor. Resist the urge to rush into the sandbox, kick over all the sand castles, and then leave it to the department manager to put them back together. This undercuts the authority of the manager and risks having her lose the respect of her team. I've said it before, but it merits repeating: An owner cannot wear his shareholder hat while serving in a functional role. If you do, it destroys the functionality of the organizational structure. That is why a consistent shareholders meeting is so important; it gives shareholders the proper forum to address their questions and concerns."

"I can see where jumping in would be tempting, because we're used to sticking our noses into every issue that comes up," Rashelle admitted. "Old habits die hard."

Empowered by the candor generated during this process, Kyle stepped up and asked a great question: "Rashelle, how do you want us to handle it when you jump into our sandboxes with your shareholder hat on?"

"I appreciate your honesty, Kyle," she replied. "I would like you to talk to me one-on-one when that situation arises. Just let me know you are on the issue and I will step back. Is that fair?"

"That is very fair," Kyle said.

This was exactly the type of productive interplay you look to generate in a team planning session. I couldn't help but smile. The team was proving its ability to talk through sensitive issues without suffering a breakdown in communication. That's the sign of a true team.

Shareholders who hold leadership roles in organizations need to be cautious when it comes to wielding their power. While someone with Eric's strong behavioral tendencies, for example, might be tempted to play his shareholder card and trump a tactical decision made by other team members, it's crucial that he understands how counterproductive that behavior would be. It would blow up the structure of the organization. This is a key point for every shareholder to consider.

I have this discussion virtually every time I encounter shareholders who are responsible for tactical execution. Sometimes I'll even go so far as to make hats that say "Tactical" and "Shareholder" to drive home the point that they can wear only one hat at a time. That's a very powerful illustration. If you are a business owner or shareholder, you must understand the difference between your shareholder hat and your functional hat. You cannot wear your owner/shareholder hat while serving in a functional role. It is acceptable to help with follow-through by removing obstacles or providing the necessary resources to implement an idea, but let the manager do her job and lead her department. Resist the urge to become too involved.

SKILL SET VOIDS

After completing the functional organizational structure and discussing the company leader's action plan to complete the structure, many times a leader will seek input from the planning team on any possible skill set voids in the organization. This discussion provides helpful input to the leader on how to complete the new organizational structure. Again it is critical that you use no names during the skill set void discussion. The Connecting Cultures planning team had been incredibly candid with each other during the process, so Rashelle felt it was healthy to get their input on what skill set voids they had in the organization. The advisor can play a key role in effectively facilitating this discussion or decide not to have it at all.

"I would really value your input on possible skill set voids in our company," Rashelle said.

Not hesitating for a second, Kyle was ready to provide some input. "I think we are desperately missing a true accounting skill set," he said. "We need to increase our financial understanding of our business and make more informed decisions. Many times we make decisions just on gut feel, but we need to combine that gut feel with the financial facts of the situation."

"I agree," Rashelle said. "In the past I have made too many decisions without the proper financial analysis. Based on the growth this plan will create, that has to change." The rest of the team nodded in agreement and Rashelle, encouraged by the productive discussion, asked, "Are there any other skill sets we are missing that are needed to deliver our competence and achieve our vision?"

"From my perspective, I think that covers it," Kyle said.

"Me, too," Erin jumped in.

Rashelle wrapped up the skill set discussion by thanking the team for their input and stating that she was looking forward to their one-on-one discussions.

SYSTEMS AND PROCESSES

"The next topic on the agenda involves deciding which systems and processes the organization needs to implement so it can build the competence and achieve its vision," I said. "A focus of the first-year process is implementing documented systems so you can run the business more efficiently."

"We need to look at our after-hours process in connection with the interpreters," Rashelle commented. "They feel we're dictating to them right now. That's because there are too many variables and not enough processes in place. We need to get them involved in projects so there is some buy-in from that group. Consistency is the key word for me right now. Having consistent processes is what gives our interpreters job security and the safety net that's not available at other places."

The team also recognized the need to create an interpreter development plan, which required some serious brainstorming.

"Is there a classic interpreter behavioral style?" I asked. "We'll need to benchmark the interpreter position to define what an optimum performer looks like."

"My guess would be high I (influence) and high S (steadiness)—definitely not aggressive," Rashelle answered. "We're going to write a white paper on a benchmark for a health care interpreter."

"Then let's put that on our action plan list right now," I said. "You also need to determine the best ways to build a steady flow of quality interpreters. Should you have a booth at job fairs? Should you connect with organizations that cater to the Hispanic population?" A solid recruiting plan should be one of the HR responsibilities. Always capture these ideas with action plans.

Erin and Rashelle led a discussion into best practices for hiring interpreters. They agreed the best course of action would begin with a phone contact, followed by an in-person interview, behavioral assessments, and a second in-person interview with customized questions based on the behavioral assessments.

Next, the team discussed ways to address the more challenging aspects of health care interpreting. The discussion focused on what the team perceived to be the major reason for voluntary interpreter turnover.

"I am guessing it's from burnout based on the intensity of health care interpreting," Erin said.

"You are probably right," Rashelle said.

Erin concluded, "Our training needs to address how interpreters can manage stress and avoid the burnout from the intensity of the interpreting encounter."

The team agreed that tracking voluntary and involuntary interpreter turnover could shed some light on whether Connecting Cultures was getting a positive return on its investment for training, and on how well it was addressing interpreter burnout. They captured action plans to address these issues.

COMMUNICATION SYSTEM

"I believe that one way to improve our retention is to improve our internal communication. In fact, improving our internal communication system

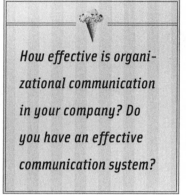

How effective is organizational communication in your company? Do you have an effective communication system?

has to be one of our most important goals," Rashelle said. "But we need to find a balance between keeping everyone informed and having too many meetings."

One of the most common issues brought up in any organization's preplanning interviews is poor or ineffective communication, and Connecting Cultures was no different. That's why we consider the development of a communication system to be a transitional issue. Among the keys to achieving the vision is ensuring all employees understand where the organization is going and their role in making it happen.

There's nothing more frustrating than going from one meeting to the next, spinning your wheels through the day and getting nothing of substance accomplished. By the same token, meetings to accomplish specific tasks serve to move departments forward and companies toward their vision. I suggested to the team that the simplest and most effective method to improve a meeting is to use an action plan register. It creates a culture of discipline and accountability. Reviewing the action plan register is also an effective start to each meeting.

The planning team agreed to the following communication system going forward:

✔ **COMPANY MEETING**—Held twice a year to update all employees on plan execution and company performance; forum for Q&A and to seek new ideas. The company leader is the owner of this meeting.

✔ **PLAN EXECUTION REVIEW MEETING**—Held once per month for the planning team to review company financials, action plan register, and measurement matrix, and discuss any strategic updates or changes. The company leader is the owner of this meeting, and the advisor should attend. This meeting will be discussed in more detail in chapter 20.

✔ **SHAREHOLDERS MEETING**—If applicable to company, held monthly, immediately following the plan execution meeting.

✔ **LEADERSHIP TEAM MEETING**—Led by the company leader, the team agreed to meet every Friday to establish the coming week's priorities, make strategic decisions, provide input to colleagues, and agree on items that department leaders should communicate at department meetings. Without a leadership team meeting, the organization drifts like a ship without a rudder.

✔ **DEPARTMENT MEETINGS**—Held weekly; each department will determine the appropriate day, but the recommendation is to follow the leadership team meeting on Fridays so department leaders can plan the week ahead. From my perspective, this is one of the more important meetings that takes place for each organization. This is where the rubber meets the road. All the goal setting and strategic planning in the world means nothing unless you are able to communicate them throughout the organization.

✔ **ONE-ON-ONE MEETINGS**—The department leader will determine the frequency with each direct report for a meeting to review action plans and progress on individual development plans.

COMPENSATION SYSTEM

"One of the systems I want the team to look into specifically is compensation," I said.

"More money is always a good thing," Eric said. "Let's see if we can develop a compensation process to make us all rich."

"That will come," I chuckled. "Remember, those who plan, profit. The compensation system must impact all stakeholders, including shareholders, leadership, managers, and employees. We've seen that the most effective compensation systems are performance-based. We have to evaluate your compensation systems to ensure they are motivating the organization to strengthen and deliver your competence, ultimately satisfying your customers at a higher level than anyone else. We should identify any changes needed in your compensation systems to ensure you're effectively motivating employees."

One of the most common and effective pay-for-performance plans we see is that employees throughout the organization are compensated based on profitability. It encourages every employee to make decisions like an owner or shareholder. It is especially critical at the leadership team level where important decisions are made daily. You want to eliminate the consideration of personal variables in the decision-making process and have leadership focus on what is in the best interest of the long-term profitability of the company. Typically, up to 25 percent of the leadership team members' compensation and up to 10 percent of managers' and employees' compensation is based on company profitability. Many organizations accomplish this through a bonus or profit-sharing plan. The team captured an action plan to design and implement a pay-for-performance compensation plan for the company.

• • •

By the end of the discussion, the team had come up with fourteen potential systems and processes, for which they created action plans to implement and assigned departments as owners. The systems and processes to be developed or refined included items such as the external sales process, the communication system, the compensation system, performance reports, delivery methods for the potential addition of telephonic and video services, consulting processes, and recruitment plans. The team split ownership responsibilities among the operations, human resources, finance, interpreter development, and new business development functions. These systems would be added to the departmental plans that will be discussed in more detail in chapter 19.

"Implementing all of those systems and processes will keep us busy all year," Bobbie said. "Are we supposed to have all of those ready to go right away?"

"No, this will be a work in progress for some time, I assume," I replied. "That's why it's so important to create action plan registers to track your progress. Our experience shows some of these processes will take hold relatively quickly, while others could take several months. As long as you have a plan and take consistent action, you will move the organization toward your vision."

DEVELOP A PLANNING SCHEDULE

The final transitional issue involves completing an annual business planning calendar, shown below, to ensure the organization optimizes its success year after year.

"Planning and execution must not be a one-time event, but rather a continuous, disciplined process," I said. "It's like sharpening the tip of the pencil. You accomplish this through annual strategic planning and monthly plan execution meetings. For organizations that work on a calendar-year schedule, I suggest they finalize the strategic plan in October, work on departmental plans in November, and finalize those departmental plans and budget in December."

Business Planning Calendar

January	February	March	April	May	June
Begin plan execution					
Monthly plan execution reviews	Monthly plan execution reviews	Monthly plan execution reviews	Monthly plan execution reviews	Monthly plan execution reviews	Monthly plan execution reviews

July	August	September	October	November	December
	Prepare market research & financial analysis	Start strategic planning process	Finalize strategic plan	Present plan to company & start department planning	Finalize department plans & budget
Monthly plan execution reviews	Monthly plan execution reviews	Monthly plan execution reviews	Monthly plan execution reviews	Monthly plan execution reviews	Monthly plan execution reviews

For businesses that don't follow the calendar year in their financial and planning systems, they should begin annual strategy discussions four months prior to the start of the new year, finalize the strategy three months prior, work on the departmental planning two months prior, and finalize department plans and budgets in the month prior to the start of the new year.

"As long as we have a schedule to keep us on track, we should be able to stick to that," Kyle said. "It's been too easy for us to procrastinate on planning like this because we've been so busy working in the business. This process will help us concentrate some of our energies on working on the business, which is what we really need."

I asked the team if there were any other transitional issues we needed to discuss that had not been addressed. I included all of the items that were brought up in the interviews or during the sessions. The team concluded that we had covered all of the issues they could address in the first year.

Addressing all the issues that transition you from where you are today to where you want to be when you achieve your vision is a critical step in the implementation of the plan. It is typically one of the most enjoyable parts of the process for the planning team because it is about taking action to make your company better. Through very candid discussions, the Connecting Cultures team had addressed the transitional issues that would help them take the first steps in achieving their vision.

The Scoop

1. What skill set voids do you think currently exist in your company or will need to be filled to deliver your competence and achieve your vision?

2. On a scale of 1 to 10, with 10 being very effective, how would you rate your company's communication system? How would your employees rate the effectiveness of the company's communication?

3. Does your company's compensation system effectively reward performance and delivery of your competence? How could it be changed to encourage ownership and motivation?

4. Are there any additional transitional issues you need to resolve to deliver your competence and achieve your vision?

Action Plans to Complete the Process

☐ Design the functional organizational chart to deliver your competence and achieve your vision.

☐ The leader/owner meets with each planning team member to gain the insight and information to complete the organizational structure moving forward. Identify development needs and address skill set voids.

☐ Document the systems and processes that need to be implemented to deliver your competence and achieve the vision. Assign the appropriate department as the owner of each system.

☐ Define the company's communication system.

☐ Evaluate the company's compensation plan and document action plans for improvement.

☐ Develop the company's annual business planning calendar.

☐ Address any other transitional issues needed to deliver your competence and achieve your vision (i.e., succession planning).

COMPANY GOALS AND ACTION PLANS
TO ACHIEVE THEM

Companies function like people when it comes to attaining goals. They need specific targets and a plan to attain those goals just like all of us do as individuals. The alternative is akin to navigating your ship across the ocean without a compass. You don't want to arrive at your destination by accident; you have a much better chance of success and arriving exponentially faster with a set plan to guide the way.

In the Stop Selling Vanilla Ice Cream process, the final, completed plan will include a set of company goals, and each goal will have necessary action plans to achieve it. The action plans are a result of the brainstorming that happens throughout the process, which is why it's so crucial to record them along the way. (You can download a template at www.stop-sellingvanillaicecream.com.) Some plans may be discarded, of course, but as you're nearing the end of the process, you should have a good starter list of action plans to achieve the first-year goals. The selected action plans will be put into the appropriate department plans, which I'll discuss in the next chapter.

The Connecting Cultures team had established a vision for what they wanted the company to look like in three years, but now the focus needed to shift to what they wanted to accomplish over the next twelve months—three to five goals that are attainable in the first year. The interviews provided a preliminary list of company goals and the major strategic challenges. Many times an organization's initial twelve-month goals will target most of these strategic challenges—the largest rocks in the water.

DEVELOPING THE COMPANY GOALS

The homework teams had the action plan to develop three to five company goals using the SMART approach. Recall that in our methodology, SMART stands for Specific, Measurable, Agreed-upon, Realistic, and Timely.

You have a much greater chance of accomplishing specific goals than general goals. For example, the planning team decided in the plan development phase that it wanted to increase sales and market share in the Green Bay area. That strategy decision could easily lead to a company goal to increase sales in the Green Bay market by 30 percent in the first year of plan execution. To set a specific goal, we must answer the six "W" questions:

✔ What do we want to accomplish?

✔ Who is involved?

✔ When do we want to have it accomplished?

✔ What resources will we need to achieve the goal?

✔ What metrics should we use to determine that we have met the goal?

✔ Why should this be a goal? Identify specific reasons, purpose, or benefits.

Measurable goals require concrete criteria for gauging progress toward the desired outcome. The ability to measure progress makes it easier to stay on track, reach target dates, and experience the exhilaration of achieve-ment that spurs the continued effort needed to reach your goal. To deter-mine if your goal is measurable, ask questions such as: How much? How many? How will I know when it is accomplished?

Agreed-upon goals are necessary to keep your organization's momen-tum moving in a positive direction. When you identify goals that are most important to you, it's imperative that everyone on the planning team is on the same page. This consensus makes it easier to find ways to make goals happen. You develop the attitudes, abilities, skills, and capacity to reach them. You begin seeing previously overlooked opportunities that bring you closer to the achievement of your goals.

You can attain virtually any goal you set when you plan your steps wisely and establish a time frame that makes it realistic for you to carry out those steps. I have never met anyone who didn't accomplish something by moving forward. Goals that may have seemed far away or completely out of reach eventually move closer and become attainable—not because your goals have shrunk, but because you've moved in a positive direction together and closed the gap. Making the effort to list goals has the added benefit of building self-image, either individually or as an organization. When you see yourself wor-thy of these goals, you develop the traits and confidence to attain them.

Realistic goals represent an objective toward which you are both will-ing and able to work. It's possible to have goals that are high and realistic at the same time. Only you can decide the tipping point that makes a goal unrealistic. Many people and organizations find that as long as they have incremental points at which to measure progress, they're able to attain much more lofty goals than they previously would have believed. In fact, the motivational energy required to reach a high goal can be so powerful that it makes the goal's attainment more likely than a simple goal with its corresponding low level of motivational energy.

Some of the most difficult challenges turn out to be attainable simply because they become a labor of love, anchored in a foundation of team agreement. Think of people who build or remodel their own house. It's a massive project, but they break down their progress to one board, one nail, and one wall at a time. It becomes a source of pride, and their intense motivation drives them toward ultimate fulfillment.

Your goal is realistic if you truly believe you can accomplish it. Draw on your experiences with goal attainment and ask yourself what conditions need to exist for you and your team to accomplish the goals you've set before you.

Finally, you need to ground your goals in a time frame to hold you accountable. With no time frame, there's no sense of urgency. The procrastinator in many of us will take over and postpone taking action. Anchoring your goal within a time frame sets your subconscious mind into motion to work toward attaining that goal.

It was time to hear what the teams had come up with and arrive at a consensus on three to five company goals for the next year.

"Okay, homework teams, what do you want to accomplish in the next twelve months?" I asked to get the discussion rolling. "What should be your first steps in achieving the vision during that twelve-month time frame?" After reviewing the list of company goals from the interviews and the strategic challenges, it took only a moment for team members to begin shouting out suggestions, as they could no longer contain their stored-up enthusiasm.

"Okay, let's try using the SMART methodology to assess each idea. Let's take one of your goals and make a preliminary run through the SMART standards," I suggested. "We'll likely make some adjustments down the road, but this exercise will get you familiar with the tool and make it easier to complete the remaining goals. Which one would you like to attack first?"

"How about our sales increase goal, especially as it relates to our market share in the Green Bay area?" Kyle said. "That would be the 'S' for Specific."

"Good," I replied. "Keep going down the SMART list as far as you can."

"There are a number of potential customers we could target to go with our current customers in the Green Bay market," Kyle continued. "We would want to measure our sales revenue and the number of customers in the Green Bay market. Both of those numbers would be worth measuring—that's the 'M' component—although the revenue end of the equation is the most important. As for 'Agreed-upon,' what do you think about a 30 percent increase in revenue as our target?"

"I'd like to challenge you on that one," I said. "That sounds like a pretty strong number for an area in which you already have a fairly strong presence. Are you sure that's attainable?"

"I think there is a large gap between where we are in the Green Bay market and where we could be," Rashelle interrupted. "I agree with Kyle. I think 30 percent is very realistic. We already handle one of the major health systems in town, but there are many organizations we haven't even contacted—at least not recently."

"Does everyone agree that a 30 percent revenue increase in the Green Bay market is an appropriate goal?" I asked. "Remember the team needs to agree on a goal in order for it to generate the maximum momentum."

Erin and Eric quickly voiced their agreement, and a glance around the table confirmed that the whole team was on board with this goal.

"That takes care of the 'Agreed-upon' and 'Realistic' benchmarks of the SMART tool," I said. "Now for the big question: in what time frame can you expect to make it happen?"

"That *is* a good question," Rashelle responded. "Honestly, if we make this a priority and devote the necessary energy and resources to making it happen, I think we can reach that target within a year."

"The other variable is hiring enough interpreting staff to handle the increased workload," Erin reminded the team. "It won't do us any good to pick up those new customers if we're not able to service them."

"That's a good point, Erin, and that will play a role in your planning as we move forward," I explained.

"We also need to develop and launch new service offerings, such as consulting, and generate incremental revenue growth over the next twelve months," Kyle said, moving the conversation on to other goals. "We can set a target date for receiving our first revenue from new services and measure the amount of revenue generated by each new service."

"I'd like to propose another goal," I said. "I would suggest you finish developing and implementing the organizational structure we discussed earlier, adding clear responsibilities and accountability. Remember the behavioral assessments showed you have role clarity issues at every level of the organization."

The planning team nodded in agreement.

"When there's a lack of role clarity, accountability is impossible," I continued. "You need to decide who is responsible for what. This process will make determining accountability a lot easier. Some measurements for implementation of the new organizational structure would include reassessing role clarity for those who had low role awareness in their initial assessments, and feedback from employees that they clearly understand their specific responsibilities and reporting structure."

"I'm concerned about having our operations mechanisms ready to handle this growth we're planning for," Kyle said. "Should we state a goal around that issue?"

"Have at it, Kyle," I said. "What should it say?"

"How about this: Prepare operations for organizational growth and the consistent delivery of our competence," he replied. "We can measure customer satisfaction through surveys, and enlist their assistance in tracking on-time arrivals and no-shows for our interpreters. That would also help make the value of our services more tangible in their eyes."

"That's perfect," Rashelle said.

Based on the discussions among the team, the company's goals for the next twelve months were as follows:

- ✔ Implement a comprehensive and effective company-wide communication plan: measure by employee satisfaction; employee morale and engagement

- ✔ Increase total sales, with a 30 percent increase in sales in the Green Bay market: measure by sales from Green Bay market; number of customers in Green Bay market

- ✔ Develop and launch new service offering (consulting): measure by revenue by service offering for the year; date of first revenue from new services

- ✔ Develop and implement the organizational structure with clear responsibilities, communication, and accountability: measure by date that new organizational structure is implemented; employees communicating that they clearly understand their responsibilities

- ✔ Prepare operations for organizational growth and the consistent delivery of the competence: measure by customer satisfaction ratings; on-time arrivals; no-shows.

BRAINSTORMING: ACTION PLANS TO MAKE GOALS HAPPEN

"While the goals are still fresh, let's brainstorm some action plans to make this growth happen," I said.

At this point, teams brainstorm action plans to achieve each goal, but they do not indicate an owner or completion date on the action plans. The key is to brainstorm as many action plans as possible for each goal. Then when the department leaders are developing their departmental plans, which we'll discuss next, they can review all the action plans brainstormed throughout the planning process and put the appropriate action plans in their departmental plans to achieve each goal.

For example, for its goal of increasing sales, the team listed one action plan of creating and documenting the sales process for its primary target market. Eventually, this action plan would become a part of the new business development department's plan. Filled with energy, the team went on to brainstorm seven to ten action plans per goal, making sure to work through the SMART acronym to ensure the greatest probability of success.

"We're in the homestretch," I told the team. "As the saying goes, 'the devil is in the details,' and we need to address those details next in the departmental planning process."

The Scoop

1. What are the three to five SMART goals you believe your organization needs to achieve over the next twelve months to increase its sales and profitability and take the first step in achieving your vision?

2. Did you review the strategic challenges when developing your company goals?

Action Plans to Complete the Process

☐ Define your three to five company goals.

☐ Brainstorm action plans to achieve each goal.

DEPARTMENT PLANNING TO MAKE IT HAPPEN

Rashelle owned the action plan to finalize the new organizational structure by adding names to the functional structure the team had developed. Before we could begin to define the departmental plans, we needed to know who was responsible for those departments.

Rashelle met individually with each planning team member and discussed where they saw themselves bringing the greatest value to the company and their careers. One of the most interesting meetings was with Erin, who voiced some frustration in her inability to find time to create training programs for her interpreting staff.

Erin's behavioral style shows she prefers focusing on one or two projects at a time, and her attention to detail ensures those projects are done right. Her Soft Skills Indicator results show she values having a plan and sticking to it but struggles with a lack of clarity in her current role.

This exercise is a great opportunity for her to move toward those comfort zones, where her strong skills lie.

"I do a lot of interpreting myself, and I feel like there are balls dropping all over the place because we're short-staffed," she told Rashelle. "It's too easy for me to get pulled into daily operations, to put out fires rather than work on staff development programs."

"As valuable as you are in that 'firefighter' capacity, we need to free up your time so you can work more 'on' the business rather than 'in' the business," Rashelle said. "Where do you feel opportunities exist for that to happen?"

"Well, part of this is on me, because I'm too quick to rescue a situation," Erin said. "I need to learn how to delegate tasks and responsibilities better, and basically just how to be a better leader."

"If we get you some training in these areas, do you think it would create the time you need to work on interpreter development?" Rashelle asked.

"Yes, I do," Erin responded. "And that's really what I would like to focus on at this point. Our training and development process was defined as one of our foundational strengths, and I would like to keep it that way."

"Then let's put a documented process in place to make that happen," Rashelle said. "Assuming we gain agreement from the planning team at our next meeting, I'll leave it up to you to identify the types of training you want and where to get it. We'll make this part of your individual development plan. Does that sound good to you?"

"Yes, it does," Erin said. "I just never felt the freedom to request it until now. We're all so busy with our daily duties that I didn't feel comfortable bringing it up."

After meeting with each planning team member individually, Rashelle was ready to reconvene the group to finalize the organizational structure and complete the plan development process.

As the planning team collected for their final planning meeting of phase 4, the team exuded a level of confidence likely unseen in the history of the company. They were ready to get to work on finalizing the plan they had developed as a cohesive team. And Rashelle was ready to discuss the structure.

"Rashelle, are you prepared to present your final organizational chart showing the functional role assignments?" I asked.

"Yes, Steve. There aren't any surprises, of course, because I've discussed this with each of you individually." Rashelle put the final organizational chart on-screen, shown on page 253, showing Kyle as head of operations and administration, Erin as head of interpreter development, Bobbie

NEW ORGANIZATIONAL STRUCTURE

Shareholders
RASHELLE, ERIC, BOBBIE, STEVE L.

President
RASHELLE

New Business Development
RASHELLE
- Sales
- Marketing

Operations
KYLE
- Scheduling
- Account Management
  BOBBIE
- Customer Service Managers
  - Translator
  - Interpreters

Interpreter Development
ERIN
- Trainers
- Educators

Administration
KYLE
- HR
- IT/Project Manager
  ERIC
- Accounting
  NEW HIRE #1
- Data Analyst

handling account management, Eric handling IT, and Rashelle as company leader and head of new business development.

"I think the planning team was correct when we discussed the accounting skill set void," Rashelle said. "As a result, we will benchmark the accounting position and execute a search to find the candidate that matches the benchmark."

"When will this organizational structure go into effect?" Kyle asked.

"Right after we present the entire plan to the organization," Rashelle said.

"Most organizations implement the structure the Monday following the plan presentation meeting," I said. "Sometimes in stages and sometimes the entire structure all at once. Waiting until after the plan presentation meeting helps any changes transition seamlessly. Remember, communication is key."

"You have developed a very focused first-year plan," I continued. "Now it's time to talk about how you're going to make it reality. The way we do this in the Stop Selling Vanilla Ice Cream process is through departmental planning, or tactical planning. I've found departmental planning is an easier term for most people to understand. Like most of the work we've been doing, these plans are about working on the business so we operate more efficiently when we work in the business."

Taking strategy from theory to tactics is where most companies fail. Many companies talk about their strategy, but few of them take the tactical steps to execute them. In fact, we estimate only three in ten companies even go through the effort of developing an annual business plan, and less than one in ten companies ever develops departmental plans to put their annual business plan into action.

> *Does each department in your company work through an annual tactical planning process? If not, why?*

This process keeps plans from becoming dust collectors. Business plans remain a living, breathing document that serves as the road map for an organization as it moves forward. It warms my heart when I see a client's business plan beaten up and covered in notes when we revisit it during the plan execution phase of the process. That means they're using it and relying on it to provide direction on a consistent basis. It also means their top and bottom lines are growing as well.

The most profitable companies in my experience are those that become experts at departmental planning. They consistently work on the business across the company throughout the year, and as a result they get better at a faster pace than anyone else in their industry. Over time, they strengthen their competence and increase their differentiation from their competition.

"Departmental plans drive the execution of the strategic plan down through all levels of the organization," I explained. "They increase the number of people working 'on' the business versus 'in' the business. As each department completes their action plans, it accelerates the success of the organization, helps prioritize weekly and daily activities, and creates a snowball effect that builds momentum toward profitable growth."

WHO DEVELOPS DEPARTMENT PLANS

"Each department leader is the owner and responsible for developing the plan for their area," I told the team, scanning the room for responses. "This allows each department to set their own stage for success. It enables them to recommend what they think needs to be done in their department to achieve the strategy."

Most department leaders have always wanted this opportunity, and this process provides it. Who better to develop the first draft of the departmental plan than the department members themselves? Each department leader and their teams need to take advantage of this opportunity.

Based on the organizational structure Rashelle had presented, the team listed the appropriate owner for each department plan:

- ✔ New business development plan—Rashelle

  - Sales plan

  - Marketing plan

- ✔ Operations plan—Kyle

  - Scheduling plan

  - Account management plan—Bobbie

  - Customer service plan

✔ Interpreter development plan—Erin

✔ Administration plan—Kyle

- Human resources plan

- IT/project management plan—Eric

- Accounting plan

- Data analyst plan

Department leaders will complete parts of the plan as well as delegate components to the appropriate individual on their team.

As we completed this step, the team was beginning to understand how the entire process ties together. It is a simple and defined process that any team can complete once they understand how all the methodologies flow together.

A side benefit of department planning is that it may filter out those who may not be good fits for leadership roles yet may be some of the organization's best task executors. Both roles are equally important to the organization. When an individual struggles to develop a departmental plan, it may be a sign she would function better outside of a management role. Certain behavioral styles are wired to lead, while other styles are more effective in an execution role.

"How involved do the owners of these plans need to be?" Bobbie asked. "Do they write the whole plan by themselves?

"The owner does not necessarily write the entire plan, but they are responsible for making sure it gets done by the due date," I said. "The best approach is a team effort driven by the leader. It's up to you as the departmental plan owner to determine how much of it you need to delegate and to whom. One of the key benefits of the departmental planning process is it involves most, if not all, members of your organization."

"Another unique aspect of the Stop Selling Vanilla Ice Cream process is that the owners present the first draft of their plans back to the planning team. Two benefits come from that first-draft presentation meeting: the planning team has the opportunity to give input and cooperate on refinements to each departmental plan; and everyone understands what each department is working on. This is an impactful day for the planning team, as you start to sense what the organization is going to accomplish when it achieves these action plans."

"I always have better ideas about how someone else can do his job," Eric said smiling.

"Well, here's your chance to do it in a professional and respectful environment," I said. "This process leads to some very healthy conflict and exchanges, because departments don't operate in a vacuum. You can discuss what help and cooperation you might need from other leaders and their departments. Every team's performance impacts other departments and the organization as a whole."

How do the department leaders in your company keep their colleagues updated on what their goals and priorities are?

"Are we required to incorporate all of those suggestions into our departmental plans?" Erin asked warily.

"Of course not, but external suggestions often will lead to subsequent decisions," I said. "Each department leader has two weeks to consider the input from their teammates and leader to finalize their departmental plans. The company leader then modifies and approves the plan and consolidates them into the annual budget."

"I'm excited to have some specific tasks on our plate, with owners and target dates," Rashelle said. "I can't wait to see what we come up with and how our organization will perform once the plans are in place."

HOW TO DEVELOP DEPARTMENT PLANS

"How extensive should we make these departmental plans?" Kyle asked.

"The first year we like to keep it simple by focusing on four key components for each department plan: education and training, action plans to achieve each company goal, key department measurements, and budget requests," I answered. "That said, the more detailed you make your plans, the better the chance things won't fall through the cracks. Typically, each department will have anywhere from ten to seventy-five action plans in the departmental plan. Many of these are the types of action plans we've been brainstorming and capturing throughout the process. When we combine all the action plans together into clear department plans, the entire organization works on the business and moves the company forward. Most, if not all, members of each department should be owners of action plans with specific completion dates. In this way, departmental plans ensure teams work 'on' the business while also completing their day-to-day tasks of working 'in' the business."

Most organizations need a taste of success early in a major process like this to propel them forward. To that end, we suggest each department include a couple of easy and visible wins in their action plans. With a couple of quick successes, the employees will fall in love with the process, and it will become a long-term part of your culture. The departmental plans will get more detailed and comprehensive with each succeeding year. Organizations at this point in the process have built an incredible amount of momentum. They will look forward to the process of making improvements every year.

"How do we come up with the action plans to include in the plan?" Bobbie asked. "You mentioned ten to seventy-five. That sounds like a lot."

"It shouldn't be a challenge," I replied. "Remember, your strategic plan already has more than one hundred action plans in it that we've brainstormed throughout the process. Once you distribute those into the appropriate departmental plans, you'll have a running start. From there, you can drill down for more detail in the four key components."

To keep it simple in the first year, the recommended department plan outline is as follows:

EDUCATION AND TRAINING: Outline the education/training needs for each or selected individuals in the department.

- ✔ Determine what type of professional development each person needs to execute the strategy and bring more value to the organization and themselves.

- ✔ Working with these individuals, use their behavioral assessment results as a foundation for creating a detailed individual development plan (see the individual development plan template at www.stopsellingvanillaicecream.com).

COMPANY GOALS AND ACTION PLANS: Develop action plans to achieve each company goal.

- ✔ Read the entire business plan.

- ✔ Review your values and beliefs statements and develop action plans to "live" them across the organization.

- ✔ Review all the action plans from the brainstorming sessions, and list the action plans that you or your department should own.

- ✔ Review weaknesses from the internal analysis and develop action plans to eliminate or minimize them.

- ✔ Review your competence hierarchy and the competitive competence analysis and develop action plans to build and strengthen your competence.

- ✔ Determine action plans necessary to ensure every member of the team understands your competence and their role in it.

- ✔ Determine action plans necessary for the department to execute in order to strengthen the competence.

- ✔ Review all the transitional issues and develop action plans to implement the new organizational structure, build or implement new systems and processes, and address skill set voids in your department.

- ✔ Develop other action plans required to achieve each company annual goal.

- ✔ Assign each action plan an owner and completion date; make an effort to ensure each individual in the department has at least one action plan to complete.

- ✔ Use the goal and action plan template to capture and monitor progress (see the template at www.stopsellingvanillaicecream.com).

KEY SUCCESS MEASUREMENTS: Determine how your department will measure its progress toward success.

- ✔ Identify those measurements that you can capture that will illustrate whether or not your departmental plan is working (see the template at www.stopsellingvanillaicecream.com). Visually illustrate how your department plan is working by color coding the measurements that are on track in green and those that are not on track in red.

- ✔ Decide how you will use measurements as benchmarks for performance reviews.

BUDGET/CAPITAL REQUEST: Define any capital or significant expense you will need to implement your plan.

- ✔ What additional expenses or capital are you requesting that is needed to execute your department plan? These requests could include expenses for training, equipment, or new employees, for example.

"One of the key steps in the departmental planning process is prioritizing the action plans by their target completion date," I continued. "Put a close-range date on more urgent action plans and a later date on less important action plans. Because there is so much to execute during the first-year planning process, organizations often toil when trying to prioritize their action plans. They also struggle because the process is new to them. But once the leaders and their teams see how these plans accelerate the success of the business, they look forward to the process every year and become experts in it."

MAKING IT A REGULAR PROCESS

"This seems like a lot of work to go through every year," Eric said. "Does it get easier after the first time through the process?"

"The first year is always the most difficult," I said, "because you have to work on the business at the same time you're working in the business.

Eventually, though, you become more efficient, both in your day-to-day work and with the planning process. I always encourage department leaders to keep a planning file in their desk so they can consistently make notes for next year's departmental plan. You will learn to adapt the departmental planning process to whatever form works best for your team and your organization. Regardless of the final version you use, it's important that every year the organization identify its key strategic challenges and resolve them through the development and execution of the departmental plans."

"That goes back to your analogy about eliminating the large rocks blocking our boat's path, right?" Rashelle said.

"Exactly," I said. "Each year you'll be able to lower the water level a little more and expose the next layer of rocks on which to focus your efforts."

The team set the due date for first drafts of the departmental plans for six weeks after the leadership team's presentation of the strategic plan to the entire company. Revisions to the departmental plans and the final budget wrap-up were planned for two weeks after that, followed by monthly plan execution meetings to track progress on company goals.

"The departmental plans create company-wide involvement, buy-in, and accountability," I said to conclude the discussion. "Before long, you'll see the entire organization working together to remove those rocks, accelerating your progress and increasing the differentiation over your competition. You'll get more business and get paid more for it."

"That's what we're hoping for!" Rashelle nearly shouted.

The Scoop

1. If you are a department leader within your organization, how would you involve members of your team in creating the department plan?

2. What professional development does each member of your team need to increase individual, team, and organizational performance?

3. Which people in your department could be depended on to own certain action plans? Which action plans would you own?

4. How would you work to make department planning a consistent process in your department or company? What hurdles might you have to overcome?

Action Plans to Complete the Process

☐ List the department plans that will be completed and identify the owner of each plan.

☐ Finalize the outline for all department plans.

☐ Provide each department leader with the process and templates to develop their plans; resolve any questions.

☐ Read the entire business plan prior to developing the first draft of your department plan.

☐ Complete the first draft of your department plans.

A PROGRAM TO ENSURE EFFECTIVE
PLAN EXECUTION AND ACCOUNTABILITY

All the strategic planning, discussion, and departmental planning in the world mean nothing unless an organization actually takes action to move its business forward. To ensure this takes place, the Stop Selling Vanilla Ice Cream process includes a plan execution program that systematically guides an organization toward its vision.

A successful plan execution program does the following:

✔ Guides timely execution of the strategic and departmental plans

✔ Keeps the organization focused on the strategy and working on the business

✔ Promotes a culture of discipline and company-wide accountability

✔ Drives completion of projects and eliminates complacency

✔ Consistently builds the talent of the organization through the completion of the individual development plans

✔ Ensures the plan is a living document used as a tool to manage your organization

✔ Creates breakthroughs via the combined impact of increasing your strategy and talent simultaneously

✔ Dramatically increases the probability of increasing sales and profits

To gain these benefits, follow the five steps of the plan execution program:

✔ Completion of the strategic plan

✔ Presentation of the strategic plan to the company

✔ First draft of department plans are presented to the planning team

✔ Budget and department plans are approved by shareholders after discussion and any requested changes

✔ Monthly plan execution meetings

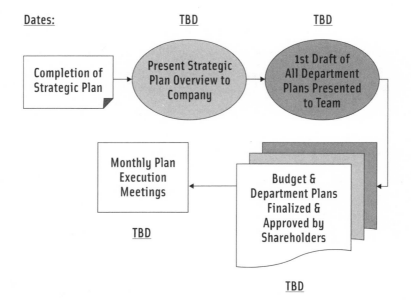

The plan execution program is relatively straightforward, but it eliminates the tendency for some team members to get distracted as soon as they leave the room and return to their regular daily activities.

COMPLETION OF THE STRATEGIC PLAN

Within five to ten business days after the last planning meeting, the strategic plan should be completed. Each planning team member should receive a copy of the strategic plan in a binder. A hard copy of the plan in the hands of each planning team member and department leader is essential. When it's sitting on your desk, it's hard to ignore.

The department leader also needs a copy of the plan to share with his or her team and use as a basis for developing the department plan. It is important to reinforce the confidentiality of the strategic plan, and the department leaders must use their discretion when sharing it with their teams.

As soon as teams accomplish even a few action plan items—especially visual items such as updating a logo or website—they feel the momentum shifting in their favor and their energy level really catches fire. I could sense that happening already with the Connecting Cultures team.

PRESENTING THE PLAN TO THE COMPANY

"When do we present the plan to the rest of the company?" Bobbie asked.

"Perfect timing, Bobbie," I said. "Our next task is to schedule the plan presentation events for the rest of the organization."

"Did you say presentation events—plural?" Rashelle asked.

"That's right," I said. "The presentation should be a special event, and you may need more than one event to cover every work shift. I encourage you to market this internally as a celebration to build excitement and set the stage for positive change. Change is hard, even when it's a good change, so you'll want to be understanding if everyone is not as fired up about this plan as you are—at least not initially.

"There will be a fair amount of uncertainty from your employee base as the company presents its first ever strategic plan. You will want to help everyone understand just how important this plan is to their future and that of the organization. I've seen employees be rather quiet during the first year's presentation. They become more involved as their engagement with the plan and their familiarity with the process ramps up later on. The departmental planning process serves as an effective tool in strengthening and uniting the members of each department.

Do you keep all employees informed on the strategy and vision of the organization? How can you increase the engagement of your employees so they can take part in helping the organization achieve the vision?

"Try not to be overly concerned with how employees react to your presentation. It will be a lot for them to comprehend, and they'll need time to process everything. It's natural for their primary thoughts to focus on how this plan affects them. It is an evolution to get to the point where everyone is involved in the plan and its execution."

"I can already picture how some of my interpreters will react to this shift," Erin said. "Some of them are better at dealing with change than others."

"And that's completely natural," I said. "As planning team members and departmental leaders, you can smooth the transition by demonstrating your excitement about the plan and the process you'll follow to achieve success. I used to take some ribbing from my colleagues at EnzoPac that I couldn't step into the plant without taking at least an hour to come back. That's because employees would consistently pull me aside with new ideas for the strategic plan and company. You'll find that some of the best ideas come from your employees on the floor and in the field as they become more engaged with the process."

Following is a recommended agenda for the plan presentation to the company. You will need to decide who is going to present which parts of the plan to the company. Each member of the planning team should present a component of the plan to show that the plan was created by the team, the team is unified around it, and each member of the team is excited to get the rest of the organization involved in the process.

PLAN PRESENTATION AGENDA

1. Review agenda
   a) Opening remarks
   b) Meeting objectives

2. Overview of planning process
   a) Planning team
   b) Planning process
   c) Company strategic challenges

3. Overview of business plan
   a) Values and beliefs statements
   b) Competence hierarchy and mission
   c) Brand and positioning strategy
   d) Vision and measurement matrix
   e) Organizational structure
   f) Company goals
   g) Communication system
   h) Plan execution program

4. Review department planning process
   a) Outline
   b) Responsibilities

5. Review timetable to plan execution
    a) Review timetable
    b) Next company meeting/plan execution update

6. Question and answer/open discussion

"How quickly can we expect the employees to begin buying into this plan?" Rashelle asked.

"Most of them will jump on board immediately," I said. "At the end of the plan presentation, encourage everyone to play an active role in developing and executing the departmental plan for their area. Encourage them to provide ideas and input to their leaders, and generate excitement by telling them this is their opportunity to provide input on how their department can improve. I'm sure many of them have always wanted this opportunity. This is their chance. Start their minds working by letting them know their department leader will pull them together in the very near future to prepare the departmental plan."

FIRST DRAFT OF DEPARTMENT PLANS PRESENTED TO PLANNING TEAM

After the presentation of the strategic plan to the company, the department teams began working on the development of their department plans. "We suggest starting the departmental planning process as soon as possible after the presentation meetings to capitalize on the momentum they generate, and then present the first draft of those plans to the planning team," I told the team.

"I can see where those departmental team meetings could be very interesting," Kyle said. "A lot of people have never been involved in planning at any level—particularly the interpreters. This will be a major change for them, but one I think they will appreciate and take advantage of."

The presentation of the department plans to the planning team typically is four to six weeks after the plan presentation to the company. The day the team members present their department plans back to the planning team is a memorable day.

BUDGET AND DEPARTMENT PLANS APPROVED BY SHAREHOLDERS

After the strategic and departmental plans are complete, all the capital and expense requests are rolled up into the annual company budget. At that time the shareholders (if applicable) will provide input to finalize the business plan and approve the annual budget to support it. The shareholders may request some further adjustments from the planning team before approving the strategic plan and budgets. Then, it's on to plan execution, where the rubber hits the road. That's where you'll begin working on the business by executing the plan, with monthly plan execution reviews to make sure you're on track.

PLAN EXECUTION MEETINGS

The last step of the plan execution program is the plan execution review meetings. The plan execution review meetings are a component of the communication process we reviewed in chapter 17. However, as they are the most important element of the plan execution program, we wanted to expand on them in this chapter.

"When the team first meets to review the completion of action plans, I suggest you consolidate all the action plans from the strategic plan into one action plan register, shown on the next page, for the entire plan. (You can download the template at www.stopsellingvanillaicecream.com.) Then, take that consolidated action plan register, shown on the next page, and draw a line at that day's date," I said. "All action plan items above the line are due and should be discussed for completion. Discuss all the items below the line at a later date, since they are not due yet. Review the measurement matrix for any red flags that indicate the strategy isn't working, and discuss

ACTION PLAN REGISTER FOR STRATEGIC PLAN

COMPETENCY:

Department	Mgr.	Company Goal					Action Plan Owner	Task or action	Measurement	Budget	Due Date	Date Completed
		1	2	3	4	5						

possible strategy adjustments or additional action plans based on measurements as you progress through the year." Measurements that are on budget should be color coded in green, and measurements that are not on track should be color coded in red.

"What happens if we can't get a certain action plan completed by the due date?" asked Erin.

"If you can see that you won't complete an action plan item on time due to a variable outside your control, you must inform your team in advance that the item needs a new completion date," I explained. "Life happens, but you do not want the act of changing due dates to become a habit. Each team member must be proactive in communicating about their action plans.

"We need to determine who should own these plan execution review meetings," I said.

"Shouldn't that be me, as the president?" Rashelle asked. "After all, this is the highest level of strategy."

"The leader is always the owner of the plan but isn't necessarily the person to schedule the meetings," I noted.

"Rashelle, keeping schedules isn't one of your strengths," Bobbie said.

"Oh, c'mon," Rashelle said. "I'm not that bad."

"We, as the planning team, will need to hold you accountable to make sure these monthly meetings happen," Bobbie pushed. "Will you be okay with that?"

"Yes," Rashelle answered. "But I don't think I'll have an issue scheduling and keeping these review meetings; I really want this to happen."

"Who will attend the review meetings?" I asked.

"The attendance list should include the planning team, shouldn't it?" Rashelle asked.

"That's the case with most of the organizations we work with, but it's still something worthy of discussion," I responded.

The team briefly debated inviting additional personnel to the meetings but quickly settled on the planning team roster as the most logical participants. They also made a commitment by establishing a regular time in the third week of each month for the meetings. This would allow time to prepare a review of the previous month's financial statements.

DEFINING WHAT ACCOUNTABILITY MEANS TO THE TEAM AND THE ORGANIZATION

The next step in finalizing the plan execution review meetings is discussing how the organization is going to define accountability. Organizational accountability is one of the most daunting challenges for many organizations. By its very nature, accountability conjures up visions of conflict, and that's something many people strive to avoid. However, accountability is an essential component to ensuring your organization takes the steps necessary to deliver the mint chocolate chip ice cream that will accelerate your business growth. Human nature is such that we require accountability to consistently and predictably complete our assignments. Absent that accountability, and it's too easy to take the path of least resistance and let things slide.

"I think people should just be able to do their jobs," Rashelle said. "Is that too much to expect?"

"Of course not," I responded. "However, people may view the tasks involved with strategic planning to fall outside of the regular scope of their jobs, at least at a subconscious level. They're so used to working in the business that it's a major shift for them to work on the business. The Stop Selling Vanilla Ice Cream process provides a framework that makes accountability much easier to implement. It all begins with the team development process and developing the plan together. The process itself creates the foundation for effective accountability with a minimal risk of conflict. The most effective teams we work with have the ability to hold each other accountable without taking it personally. Healthy conflict is a characteristic of high-performing teams because it challenges the status quo. And high-performance teams also recognize that accountability cannot be delegated to someone else. Accountability is at the core of an effective team.

"Remember the velvet hammer analogy that I use to describe how I gently hold people accountable while avoiding the tendency to make them feel defensive? The objective of the velvet hammer approach is to professionally and respectfully hold someone accountable without making him or her feel defensive. Members of a leadership team can use that same concept to hold people accountable within an organization. In fact, a lack of accountability can hurt an organization in more ways than one. In addition to treading water with regard to goal attainment, the company risks losing some of its higher performers because they get frustrated when individuals fail to deliver on commitments and then suffer few, if any, consequences. It is the responsibility of each team member to ask this question at the end of each discussion: What are we going to do about it?"

The action plan register remains the simplest and most effective tool I've come across to aid in accountability. Try this in your next team meeting: pull out an action plan register and write down a specific task whenever anyone agrees to get something done. Note the owner of that task and ask for a completion date. This doesn't necessarily mean the owner of the action plan item will complete the task herself, but it does mean she is responsible for getting it done and will be held accountable when that target date arrives. The action plan register should become a perpetual document, ever changing and never devoid of tasks in need of completion.

"Accountability is absolutely necessary to ensure the organization continues moving forward," I said. "When handled properly, such as through the use of the action plan register, accountability becomes the foundation for a high-performance culture."

"I hate to admit it, but I'm someone who needs to have accountability," Eric said. "That's probably why I was a higher performer in the military than I am in a civilian organization like this. There is major accountability in the military and a definite chain of command."

"Then you should flourish with this plan execution methodology," I said.

"Eric isn't the only one that needs to be held to the fire," Rashelle said. "I'm the same way. And it won't look good if I don't set a good example as the president of the company."

"That's absolutely right," I said. "Your company will emulate the degree to which you, as the leaders of the organization, handle accountability."

The plan execution program creates the most effective form of accountability, and

How does your organization hold people accountable for fulfilling their commitments to their teams, departments, and to the organization as a whole?

that's team accountability. A combination of psychological and practical components makes this tool work:

✔ No one wants to let his or her team down.

✔ Coming to meetings with your action plans complete, except in those rare instances when a completion date needs to change, becomes part of the rules of engagement, and more important, part of the culture.

✔ Once accountability is in place for the planning team, you can then focus on implementing it across the department teams.

However, if the team accountability approach isn't working, then we move on to structural accountability. Structural accountability means the leader holds each of her direct reports accountable. This option comes into play when someone consistently does not complete his or her action plan items in the time frame intended. The leader then needs to step in and take action.

"I hope we can handle most of our accountability issues through the team accountability option," Bobbie said. "I think that would be less stressful on everyone involved compared to having to bring the leader into the situation."

"Most organizations find that's the case," I said. "However, sometimes accountability becomes a performance issue that impacts the entire organization, and the appropriate leader at whatever level of the organization needs to step in and address the situation with a plan."

"Since this is our first time through the plan execution process, I'd feel most comfortable if you'd at least guide us for a while," Rashelle said. "We have a great plan, and I don't want to chance making a mistake at this point."

"You do have a great plan," I noted. "The ultimate value of that plan is not measured by the written plan itself but by the results generated through the execution of that plan."

The team enthusiastically began discussing the nuts and bolts of its ideal plan execution program. Kyle accepted responsibility for bringing updated company financials to the monthly plan execution team meetings, along with the action plan register and an updated measurement matrix.

"Compared to when we first met and started this process, the idea of executing our strategy is a lot less intimidating now," Erin added. "Now I am confident that we can do this!"

The Scoop

1. What measures would you take when rolling out a new strategic plan to build buy-in across the organization? What is the plan to present the strategic plan to all team members in the organization to build excitement and motivation?

2. What improvements to the strategic plan resulted from the first draft of the department plans being presented to the planning team by the department leaders?

3. If applicable, what changes did the shareholders/owners request in the plan? Which items were not approved in the budget presented to support the plan?

4. How could your organization build and promote a culture of accountability? How do your team and organization define accountability?

Action Plans to Complete the Process

☐ Define the dates for each step of the timetable to plan execution.

☐ Provide a completed strategic plan binder to each planning team member.

☐ Finalize the agenda for plan presentation to the company and determine who is going to present each component.

☐ Provide input for improvement in the department plans as they are presented to the planning team by the respective leader.

☐ Finalize each department plan and its capital/expense requests.

☐ Finalize the annual budget that considers all the capital and expense requests from the department plans. Is the budget realistic and reasonable?

☐ If applicable, gain approval on the strategic plan and budget by shareholders.

☐ Define what accountability means to the team and the organization.

☐ Consolidate all the action plans from each department plan into the action plan register for the entire strategic plan.

☐ Define the process to ensure accountability across the planning team, departments, and the company.

CONCLUSION

WRAPPING UP PLAN DEVELOPMENT, ON TO PLAN EXECUTION

"Before we unleash your plan on the world, I sense it would be wise to highlight a few key points to remember as you execute the plan," I said.

"I think we could use a summary to wrap up what's been a fascinating, life-altering process," Kyle said.

A road map can play an important role in keeping the team on track. Without one leading to a consistent endpoint, you run the risk of team members bolting in multiple directions the second they walk out the door.

"Here are five points for you to keep in mind as you go forward," I began. "The first is to *focus on building your competence.* As you progress through the action plans and departmental planning process, always ask the question, 'Does this build our competence?' If it doesn't, ask yourself, 'Should we be spending time on this activity?'

"Use that question as a filter in determining whether a particular piece of business is a profitable fit for your company. In deciding where to allocate capital investments, be sure to invest your human and financial resources into action plans that will strengthen your competence and increase your differentiation. Also, eliminate distractions by focusing your team and the organization on strengthening and delivering your competence. That will keep you zeroed in on what will drive sales and profitability.

"Second, *live as a team member*. That might sound obvious, but for some of you it will mean making a shift from an individual focus to one in which others will hold you accountable. Remember that a true team member recognizes the importance of holding each other accountable and will value that in his teammates. Support each other even while you challenge each other, and be a cheerleader for individuals, teams, and the organization. If you bring an issue to the table, make an effort to bring a recommended solution and next steps to discuss. Without a recommended solution, after a while it just becomes complaining."

"I think we're all a little guilty of that," Rashelle said. "But we've grown so much through this process as individuals and as a team that I don't think that will be as much of an issue going forward. Just the action plan register alone will keep us on track more than we've ever been before."

"I'm glad you think so," I said. "The tools contained in the Stop Selling Vanilla Ice Cream process provide your company with a formal planning structure that you can implement year after year. Your results will improve exponentially as you build momentum and people get excited about the process and the progress. The momentum that it creates is like a snowball rolling downhill. It gradually picks up speed and gains mass, and before you know it, you have an energetic team that's leaving competitors in its wake."

"I am so excited to watch that happen," Bobbie added. "It's been a long climb for us, and we needed this process to get the ball rolling."

"The third point I'd like to leave you with is to *focus on skill sets*," I continued. "Make sure each individual has the appropriate skill set for her position. Even if you like the person as an individual, you will be doing a disservice to them and the organization if you put her in a position for which she is not equipped. This can be especially difficult in family businesses. This focus will minimize personnel issues in the long term because you won't have to deal with employees mismatched to their job duties. Leadership has the responsibility to set up each employee for success, and you accomplish this by putting them in a position that matches their skill sets. I refer to this ideal position as that employee's home."

Bobbie's renewed interest in the business since we identified a position that better fit her skill set is one of the more visible benefits of the process. Leveraging and motivating existing talent can be worth its weight in gold if individuals like Bobbie and Eric find a place to maintain that motivation and contribute their extensive knowledge base to the success of the company.

"My fourth point is to *execute with passion*," I said. "Now that we've gone through this process, you know where you want to go. So be a leader! Consistently communicate the vision of the organization to your teammates and encourage them to reach for it every day in their decisions and hard work. Concentrate on building a culture of coaching and development in your company.

"And finally, *have fun with your successes*. Celebrate them and recognize the hard work that everyone contributes. Create a 'we are in this together' mind-set, and the momentum you'll generate will amaze you."

"I just can't wait to get going," Rashelle said. "We have some very talented people, and I want all of them to be a part of it moving forward."

"I'm also eager to see where your hard work will take Connecting Cultures," I said. "Congratulations! You've made it through a challenging few weeks in which we've asked you to stretch beyond your comfort zones, and now you're ready to set sail. Thank you for your patience and hard work, and I'll see you next at the plan presentation to the company.

"One last question: Are you ready to stop selling vanilla ice cream?"

"You know we are, Steve!" Rashelle answered. "We've never been so ready in our company's history."

AN UPDATE FROM RASHELLE

A few months after we moved into the plan execution process, I asked Rashelle if she would consider providing an update on Connecting

Cultures that I could use in the book, offering her perspective of the process to readers. Rashelle was quick to accept the opportunity. I'm confident you'll sense her enthusiasm and gain a better understanding of the impact the process can have for your business.

Dear Steve,

Connecting Cultures—like most organizations, I am guessing—never spent much time planning. For many years, I felt overwhelmed and consumed by the need to respond to situations, but always hoped things could be different. We followed a reactive, firefighter approach to running our business versus the more proactive approach we learned with the Stop Selling Vanilla Ice Cream process.

When I read the manuscript of this book for the first time, I found myself reflecting on how much our team has changed since those sessions occurred. There is a sense of ownership and pride among the team members now that trickles down to the entire organization.

Seeing Bobbie and Eric take ownership of the success that Connecting Cultures achieves has helped relieve much of the pressure I used to feel. The behavioral assessment session is one of my special memories from working through the process. I enjoyed watching walls come down and seeing a group of individuals develop into a high-performance team. The self-awareness of style we gained in going through this portion of the process has been very helpful. As a team, we've all learned to communicate better, even giving each other a heads-up when we can sense certain behavioral traits more in play.

A statement such as, "My D (dominance) is high today," might sound funny, but it's not that uncommon with our group of strong individuals. Especially with Kyle and me, we are more aware of each other's styles now and have a better perspective of where the other is coming from. As a team, we're more conscious of behavioral styles and how they affect our interpersonal communications. In fact, we're using behavioral assessments for the continuous development of our team and to improve communication company-wide. We also use them to make sure we hire the right person for any new positions the first time.

I was pleasantly surprised in reading our story again that I found myself coming up with new ideas that we could apply to things we're doing today. That's the thing about planning—it never ends. With the right process, there are always opportunities for your organization to develop and grow. We now have that process and will continue to use it every year to optimize the success of Connecting Cultures and its team members.

As an entrepreneur, I am constantly coming up with new ideas. I can't help it! As you saw with my behavioral style, I've often ignored process and procedure to jump around to what I felt was important in the moment. I struggled with the feeling that the organization was not moving fast enough; that we were not taking advantage of the opportunities in the market. As I am sure is the case with many leaders, I felt like I was on an island.

However, the planning process has grounded me. I am able to trust the team of people around me and understand the strengths they have that add value to our company. They are my sounding board, and I know they care about Connecting Cultures' culture and success. This trust and understanding exists because we were able to step away as a team and communicate our behavioral styles directly through a unique team development exercise. The behavioral assessments add tremendous value to our talent management process, and they're fun and intriguing, too.

This process has changed my life. It gives me the structure I need to gain perspective and pause for reflection before moving forward. I shoot from the hip less than I did, and I give more consideration to all aspects of the business, especially how potential changes will affect people and impact resources. There are so many variables that affect a business, and each day brings on new challenges. Without a plan, you get bogged down in solving day-to-day problems and working "in" the business. There is little focusing on the future—the future that will bring you success.

I've also come to place significant value on the combination of strategy and talent, and the breakthroughs it has created for me, our team, and the organization. Connecting Cultures now has a clear path that was laid out by a team that I trust. This path can change, but any change happens with an end goal in mind. Planning is something that needs to happen repeatedly to keep the business driving forward. This forward movement is challenging and exhilarating, and the rewards are endless.

Connecting Cultures just celebrated its thirteenth year of business as of this writing, and as I reflect back, it has been a roller-coaster yet rewarding journey. Becoming your own boss starts with a great idea, talent, or passion. That is the easy part. Too often you see talented people with great ideas fail as business owners, and it's because they don't invest the necessary resources to develop their business plan. Many don't know where to start. The Stop Selling Vanilla Ice Cream process gives you that starting point.

Whether you're a leader in an established organization, a divisional or department leader, a small-business owner, a future entrepreneur, or an individual, the Stop Selling Vanilla Ice Cream process can help you achieve your goals. You may not even know what those goals are, or you may have some goals and don't know how to achieve them, but planning is valuable regardless of where you are in that process.

I have enjoyed watching the cohesive efforts our team has made to move the company forward. The interpreter benchmarking effort is one of our shining successes. We have developed a description of what the optimum performer looks like for interpreting in a health care setting, and no one else in the country has that. We found that an interpreter's motivators are the most important part of an individual's makeup; more specifically, their desire to help people (social) and their system of living (traditional). We have assessed ninety interpreters across the country to this point, and 80 percent of them had those two as the primary characteristics on their behavioral assessment reports. Companies armed with this information can make better hires, and this tool is a major part of our consulting practice.

Everyone is a leader now, and no aspect of the business is dependent on the presence of one particular person. We now have a clear differentiation in the markets in which we compete, which has led to unprecedented sales growth and profitability. I wish you the best in your pursuit to stop selling vanilla ice cream. As SM Advisors says, "Those who plan, PROFIT!" I am living proof of that.

My best,
Rashelle

I vividly remember the first time I had the chance to play a lead role in developing and executing a strategic plan for a company. We couldn't find a simple process to implement the fundamentals of strategy and talent into our organization. So over the last twelve years I have fine-tuned a process that you and your team can now implement into your business or department.

The level of success you want to achieve in your life is under your control. And the only person holding you back from optimizing your success, however you define it, is you. Set the dates for your planning process today and keep us posted on your success.

It's time to stop selling vanilla ice cream.

ABOUT THE AUTHOR

Steve Van Remortel, entrepreneur, professional speaker, strategist, certified behavioral analyst, author and columnist, is inspiring business leaders in all types of organizations with the profit-critical message of business differentiation. His no-nonsense approach motivates businesspeople to take action, and his step-by-step process arms them with tools for creating real differentiation that leads to consistent and significant increases in sales and profitability. The Stop Selling Vanilla Ice Cream process focuses on creating individual and organizational performance breakthroughs through the optimization of strategy and talent—his two professional passions.

Steve has spent most of his professional life as a business owner, executive, and advisor, working primarily with privately held organizations. As founder and chief strategist at SM Advisors, he has personally completed more than 1,000 planning sessions across more than 300 different industries. The Green Bay Area Chamber of Commerce recognized his contributions to the business community by naming him the 2010 Business Person of the Year.

He earned undergraduate degrees in marketing and organizational communications and an MBA in strategic management. Steve is also a certified professional behavioral analyst (CPBA).

He lives in Green Bay, Wisconsin, with his wife, Lisa, and four children. And for the record, his favorite ice cream flavor is chocolate chip cookie dough.